The Political Economy of the Middle East

Series editors
Rory Miller
School of Foreign Service
Georgetown University
Doha, Qatar

Ashraf Mishrif
Institute of Middle Eastern Studies
King's College
London, UK

This series explores the nature of Middle Eastern political regimes and their approaches to economic development. In light of the region's distinctive political, social and economic structures and the dramatic changes that took place in the wake of the Arab spring, this series puts forward a critical body of high-quality, research-based scholarship that reflects current political and economic transitions across the Middle East. It offers original research and new insights on the causes and consequences of the Arab uprisings; economic reforms and liberalization; political institutions and governance; regional and sub-regional integration arrangements; foreign trade and investment; political economy of energy, water and food security; finance and Islamic finance; and the politics of welfare, labor market and human development. Other themes of interest include the role of the private sector in economic development, economic diversification, entrepreneurship and innovation; state-business relationships; and the capacity of regimes and public institutions to lead the development process.

More information about this series at
http://www.palgrave.com/gp/series/14415

Ashraf Mishrif • Yousuf Al Balushi
Editors

Economic Diversification in the Gulf Region, Volume II

Comparing Global Challenges

palgrave
macmillan

Editors
Ashraf Mishrif
Institute of Middle Eastern Studies
King's College London, London
United Kingdom

Yousuf Al Balushi
Supreme Council for Planning
Muscat, Oman

The Political Economy of the Middle East
ISBN 978-981-10-5785-4 ISBN 978-981-10-5786-1 (eBook)
DOI 10.1007/978-981-10-5786-1

Library of Congress Control Number: 2017951402

Printed on acid-free paper

This Palgrave Macmillan imprint is published by Springer Nature
The registered company is Springer Nature Singapore Pte Ltd.
The registered company address is: 152 Beach Road, #21-01/04 Gateway East, Singapore 189721, Singapore

Acknowledgement

We are delighted to have put together this highly valued work on the role of the private sector in the economic diversification in the Gulf Cooperation Council countries. This original research and invaluable insights brought forward by leading experts from various disciplines and professions makes this volume truly interdisciplinary and offers a realistic vision on the current stages of economic development in the Gulf region.

The production of this work is made possible with the generous contribution of the authors, who committed their time and efforts to present their work and share their views on this timely topic. We are extremely grateful to all the contributors of this volume, without whom this book would not have been available.

Special thanks goes to the Gulf Research Centre for organizing the workshop Economic Diversification: Challenges and Opportunities for the GCC held in Cambridge University, UK, in August 2015. We appreciate their generous financial and administration support, and their commitment to advance knowledge in humanity and social science in the Gulf region. We also appreciate the generosity of everyone who has given us his or her support.

We, the editors, believe that the work and experience in publishing this book will be useful to all stakeholders, particularly decision-makers, professionals, academics, postgraduate and undergraduate students, particularly in the GCC. The book intends to attract different readers from different backgrounds, including international and regional organizations promoting economic diversification, government departments concerned with policy formation and implementation, and academics and research institutions.

Contents

Notes on Contributors

Said Al Saqri is the President of Omani Economic Association. Al-Saqri received a PhD in economics from Victoria University in Australia in 2010 and a master's degree from Boston University in 2000. He previously taught at Sultan Qaboos University and the Center for International Studies in Oman. He published several studies on the relationship between natural resources and development.

Nouf N. Alsharif is a lecturer at Prince Sultan University and is currently a PhD candidate in economics at the University of Sussex. Her interests are development in resource-rich countries and economic diversification. Previously, she worked as an economist in the private sector. She also served as a board member at the Saudi Economic Association between 2011 and 2014.

Náder Alyani is an associate of the ESRC LLAKES Centre, UCL IOE, University College London, and faculty member at College of Business Administration, Prince Mohammad bin Fahd University (PMU), Khobar, Saudi Arabia. He is the Gulf region lead at Menas Associates and a Fellow of the Royal Geographical Society, with interest in economic geography of innovation, human capital development, learning for sectoral growth policies and managing policy risks.

Veronika Cummings is a Professor for Human Geography at Johannes Gutenberg-University Mainz and Associate Scholar at the Middle East Institute of the National University of Singapore. Her current research covers social and political aspects of international migration, economic diversification, national identity, and the question of the Urban in the modern Arab Gulf States (GCC).

Sterling Jensen is an Assistant Professor of Security and Strategic Studies at the UAE's National Defense College in Abu Dhabi where he has been Course Coordinator for Economic Statecraft and International Context. His doctoral dissertation, taken at King's College London, focused on Iraqi narratives of the Anbar Awakening. He has an MA in International Relations with a specialization in emerging markets from Johns Hopkins' SAIS in Washington, DC.

Harun Kapetanovic is the Economic Adviser at the Government of Dubai. Previously he held positions at the DIB Capital, Dubai Islamic Bank, Islamic Development Bank and the World Bank. As a Chevening Scholar, he holds MSc in International Securities, Investment and Banking, Henley Business School, University of Reading. He is a PhD candidate at King's College London.

Maike Laska-Khalil is managing partner at ARGUMED Consulting Group, an internationally active, well-established engineering firm specialized in industrial safety and environmental protection. With degrees in Business and Innovation Management from Constance (Germany) and Oxford (UK), Maike is currently wrapping up her doctoral thesis at the University of Fribourg in Switzerland, examining success factors of small- and medium-sized joint ventures with great cultural distance.

Minju Lee earned a Master's degree in Gulf Studies at Qatar University. Her essay 'South Korea's Diversifying Economic Cooperation in the Gulf' was published in the essay series of Middle East-Asia Program of The Middle East Institute (Washington). Her research interests cover diverse topics, ranging from Gulf politics and the international relations of the Gulf, to sectarianism, political Islam, energy policy, and Islamic feminism.

Ashraf Mishrif is Senior Lecturer in Political Economy of the Middle East at King's College London, where he was also Senior Research Fellow in the Middle East and Mediterranean Studies Programme. Prior to that, he was Senior Lecturer in international business and finance at Anglia Ruskin University (Cambridge) and the University of Greenwich (London), UK. He has authored a number of books, book chapters and scholarly papers, including the *Political Economy of Islamic Banking and Finance in the GCC* (Gerlach Press, 2015) and *Investing in the Middle East: the Political Economy of European Direct Investment in Egypt* (I.B. Tauris, 2010).

Daisuke Yamamoto is Deputy Director General Senior Economist of Sojitz Research Institute, Ltd., the research wing of general trading company, Sojitz Corporation. While doing various economic, political, and industrial researches, he is a member of the Trade Development Study Committee and the Special Research Committee of Japan Foreign Trade Council.

About the Editors

Ashraf Mishrif is senior lecturer in political economy of the Middle East at King's College London. He was also senior lecturer in international business and finance at Anglia Ruskin University and the University of Greenwich, UK. Dr Mishrif has held a range of executive and advisory posts, including cultural advisor for the Egyptian Embassy Cultural Bureau in London and a member of the Academic Board of Directors at the Boston Business Management School, Singapore. He provides advisory services to companies, government departments and international organizations, including UNCTAD. His research interests include political economy of the Middle East, foreign direct investment, international trade, economic transitions in the Gulf and the wider MENA region. He authored a number of books, book chapters and peer-reviewed papers, including Investing in the Middle East: the Political Economy of European Direct Investment in Egypt (I. B. Tauris, 2010); and the Political Economy of Islamic Banking and Finance in the GCC (Gerlach Press, 2015).

Yousuf Al Balushi is an experienced economist with over 20 years of professional experience at the Central Bank of Oman and the Supreme Council for National Development and Planning of Oman. He obtained his PhD from King's College London. His research interests cover monetary and fiscal policy, foreign trade, foreign direct investment, and private sector development.

List of Figures

List of Tables

CHAPTER 1

Challenges of Economic Diversification in the GCC Countries

Ashraf Mishrif

Efforts by the Gulf Cooperation Council member states (GCC) towards economic diversification have intensified in the wake of the sharp decline in oil prices by 75 per cent—from US$115 per barrel in June 2014 to around US$27 per barrel in January 2016. Despite financial wealth and relative economic and political stability in most GCC countries, the decline in oil prices has exposed the structural weaknesses of Gulf economies in their heavy dependency on oil and gas and inevitability of bringing about radical changes in the economic system. In the first volume of this work, we acknowledged the political will of these countries to diversify their economies by shifting resources and investments from the energy sector to non-hydrocarbon sectors. We stressed the vital role of the private sector as an engine of growth and effective tool for economic diversification and development. The dynamism, flexibility and creativity of private sector enterprises to take advantage of the available business opportunities allow the private sector to engage actively in all sectors and industries through

A. Mishrif (✉)
King's College London, London, UK

A. Mishrif, Y. Al Balushi (eds.), *Economic Diversification in the Gulf Region, Volume II*, The Political Economy of the Middle East,
DOI 10.1007/978-981-10-5786-1_1

either outsourcing and contracting from state-owned enterprises (SOEs), public-private partnerships (PPP), small- and medium-sized enterprises (SMEs) or start-ups and micro-companies. Analysis also showed that private enterprises are more flexible and capable of operating outside their national borders by taking advantage of the dynamics of regional integration in order to maximise their profits and market shares.

In this second volume, we explore the key challenges that could face GCC countries in their efforts to diversify their economies. Indeed, the challenges are numerous as diversification is a long-term process and hence requires long-term strategies to bring about noticeable changes in the economic system. The first and foremost challenge is the resource curse and Gulf development model. In fact, the huge increases in oil prices since the early 1970s have led to huge investment in the energy sector and related energy-intensive industries such as petrochemicals, chemicals, fertilisers and aluminium (Auty 1990). More recently, GCC countries have made significant investments in infrastructure, with construction and real estate sectors leading by far all other economic sectors in terms of investment and growth. This limited pace of development raises serious questions about: why have the high expectations for resource-based industrialisation not been fulfilled in the Gulf region? Why have the GCC countries, despite the abundance of capital and cheap energy, failed to develop an industrial infrastructure that could form the base for industrial and technological development, and why have their industries remained uncompetitive in the global markets, except for the petrochemical industry that is still heavily subsidised? The fact that most GCC countries import almost 98 per cent of their needs from international markets also questions the wisdom of the Gulf development model and its consequences for sustainable development in the oil-rich GCC countries. There is no straightforward answer to these questions, but a possible explanation for the failure of GCC countries to develop an industrialisation programme could be their desire to create a service-based economy. Diversification then means the allocation of resources to education, health, financial services, tourism, aviation and real estates. Diversification could also be seen by Gulf countries as long-term strategy, and hence there is no rush to disrupt their economic system as long as oil rents will continue to be the main source of government revenues for the foreseeable future (Luciani 2012).

Rentier State Model and Development in GCC Countries

The rentier state model of development in the Gulf region has its own limitations. The first and foremost challenge is the issues of governance, resources allocation and wealth distribution in the GCC countries. There is a common perception that the abundance of resources often leads to bad governance. This hypothesis is widely tested in countries where governments failed to utilise their national resources to boost their economic, political and social development (Gelb 1988; Auty 1990; Salame 1994; Schlumberger 2007; Ross 2012). Such perception applies to many countries in South America, Africa and Asia, including the Middle East region, where the levels of development are probably among the lowest in the world. Literature attributes much of this connection to the link between resource revenues and authoritarian rule, where political regimes use the resource rents to consolidate their power through either use of government expenditure to buy off opposition or providing better opportunities to deliver services and engage in mainstream policies. This may have been the case in most Middle Eastern countries; and for this challenge to be overcome, these countries should develop their institutional structure and governance mechanisms to interrupt the connection between resource revenues and authoritarianism and between resource rent and increased corruption. Good governance can guarantee the creation of a system, where resource revenues are channelled into the economy for consumption and investment, which will consequently increase economic growth and development.

The rentier state model in the Gulf region is naturally associated with the lack of fiscal policy or absence of taxation because of the abundance of resource revenues and unwritten social contract, where citizens receive rent for loyalty. Luciani (2012) argues that oil has generated huge rent for GCC countries and that the ability of the state to easily capture this rent has enabled these countries to control, spend and distribute their revenues without resorting to impose taxation on their citizens. Nevertheless, current economic conditions indicate that the continuity of this pattern of governing is no longer possible in the wake of declining oil prices and increased budget deficits in all GCC countries in 2015 and 2016. According to Alp Eke, senior economist at the National Bank of Abu Dhabi, GCC economies could incur a net foreign asset deletion of about US$390 billion and a budget deficit of US$300 billion in 2 years (Gulf Base 2016). With the fiscal space of GCC countries' net oil energy revenues reduced significantly, these countries are expected to have an average budget deficit of 11 per cent of GDP in 2016 and 8 per cent in 2017, with Saudi Arabia, Bahrain and Oman suffering the largest shortfalls in revenues.

Consequently, GCC countries had to borrow around US$318 billion through issuance of local and international bonds to finance their fiscal deficits as a result of lower oil prices between 2015 and 2016, a significant jump from the US$72.1 billion borrowed between 2008 and 2014 (Gulf Base 2016). With oil revenues represent around 80 per cent of government revenues in GCC countries, the impact of prolonged lower oil prices could further worsen the fiscal situation. Investment analysts also expected public foreign assets to decline substantially over the next 5 years. In 2016 and 2017 budgets, most GCC countries have cancelled or postponed a large number of mega infrastructure projects and introduced rigid measures to contain the fiscal shortfalls. Among these new measures are reducing government expenditure by implementing structural reforms, issuing foreign and local debt and improving revenue-generation methods through tax and fee collection. Part of these measures is the decision to introduce 5 per cent value-added tax (VAT) in 2018, which could increase to 10 per cent in the future owning to sustained fiscal deficit for the next 5 years (Gulf Base 2017). The VAT, which exempts foodstuffs and other services such as healthcare and education, will have only a marginal effect on consumers and inflation, but it will be an important step towards diversifying government income and increasing non-oil revenues. Of course, the introduction of VAT is part of a wider fiscal consolidation plan that includes also subsidy cuts and public sector freezes in the GCC countries, but the political implications of this step could be significantly huge in the way these countries are governed in future. According to International Monetary Fund, introducing the VAT in GCC countries will have limited fiscal impact on GDP, as United Arab Emirates (UAE) is likely to raise only 2.1 per cent of GDP from tax, compared to 2 per cent in Kuwait and 1.1 per cent in Qatar. What remains unclear is whether further measures such as income tax will follow this step at a later stage, and how this will affect the nature of the social contract and potential increase of citizens' assertiveness of political rights.

Diversification Outside the Energy Sector

One of the main challenges of economic diversification is to diversify from oil and gas to non-hydrocarbon sectors and industries. The challenges lie in the nature of GCC economies, where oil and oil-related products, and to some extent gas, are the only tradable commodities to be sold internationally for rent revenues. In the GCC countries, where oil rents account for almost 80 per cent of government revenues, this tradable sector receives most government attention, and significant investments are made in this sector, often at the expense of non-tradable sectors that produce for local consumption. Luciani (2012) argues that not only the discovery of oil and gas but also any significant rise in their international prices often results in the demise of traditional productive activities in the GCC countries. This is true, when an increase in oil revenues generates growth in GDP and expenditure, while the cost of production of non-tradable products is higher than importing them from the international market. This so-called Dutch Disease is theoretically ration in international trade theory and empirically notable in the GCC countries, where the discovery of oil and increase in its production and export in large quantities have led to deindustrialisation and disappearance of traditional industries such as pearl fishing. This means that the cost of production in GCC countries would be high that no industry might become internationally competitive. The cases of oil-related industries such as petrochemicals, chemicals, fertilizers, aluminium and steel are clear examples of industries that are exceedingly dependent on state subsidies to survive domestically and compete internationally (Hvidt 2013). For all GCC countries, oil and gas are capital-intensive state-run industries; hence, diversification in the energy sector sustains the leading role of the state in development, a role that is sustained through heavily subsidies to these major oil-based energy-intensive industries that create jobs for the internal market and develop competitive advantage in the global market. Investment in these oil-related industries is unlikely to reduce the dependence of the state on the hydrocarbon sector because their production depends largely on the availability of low-cost energy. We also argued in the first volume that investments in renewable energy may provide a new opportunity for diversification from fossil fuel to non-fossil fuel energy, but shifting capital from fossil to non-fossil fuel is unlikely to reduce the role of the public sector in the economy because renewable energy is capital-intensive and run by large state-owned enterprises (Mishrif 2017). This concludes that diversification in energy is unlikely to reduce the dependence of the state on the hydrocarbon sector.

Nevertheless, one cannot underestimate the efforts of GCC countries to invest a substantial portion of their expenditures in predominantly non-tradable sectors, including infrastructure, real estates, consumer services and social services such as education and healthcare. Such investment contributes directly and indirectly to real improvement in the physical infrastructure and human capabilities, hence creating the conditions for a competitive business environment.

In sectoral terms, diversification should take place in non-hydrocarbon sectors that are largely underdeveloped. With most GCC countries eyeing the development model of Asian tigers, whose development has depended largely on successful industrialisation, one could argue that the industrial sector could be a major force for economic development and growth and a step towards catching-up with the small Asian tigers. O'Connor (2007) argues that industrial development may not be the only way to a developed country standard of living, but it is a well-proven one. For the GCC, industrialisation is a challenging and lengthy root for economic development, but it is inevitable for sustainable economic development. Mueller (2012) identifies three advantages of the development of manufacturing industries:

1. Manufacturing industries are essential ingredients of social and economic development. He argues that manufacturing is a driver of productivity and that countries with large manufacturing sectors grow faster and more capable of taking advantage of new opportunities than countries with small sectors or narrow range of products.
2. If GCC countries are aiming to create knowledge-based economy, manufacturing industries are the main source, user and diffuser of technological progress. Even if they aim to develop a service-based economy, the development of modern services in areas such as finance, insurance, logistics, communications and education is stimulated largely by the needs of rapidly developing manufacturing enterprises.
3. Manufacturing could be a major factor to create competitive advantages, particularly where competitiveness of GCC products in international markets is determined by comparative cost advantage rather than technological superiority.

In fact, the manufacturing sector in the GCC countries is slowly catching-up, because of the dominance of the energy sector and services in comparison to industry, which has limited size and low investment. In 2008, manufacturing value added accounted for only 9 per cent of total GDP in the GCC countries. In the same year, the share of manufacturing to GDP has ranged between 5.59 per cent in Kuwait and 13.81 per cent in Bahrain, which has the least hydrocarbon resources. Saudi Arabia and UAE account for about three-quarters of the GCC's total manufacturing output, with most non-oil factories operate in the building materials and food processing. Mueller (2012) argues that production capacities of steel, aluminium, cement, fertilisers and plastics are currently undergoing substantial expansion and can be leading manufacturing industries in the diversification of GCC economies. While these are capital-intensive, energy-intensive, state-run industries, the potential for expansion and development is conditioned with high oil prices and significant investment made into these industries. Beblawi (2011) suggests import substitution industries for diversification because this type of industries provides a diverse set of activities, most commonly manufacturing of building materials and food processing. He argues that these industries often attract SMEs that are labour intensive and contribute to development outside the energy sector. The development of import substitution industries could offer greater opportunities for investment in manufacturing, tourism, finance, banking, insurance, financial services, construction and real estates. For example, most GCC countries consider tourism an industry that can increase foreign direct investment (FDI), increase GDP and reduce the level of dependence on a narrow, primary product range of goods. These industries do not only facilitate the expansion and growth of the private sector, but they also enable the government to spread the risk of possible economic shocks and volatility in oil prices while creating a variety of income revenues.

Hertog (2012a) provides different views on Gulf industrial development. He argues that the nature of state-led development in the GCC countries allows for the development of public industry that is driven by state-owned enterprises (SOEs). The common perception that traditional SOEs are largely characterised by inefficiency, corruption, mismanagement and misallocation of resources in many oil-producing developing countries, such as Algeria, Iran, Libya, Nigeria and Venezuela, does not necessarily apply to the GCC countries. Gulf SOEs are relatively modern, financially sound, technologically developed and their management is structured in line with international corporate practices. Another characteristic of Gulf SOEs is the quality of leadership that is often selected by the ruling families, taking into account the managerial capabilities and a degree of accountability of the chief operating officer (CEO) who is often expat with a global standard to company chairperson, who is often a member of the ruling family. So, the pressure is always there on CEOs, who are highly paid and internationally recognised, to deliver their best and take their companies to new highs. Gulf SOEs are politically and socially important because they are the main vehicle for employment of the majority of nationals, while less than 10 per cent of nationals work for local private sector companies.

There are also a number of successful industrial SOEs in various GCC countries, including Saudi Basic Industries Corporation (SABIC) in Saudi Arabia, Industries Qatar in Qatar, Abu Dhabi Basic Industries Corporation (ABBIC) in UAE, ALBA in Bahrain, DUBAL in Dubai and EMAL as a joint venture of DUBAL and Mubadala in UAE. Most of these companies have followed the SABIC model of build-up, transformation and becoming global SOEs while providing a good industrial base for expanding and developing the industrial sector in their countries. Such industrial base is fundamental for the utilisation of existing business clusters and creation of new free zones while implementing long-term industrial strategies and policies, with the aim of increasing the share of industry in export outputs and real GDP.

Morakabati et al. (2014) take us to another level of diversification that promises growth in income revenues. They stress the importance of export diversification and underline the association between the diversification of exports and economic development. Their analysis raises the question of whether export diversification is a natural outcome of the development process or whether the development process leads to diversification. They argue that export diversification is a growing trend in most developing countries: 80 per cent of these countries were exporting primary goods some 50 years ago, while currently 80 per cent of them export manufactured goods. They also highlight the tendency among these countries towards developing capabilities in the export of services, particularly after the introduction and implementation of General Agreement on Trade in Services in 1995. UAE's Etisalat, Saudi Telecom and Ooredoo of Qatar are examples of export of services in the telecommunication industry in regional and global markets. This argument poses a challenge of diversification to the GCC countries, but it offers hope and promises a brighter future if these countries realise that dependence on a narrow range of exports makes the country susceptible to the negative effects of price shocks, which in turn destabilise the economy and discourages investment (Shuai 2013). Apparently, export diversification requires the creation of a wide range of industries and services through specialisation and development of human and technological capabilities that are relatively underdeveloped.

Human Capital Development and Labour Market

Today, GCC countries have more financial capabilities than ever before, but they face major challenges in human capital development, particularly levels of labour productivity and participation of nationals in the private economy. Although Arab human development reports have recently indicated significant progress in most human development indices (HDI) in the GCC, particularly in areas such as school enrolment, life expectancy and access to basic services such as education and healthcare, there have been some concerns about the quality of education and labour market in this region. In education, significant investment has been made in building schools, colleges and universities, as well as state-of-the-art education cities in Qatar, Saudi Arabia and UAE. Most educational establishments are provided with high-tech audio visuals, laboratory equipment and information technology facilities. The vast portion of investment in education has been made in physical infrastructure; yet more investment is needed to develop the education system in a way that equips students with the hard and soft skills required by the increasingly competitive labour market. Therefore, education reforms in the GCC have recently begun to focus on incorporating "new policies, regulatory measures, creation of academic accreditation and quality assurance bodies, funding schemes and research enhancement initiatives" (Abouammoh 2012).

In higher education, the increase in the number of universities has resulted in growth in student enrolment rate by an average 5 per cent per annum in the GCC countries. There are demographic and gender imbalances, most notably in the percentage of male and female students enrolment in higher education. Statistics show an average 60 per cent of all enrolled students in all GCC higher institutions are females. This figure corresponds to the percentage of females in both Saudi and Qatari higher education. In UAE, female participation is much greater as males represented only 27 per cent of all students enrolled in higher education,

24 per cent of all Emiratis attained first degree and 26 per cent of all students received science and engineering degrees in 2008–2009. Another major imbalance is that despite the greater participation of females in higher education, unemployment rates among females are much higher than among males. This could be attributed to societal factors such as old traditions and conservative customs claiming that the right place for woman is home, educational factors such as limited availability of certain programmes and specialisation provided by universities or job market biased towards males in the GCC countries. Whatever the reason is, the low level of female participation in the labour market has deprived GCC economies from a highly qualified and significantly important segment of the society, that if utilised efficiently could have direct positive impacts on productivity and overall GDP.

Another major challenge facing economic development and diversification is the demographic structure of the GCC countries. Only Saudi Arabia and Oman have majority nationals, which accounted for 69 per cent in both countries in 2010. Meanwhile, the percentage of nationals to foreigners recorded 13 per cent to 87 per cent in Qatar, 18 per cent to 82 per cent in UAE, 40 per cent to 60 per cent in Kuwait and 51 per cent to 49 per cent in Bahrain (Fargues and Brouwer 2012). This data shows that GCC countries have smaller national populations compared to foreigners and extremely low population density, with the exception of Bahrain that ranks among the 25 most densely populated countries in the world. Such low population density resulted in heavy dependency of GCC countries on foreign workers in economic development. The high growth rate in the number of foreigners and their contribution to economic development are very significant; as a result, numerous social problems have emerged such as the so-called *bidun*, persons without citizenship, whose number is estimated around 100,000 in Kuwait.

Despite such considerable demographic challenges, increasing the participation of nationals in the private labour market is a critical socio-economic challenge for GCC governments. Hertog (2012b) argues that labour market nationalisation has been effected through quotas and prohibition rather than genuine national employment by acquiring the skills and specialisations needed in the marketplace. This makes large-scale job creation for nationals unrealistic because of the large wage differentials between local and foreign workers, and higher job mobility and better labour rights for nationals make them less attractive employees. Reasonable adjustment in the GCC labour market is challenged by the high degree of segmentation in this market. Indeed, nationalisation may have succeeded in the civil service and the public sector, where most nationals are now concentrated, because of privileges such as job security, social status, shorter working hours, and financial incentives. The concentration of nationals in the civil service and the public sector has negatively affected labour productivity in this sector vis-à-vis that in the private sector. Another element of segmentation is the wage and benefits differentiation between nationals and foreign workers. Nationals are more expensive to employ than foreigners due to higher wage expectations that can be three or four times as high as those of foreigners. Differentiation is also visible in the widening gap between high-level and low-level wages and between the wages of men and women in the labour market. Such differentiation could have adverse socio-economic consequences, including widening the gap between rich and poor and the erosion of the middle class in more populated countries such as Saudi Arabia and less resourceful countries such as Oman and Bahrain.

Employment in the private sector is considerably difficult for GCC nationals. As explained above, the percentage of education participation is high among GCC women; and despite attaining higher qualifications, women are less successful than men in securing jobs in the private sector. This does not reflect the nature of labour market mechanisms in any way, but an interpretation of how culture, tradition, institutional and legal environment affect the labour market in this region. As for men, one could argue that the availability of cheap, high-skilled foreign labour may have affected the supply side of the labour market and made private employers disinclined to employ nationals. In fact, while nationals are less willing to accept low wages, they are less experienced and lack practical qualifications, specialisation and skills that make them competitive vis-à-vis their foreign counterparts. Private employers often complain about the motivation factor when it comes to evaluating the performance and productivity of local employees. Meanwhile, the legal system through labour sponsorship schemes enables employers to hire and fire and control foreign workers easily in a way that make them more attractive employees than nationals. While the aim of labour market policy is to reach full employment, there is little room to argue that labour market nationalisation has succeeded in the GCC, in light of the declining productivity rates, particularly in the public sector, low percentage of GCC citizens as labour market participants and underutilisation of national labour potential that is unsustainable in the long run. The success of labour market nationalisation is most likely to succeed if GCC countries make reasonable adjustments in their labour market through an increase in the price of foreign labour and creation of internally liberalised labour market (Hertog 2012b).

Addressing Challenges Through Learning from Global Best Practices

National and regional markets do often have their own characteristics and dynamics, which differ considerably from other countries and regions. That nature and structure of the GCC markets are unique in many ways due to specific political, economic, demographic and social conditions. The success of diversification in one country does not mean that the set of policies adopted in that country will succeed in another. The mixed results of general packages such as economic reforms and structural adjustment programmes introduced by the IMF and the World Bank in developing countries show that no one size fits all when it comes to economic development. So, what concerns us here is not whether diversification will succeed or fail, but how GCC countries can address the key challenges of diversification. To achieve such an objective, we put together a selection of case studies that are most relevant to GCC economies and are likely to provide new insights on how other countries have succeeded in overcoming major structural weaknesses in their economies. This volume is not concerned with finding short-term solutions for the volatility in international oil prices, which has declined sharply since July 2014. Rather, it is concerned with dynamic changes in the business cycle, diversifying the economic base and adjusting the state-led development model in a way that can lead to long-term sustainable development.

In this respect, we devote the following two chapters to look at the effects of resource abundance and rent resources on economic diversification. Economic analysis shows that GCC economic cycle is driven by the hydrocarbon sector and that all other economic sectors are highly dependent on investment generated from production and export of oil and gas. This economic cycle has not fundamentally changed in the past 50 years and is unsustainable in the future; this has now forced GCC countries to seek means through which a reallocation of resources and investment from oil to non-oil sectors could break this cycle and inject life in non-oil sectors for employment and income generation. Nouf Alsharif (Chap. 2) examines the impact of natural resource rents on diversification in exports, in employment and in value added in 136 countries, including GCC countries, between 1962 and 2012. Alsharif finds a significant negative relationship between resource rents and economic diversification. Although the results are heterogeneous across different country groups and resources, GCC countries are not an exception as they follow the high resource-dependent group. The study shows that the higher the resource dependency, the less likely the country will diversify its economy through development in comparison to less resource-dependent countries. In addition, Said Alsaqri (Chap. 3) examines the linkages and interdependency between the oil sector and non-oil sectors such as the agriculture and fisheries, manufacturing and services. Alsaqri tests how sensitive and dependent these sectors to oil sector and oil price change and how they increase or decrease in the face of changing government expenditure. The study finds that all non-oil sectors are sensitive to changes in oil prices, particularly in GCC countries that are characterised by large fiscal and current account deficits because of the recent decline in oil prices. Although the study highlights the negative impact of interdependency between oil and non-oil sectors on the economic performance and development in the GCC, it calls for further investigations on how the oil sector will affect the macroeconomic dynamics of the GCC countries.

Giving the political, economic, social and demographic similarity and historical and geographical ties, the UAE is the most diversified economy among the GCC countries, and its economic development model is worth examining in this context. Sterling Jensen (Chap. 4) focuses on UAE's economic diversification strategy and its policy implications. The study argues that UAE has seriously begun its diversification to decrease its dependency on oil since the 1980s, when the oil prices stood at US$9 per barrel. It argues that while some emirates have diversified quicker than others, this diversification strategy has come at the cost of other important national objectives such as preserving the national identity and Emiratisation. It explains in detail the policy implications of the diversification strategy and trade-offs to pursuing diversification in its trade, manufacturing, finance, services, tourism and the defence industry sectors. The chapter concludes that the success of the UAE economic diversification strategy relies on the government's ability to incentivise the Emiratis to leave relatively the public sector and increase labour productivity in the private sector. Ashraf Mishrif and Harun Kapetanovic (Chap. 5) get more specific and examine the economic diversification model of Dubai. They argue that the uniqueness of Dubai's model lies in its business openness and integration into the global economy rather than oil dependency.

In line with the argument presented above by Alsharif, the decline of oil contribution to Dubai GDP from 5.48 per cent in 2000 to 1.4 per cent in 2013 could have been a facilitator rather than a hindrance to the city's economic growth and development. In contrast with the prevalent views on various inefficiencies associated with resource-rich economies, Dubai's model of development rests on the government leadership with specific governance and state entrepreneurship models, inward investment orientation, unhindered access to capital and labour markets, protectionism and legal dichotomy and policy of systematic diversification. This model offers a promising future for Dubai, where most key elements of Dubai's model are synonymous to the economic systems and conditions of the GCC countries.

At the regional level, there is a potential to learn from the experience of other regional countries, which have gone a lengthy way in their economic development and diversification path. In a comparative perspective between Iran, Saudi Arabia and UAE, Náder Alyani (Chap. 6) explores the need to integrate sectoral learning and skills development into sectoral policies, particularly in priority sectors with significant potential to contribute to economic diversification while simultaneously moving towards sectoral specialisation. Alyani provides a circumscribed review of the creative sector as a potential employment-creating sector, specifically in the digitised creative segment in Iran, Saudi Arabia and UAE, focusing on the learning and upskilling required for innovating in the nascent creative subsectors. Alyani also explores the in situ learning episodes within a conceptual model, pointing to the prominent use of skill webs as a means of in-project upskilling and a resource for development of inter-professional learning and judgement capability, which forms a core ingredient for innovation.

At the global level, this work examines some interesting global best practices through detailed analysis of case studies on successful diversification from Germany, Japan, Singapore, Malaysia, Taiwan, and South Korea. Maike Laska-Khalil (Chap. 7) analyses the success factors in small- and medium-sized joint ventures with high cultural diversity through the lens of Saudi-German business cooperation. The study explains how entry into foreign markets represents a challenge, especially for SMEs, not least due to financial and human resource constraints. Despite the increasing popularity of international joint ventures (IJVs) as an internationalisation strategy, their effectiveness has been generally underexplored, with researchers tending to focus on ventures established by large firms, the results of which are not entirely applicable to SMEs. Laska-Khalil integrates existing research results to identify crucial success factors for SME IJVs. To take the practical relevance of this study into consideration, a causal model is developed based on the results of a well-designed, comprehensive meta-analysis. The study demonstrates that inter-company cooperation in SMEs joint ventures with high cultural diversity can facilitate diversification through learning and exchange of variables that are crucial for the economic development of a rentier country such as Saudi Arabia.

Daisuke Yamamoto (Chap. 8) provides another important case study, which looks at the shape and background of East Asia's economic development model. He compares situations in the GCC and East Asia and examines paths the GCC should go through to industrial diversification. He employs the Asia's flying geese paradigm to explain the way that Japan acted as leader of Asia's economic development in the 1970s and the 1980s, followed by similar developments in South Korea, Taiwan, Hong Kong and Singapore. The flying geese model is attributed to the existence of consumer markets for Asian products, the region's plentiful and cheap labour, transfer of technology from Japan to Asian countries, the era of cold war mentality and more recently by the division of labour across countries through global supply chains and the creation of a logistics network that supports these chains. The current situation in the GCC region is quite different from what Asia experienced; hence, GCC countries should not aim for the same industrialisation-fuelled economic growth that once took place in Asia. Rather, these countries should utilise their abundant capital reserves from oil and gas to promote capital-intensive or knowledge-intensive industries. While providing several case studies that could serve as models for the GCC countries, the study also considers practical measures of how governments can contribute to the region's industrial development while summarising basic policy and explicit means for diversifying the GCC economy. In terms of concrete methodology, the study touches on the general promotion of industry, strengthening and stimulating oil- and gas-associated industries through M&A, promotion of knowledge-intensive industries and creation of the soft and hard infrastructure necessary to make these methods viable.

Minju Lee (Chap. 9) examines the current challenges facing the GCC economic diversification and relates the Korean experience of economic breakthroughs to the GCC countries' strategic planning for the next phase of diversification towards a sustainable growth. Her study aims to compare key characteristics of economic diversification model of South Korea and the GCC countries while attempting to extract useful meanings from the Korean experience and generalising them to the GCC vision of economic diversification. In doing so, Lee explains the rationale of the newly formed collaborative partnership between South Korea and the GCC countries, with the aim of supporting the latter countries in their economic diversification. While providing an overview of Korean industrialisation and economic development since the 1960s, Lee pays particular attention to the similarities and differences in economic diversification in the GCC and the Korean experience and lessons learned from this experience for sustainability of the GCC economies through diversification.

Veronika Deffner (Chap. 10) finally provides a critical analysis of the Singaporean model, a model that is one of the most sought-after models of an advanced diversified service economy. While examining the economic diversification and nationalisation strategies in the GCC and Singapore, Deffner argues that due to rapid modernisation and high dependence on foreign-imported workforce and expertise, both the economies of the GCC and the most advanced economies of the Association of South East Asian Nations (ASEAN) are currently tackling similar political, economic, social and demographic challenges. She draws a similarity in the way the GCC countries are trying to diversify their economic revenues by reducing the high dependence on the hydrocarbon sector, whereas Singapore, as the most developed economy in ASEAN, is implementing policies to diversify from its strong economic foothold the financial service sector. She places a great significance of the development of national human capital as key for a successful and, thus, sustainable diversification process for the GCC and Singapore, whose advanced and swiftly modernised economies require a capable workforce that is sufficiently skilled and experienced. Singapore represents an interesting case for the GCC as both regions have made great efforts to develop their economic ties, both in scope and depth, in the past decade. It could offer experience and general features for the strategic planning and implementation of diversification, particularly in the areas of education, R&D, and innovation that are vital for developing GCG national workforce, as well as balancing between the persisting need of high-skilled foreign workforce and the demands for greater employment opportunities for their national citizens. Deffner provides her analysis with reference to the Sultanate of Oman and Singapore's economic structure and its strategies for dealing with similar, though different diversification challenges; but both are finding it difficult to find a balance between economic diversification and human resource management.

Concluding Remarks

This introductory chapter has provided an overview of some of the most challenging aspects to economic diversification in the GCC countries. It identifies three major challenges facing GCC countries in their economic diversification: the nature of the rentier state and all attributes and limitations associated with this model; the capacity of the state to diversify the economy outside the energy sector; and the appropriate means and policies to overcome obstacles facing human capital development. Indeed, GCC countries have made significant progress in their economic growth, but some critical challenges have remained tenacious and continued to undermine the diversification process across the region. Challenges of diversification are not limited to the GCC countries; they exist in most developed and developing countries in various forms and degrees and require differing strategies and policy appropriate to the political and economic settings of the respected country.

Today, the GCC is fortunate by the availability and richness of successful experiences and global best practices in economic diversification. Contrary to the common perception that the abundance of nature resources is often associated with bad governance, the chapter demonstrates a number of case studies from within the GCC region and globally that resources could be a bless and contribute directly to economic development and diversification by allocating resources to the most productive sectors of the economy. Dubai's model of economic development provides some insights and guiding principles for other GCC countries, some of them share the basic characteristics of Dubai's experience. Although GCC countries experience similar economic structure and levels of economic growth, they have the potential of learning from the experience of one another on bilateral and regional levels. Globally, the GCC is increasingly looking east; hence, the experiences of highly advanced economies of Japan, South Korea and Singapore provide new opportunities for the GCC countries not only to enhance their economic ties with these countries but also to emulate some of the successful elements of their strategies and policies in economic diversification.

References

Abouammoh, A. M. (2012). Higher Education in the GCC States: Reforms and Regulations. In S. Hertog (Ed.), *National Employment, Migration and Education in the GCC* (pp. 265–285). Berlin: Gerlach Press.

Auty, R. (1990). *Resource-Based Industrialisation: Saving the Oil in Eight Developing Countries.* Oxford: Clarendon Press.

Beblawi, H. (2011). Gulf Industrialization in Perspective. In J.-F. Seznec & M. Kirk (Eds.), *Industrialization in the Gulf: A Socioeconomic Revolution* (pp. 185–197). London: Center for Contemporary Arab Studies, Routledge.

Fargues, P., & Brouwer, I. (2012). GCC Demography and Immigration: Challenges and Policies. In S. Hertog (Ed.), *National Employment, Migration and Education in the GCC* (pp. 231–257). Berlin: Gerlach Press.

Gelb, A. (1988). *Windfall Gains: Blessing or Curse?* Oxford: Oxford University Press.

Gulf Base. (2016, April 13). GCC States Set to Borrow Billions to Fund Deficits. Retrieved from http://www.gulfbase.com/news/gcc-states-set-to-borrow-billions-to-fund-deficits/288882

Gulf Base. (2017, February 16). Gulf VAT Rollout at 5% in 2018 May Rise to 10% Over the Years: BMI. Retrieved from http://www.gulfbase.com/news/gulf-vat-rollout-at-5-in-2018-may-rise-to-10-over-the-years-bmi/294985

Hertog, S. (2012a). Public Industry as Tool of Rentier Economy Diversification: The GCC Case. In G. Luciani (Ed.), *Recourses Blessed Diversification and the Gulf Development Model* (pp. 115–138). Berlin: Gerlach Press.

Hertog, S. (2012b). A Comparative Assessment of Labour Market Nationalisation Policies in the GCC. In S. Hertog (Ed.), *National Employment, Migration and Education in the GCC* (pp. 65–106). Berlin: Gerlach Press.

Hvidt, M. (2013). *Economic Diversification in GCC Countries: Past Record and Future Trends.* Kuwait Programme on Development, Governance and Globalisation in the Gulf States, 27. London School of Economics and Political Science, pp. 1–49.

Luciani, G. (2012). Introduction: The Resource Curse and the Gulf Development Challenge. In G. Luciani (Ed.), *Recourses Blessed Diversification and the Gulf Development Model.* Berlin: Gerlach Press.

Mishrif, A. (2017). Economic Diversification in the GCC Countries: An Introduction. In A. Mishrif & Y. Al Bulushi (Eds.), *Economic Diversification in the Gulf Region: The Private Sector as an Engine of Growth* (Vol. I). New York and Singapore: Palgrave Macmillan.

Morakabati, Y., Beavis, J., & Fletcher, J. (2014). Planning for a Qatar Without Oil: Tourism and Economic Diversification, a Battle of Perceptions. *Tourism Planning and Development, 11*(4), 415–434.

Mueller, H.-G. (2012). GCC Industrial Development. In G. Luciani (Ed.), *Recourses Blessed Diversification and the Gulf Development Model* (pp. 139–181). Berlin: Gerlach Press.

Ross, M. (2012). *The Oil Curse*. Princeton and Oxford: Princeton University Press.

Salame, G. (1994). *Democracy Without Democrats? The Renewal of Politics in the Muslim World*. London: I B Tauris.

Schlumberger, O. (2007). *Debating Arab Authoritarianism: Dynamics and Durability on Non-Democratic Regimes*. Stanford: Stanford University Press.

Shuai, X. (2013). Will Specialisation Continue Forever? A Case Study of Interaction Between Industry Specialisation and Diversity. *Annals of Regional Science, 50*, 1–24.

CHAPTER 2

Natural Resources and Economic Diversification: Evidence from the GCC Countries

Nouf N. Alsharif

Introduction

Natural resource rents exceed US$4 trillion per year, amounting to 7 percent of world GDP. Non-renewable resource revenues are a dominant feature of 50 economies with a combined population of 1.4 billion people. There are 24 countries for which resources make up more than three-quarters of their exports, 13 countries for which resources make up at least 40 percent of their GDP and 18 countries in which resources provide more than half of fiscal revenue (IMF 2016 and van der Ploeg and Venables 2012).

Resource-rich countries have been historically heavily dependent on a limited range of natural resources, mostly for export. This limited diversification may lead to unsustainable growth, driven by a high concentration in low productivity sectors. Concentration in such sectors may lead

N.N. Alsharif (✉)
Department of Economics, University of Sussex, Falmer, UK

College of Business Administration, Prince Sultan University, Riyadh, Saudi Arabia

A. Mishrif, Y. Al Balushi (eds.), *Economic Diversification in the Gulf Region, Volume II*, The Political Economy of the Middle East,
DOI 10.1007/978-981-10-5786-1_2

to high vulnerability to macroeconomic instability, price volatility and external shocks. Many resource-rich countries aspire to a diversified economy, but many of them—especially the less developed countries—have limited experience with regard to which aspects of diversification are important.

In this chapter, we test the impact of natural resource rents on diversification in exports, in employment and in value added. By using employment data, Imbs and Wacziarg (2003) find that diversification path follows a U-shaped pattern in relation to per capita income: countries tend to diversify at early stages of development, and then at higher stages of income, they tend to specialize in certain sectors. This chapter revisits the issue using an additional perspective; we investigate the effect of resource rents on the noted U-shaped diversification pattern in employment, in addition to value added and exports. We find a significant negative relationship between resource rents and diversification.

The literature on the relationship between resource rents and non-resource economic activity focuses on the concept of the "Dutch Disease", which is a widely used term in the development literature. *The Economist* magazine coined the term in 1977 to explain the gas boom implications on the Dutch economy.

The extensive literature on the Dutch Disease is pioneered by Corden and Neary (1982) who show a decline in manufacturing employment and exports as a result of resource boom. Three factors can cause this boom: a technology-induced rise in productivity, a new resource discovery, or a rise in the commodity world price. They distinguish between two main effects of the resource boom on the manufacturing sector; the spending effect occurs when a sudden rise in the value of the natural resource exports raises real income leading to extra spending on services, which raises their prices and leads to adjustments in real exchange rates. That makes exporting non-resource commodities more difficult and makes competing with imports across a wide range of commodities harder. Foreign exchange earned from the resource exports may be used to purchase internationally traded goods, at the expense of domestic manufacturers of the goods. Simultaneously, domestic resources such as labor and materials shift to the resource sector, where the resource movement effect takes place. Consequently, the price of these resources rises in the domestic market, thereby increasing the costs to producers in other sectors. Eventually, extraction of natural resources sets in motion a dynamic that gives primacy to two domestic sectors—the natural resource sector and the non-tradable sector—at the expense of more traditional exports sectors.

Ismail and Arezki (2010) test the Dutch Disease on a sample of 32 oil-rich countries from 1992 to 2009 and find that during an oil boom, fiscal policies have helped to reduce capital expenditure. Harding and Venables (2013) find that exports of natural resources crowd out non-resource exports. They find that in countries with high income and good governance, the impact on non-resource exports becomes greater, as these countries tend to have higher manufacturing in their non-resource exports.

The "resource curse" was first noted by Sachs and Warner (1995, 2001) who show a significant negative relation between natural resource dependence and growth in GDP per capita. They also argue that resource abundance squeezes the manufacturing sector, as in the Dutch Disease model. Other studies considered oil rents specifically. Ross (2001) and Sala-i-Martin and Subramanian (2003) find a negative relation between oil rents and economic performance. Other papers show that the impact of resource abundance is mainly driven by political factors (Tornell and Lane 1999).

We also test if different kinds of resources could have varied impacts on diversification, as Bhattacharyya and Collier (2014) show that resource curse occurs in case of point resource natural resources such as minerals, but not in renewable point source resources such as agriculture and forestry.

To date, there are not many empirical studies on diversification. Few exceptions include Imbs and Wacziarg (2003) who find that employment diversification follows a U-shaped pattern in relation to per capita income: countries tend to diversify at early stages of development, and then at higher stages of income, they tend to specialize in certain sectors. Koren and Tenreyro (2007) also find the U-shaped pattern in plotting production concentration against income, but the depth of that shape varies across different income groups. Moore and Walkes (2010) find a positive relationship between economic volatility and concentration. In studying trade diversification, a number of papers find that exports are more concentrated than production, such as Hausmann and Rodrik (2003) and Easterly et al. (2009). Cadot et al. (2011) find the U-shaped pattern in export diversification, as countries tend to reconcentrate on exports after a certain point of income. Alsharif (2015) used commodity prices to instrument resource rents and found empirically that higher resource dependency leads the country to skip the U-shaped diversification pattern through development and mostly remain concentrated.

Investigating productivity growth and structural change, McMillan and Rodrik (2011) argue that in developing countries, there are large productivity gaps between different parts of their economies, and between different firms within the same part or industry. These gaps are smaller in developed countries. They acknowledge that structural change could move into different directions along with the economic development process. In resource-rich countries particularly, natural resources do not generate much employment compared to manufacturing and other tradable sectors, which takes structural changes into a direction away from productive sectors.

This chapter adds to the literature through examining the effect of resource rents on diversification. As shown above, previous literature covered the effect of development on diversification or studied the effect of natural resources on development. In this chapter, we combine the two strands of literature and study the effects of resource rents on structural change in employment and value added (internal diversification) and the effect on exports (external diversification). We examine the concentration in employment and exports in resource and non-resource, tradable and non-tradable sectors. Previous literature examined these effects separately, either structural change or exports, and as far as of our knowledge, none of them examined the effect of natural resources directly on diversification.

The rest of the chapter continues as follows: Section 2 briefly describes economic diversification. Section 3 defines the data and outlines the methods. Section 4 presents the empirical results. Section 5 concludes.

Economic Diversification: How and Why

Through the development literature, a number of studies have investigated the relationship between diversification and development. The findings vary across papers depending on the used methodological approach, the dataset and the diversification measures (De Benedictis et al. 2009). Some of these studies find a monotonic relationship between diversification and development, where countries tend to diversify moving along the development path (Stokey 1988), while other studies find countries grow into more specialization as they develop (Krugman 1987).

More recently, a growing number of empirical studies have investigated the relationship between diversification and development. The highly cited paper by Imbs and Wacziarg (2003) find a non-monotonic relationship where diversification takes a U-shaped pattern, a result found by other following papers such as Koren and Tenreyro (2007) and Cadot et al. (2011). Cadot et al. (2011) argue that diversification should not be taken as a policy objective for two reasons: first, they emphasize the importance of specialization, not diversification, following Ricardian theories which stress on the importance of specialization, not diversification. Second, they argue that by looking into exports, the Heckscher-Ohlin model implies that export patterns are largely determined by endowments, drawing the attention to factor accumulation, not diversification.

However, policymakers in developing countries and resource-rich countries are constantly preoccupied by diversification as they believe it is the path toward higher development, according to Papageorgiou and Spatafora (2012). Gylfason (2011) argues that economic diversification could stimulate growth by attracting new economic activity that avoids excessive reliance on primary production in few natural resource–based industries, thus facilitating the transfer of labor from low-paying jobs in low-skill-intensive farming and agriculture to more lucrative jobs in more high-skill-intensive occupations in manufacturing. Gylfason (2011) also argues that a dependency on natural resources could be good for growth, if well managed and used to diversify the economy. In exports, diversification may help countries to upgrade their resource-based sectors, as they move away from unprocessed primary exports to more complex products and services (Gelb and Grasmann 2010). A higher resource dependency makes diversification more difficult, but resource-rich countries still want to diversify for a number of reasons (Gelb and Grasmann 2010): First, export diversification is associated with higher long-run growth, as engaging in manufacturing enables dynamic learning-by-doing that raises productivity and income. Second, diversification exposes producers to a wider range of information about foreign markets and may open the way to other sectors. Third, diversification reduces the impact of volatile resource prices. van der Ploeg and Venables (2012) argue that to achieve diversification in resource-rich economies, public and private investments are needed to work jointly through investments in human and private capital.

Figure 2.1a shows the difference in export diversification between developed and developing countries in the sample. It shows developing countries increased their export diversification during the sample period more rapidly than developed countries. Gelb and Grasmann (2010) note that developing countries in general have had successfully diversified their economies and exports. They note that in the 1960s, about 80 percent of developing countries' exports were primary commodities, while recent figures show that almost 80 percent are industrial products (although some primary industries are classified as industrial). These

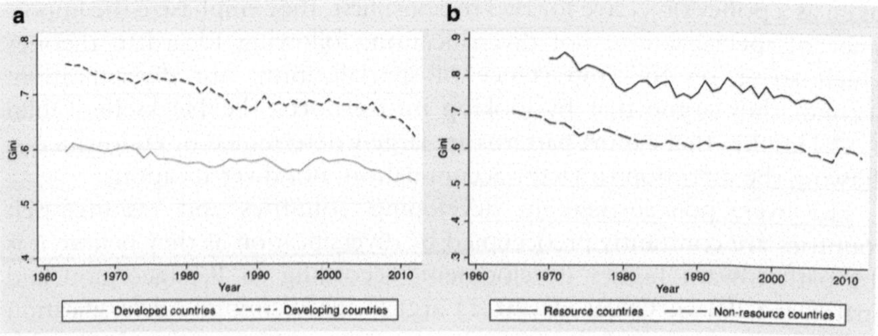

Fig. 2.1 Export diversification in (**a**) developed and developing countries and (**b**) resource and non-resource countries. Gini ranges between 0 and 1; lower Gini indicates higher diversification. Source: WITS (2013)

figures relate to the U-shaped pattern found by Imbs and Wacziarg (2003), assuming that developing countries are in the initial stage, where concentration is still high.

Figure 2.1b shows the difference in export diversification between resource and non-resource countries in the sample. Apparently, we can see the higher level of concentration in the resource countries' exports, which is mainly driven by resources.

Elbadawi and Gelb (2010) show two types of diversification—diversifying by introducing new sectors in the economy and diversifying within the resource sector. We focus on the first type in this chapter. Diversification strategies do not always succeed. Esanov (2012) lists certain criteria for successful stories: sound macroeconomic environment, designing a realistic strategy taking into consideration local factors, well-functioning government institutions, adequate financial sector and social infrastructure to support diversification efforts, and creating special incentives to facilitate export diversification.

Measures of Economic Diversification

The dataset in this study includes sectoral data on structural change measured by employment, value added and exports. The number of countries in the dataset is 136, ranging across all levels of development. The data are annual, covering the period from 1962 to 2012. There are many measures for sectoral diversification; most of them are borrowed from the income equality literature. Here we report three measures: the Gini, Theil and Herfindahl-Hirschman indices. Table 2.3 in appendix presents descriptive statistics of these measures, and Table 2.4 in the appendix presents the correlation between all the measures, which is rather high. Imbs and Wacziarg (2003) use Gini, HHI and the coefficient of variation. Cadot et al. (2011) use Gini and HHI and Moore and Walkes (2010) use only HHI. Lederman and Maloney (2003) use HHI. McMillan and Rodrik (2011) use the coefficient of variation. All three measures are calculated in this study, but we report the Gini index only due to the high correlation between the three measures. (See Appendix for full data description.)

We calculate diversity for all sectors first and then for all non-resource sectors. To get the non-resource sector values in the ILO data, we exclude "Mining and quarrying", and in the WITS exports data, we exclude "Crude material, inedible, except fuels", "Mineral fuels, lubricants and related materials" and "Commodities not classified according to kind". The UNIDO data does not cover resource sectors at all.

From Table 2.3 in the appendix, we can take that highest diversification in employment (using ILO dataset) happened in Algeria in 1984. The highest export diversification (using WITS dataset) happened in Greece 2006, while the highest concentration in exports happened in Libya between 1976 and 1981, dominated by the mineral exports sector.

Methodology

The methodology has three steps: First, we use panel data to examine the relationship between resource rents and diversification. Second, we use commodity prices as an instrument for resource rents. Third, we test the heterogeneity of natural resources in different specifications.

The employment data are from the International Labor Office for nine main sectors (1-digit level), covering the years 1969–2009, and the United Nations Industrial Development Organization (2012) for 23 main sectors (3-digit level, INDSTAT2) covering the years 1963–2010. Note that UNIDO data are partial, covering only manufacturing, employment and value added. It is included here because the value-added data shine an additional light on diversification and structural change. Exports data are from WITS for the 10 main sectors (1-digit level) covering the years 1962–2012. Income data are from Penn World Tables (PWT) version 8.0, which goes back to 1950.

Data Analysis and Discussion

Natural Resources and Diversification

We begin by revisiting the non-monotonic relationship between diversification and development uncovered by Imbs and Wacziarg (2003) and Cadot et al. (2011). Figure 2.2 shows the existence of the non-monotonic U-shaped path in our data in employment, value added and exports. The U-shape persists in diversification through all specifications even after counting for the non-resource sectors only.

Second, we examine the effect of natural resource rents on sectoral employment to test the structural change movements in resource countries. There is a large and significant negative effect of the resource rents on ILO sectoral employment diversification. Coefficients are larger within

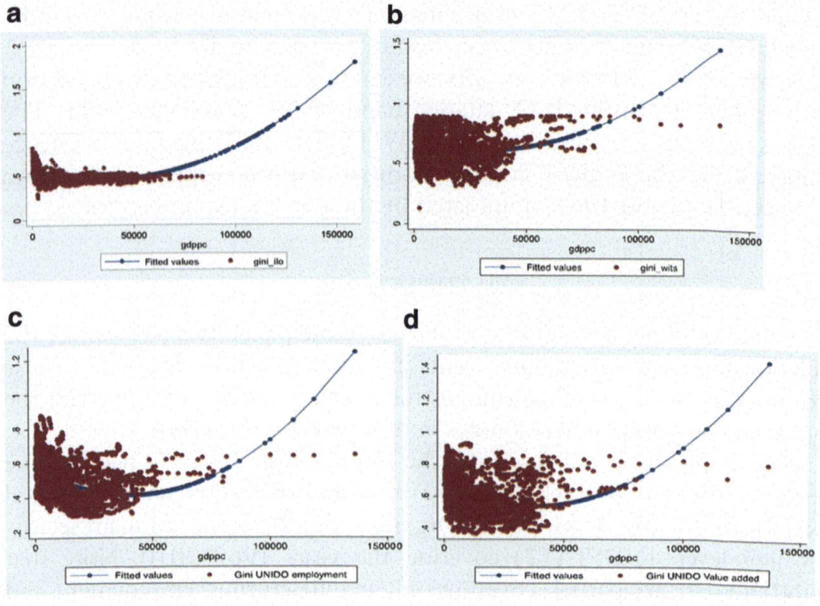

Fig. 2.2 Revisiting the U-shaped development path noted by Imbs and Wacziarg (2003) and Cadot et al. (2011) in (**a**) ILO sectoral employment, (**b**) exports, (**c**) UNIDO manufacturing employment, (**d**) UNIDO manufacturing value added. Note: The U-shaped pattern is based on our data. Countries diversify first and then specialize again through all data groups. Data sources: ILO (2012), WITS (2013) and UNIDO (2012)

the non-resource sectors, showing that employment concentration happens out of the resource sector which is usually capital intensive and does not create many jobs. The Dutch Disease theory predicts that a resource boom increases wages in the booming sector and thus increases employment in that sector affected by the spending effect. But due to the fact that the resource sector is capital intensive, employment concentration occurs in other non-tradable sectors affected by the resource movement effect.

Within the UNIDO manufacturing data, we test the effect on manufacturing employment and value added. Results show that there is a significant negative effect of the resource rents on manufacturing employment and on the manufacturing value added. This could reflect increased local demand on manufactured goods as an implication of the Dutch Disease spending effect. This result might be also affected by the low employment in the resource sector as explained previously.

We next turn from employment to exports, to test the effect of resource rents on the tradable sectors. The Dutch Disease model predicts a decline in producing tradable goods and higher exports of the natural resources. There is a significant negative effect of the resource rents on export diversification, in both full sample exports and in non-resource sectors. Concentration in resource exports examined by the total exports (All) is larger in most specifications. Less manufacturing output and other tradable goods could cause the noted higher diversification in non-resource sectors, as the Dutch Disease model predicts.

So far, the results show high concentration in employment, value added and exports as a result of natural resource rents. Figure 2.3 plots predicted Gini indices against GDP per capita for various levels of resource rents to GDP shares; it shows that the U-shaped relationship is maintained in most levels, and the steepest curve is the non-resource countries. However, this U-shaped relationship disappears in the higher levels of resource rent share in GDP (over 40 percent) where the concentration continues to increase along the development path. Accordingly, the higher the resource rent share in GDP, the less likely diversification could happen along the development path. Instead, concentration increases rapidly.

Heterogeneity Across Natural Resources

Diversification in different sectors is likely to vary across different kinds of natural resources, since commodity prices are heterogeneous. We test the diversification affected by two groups of resources: oil and gas, and forestry.

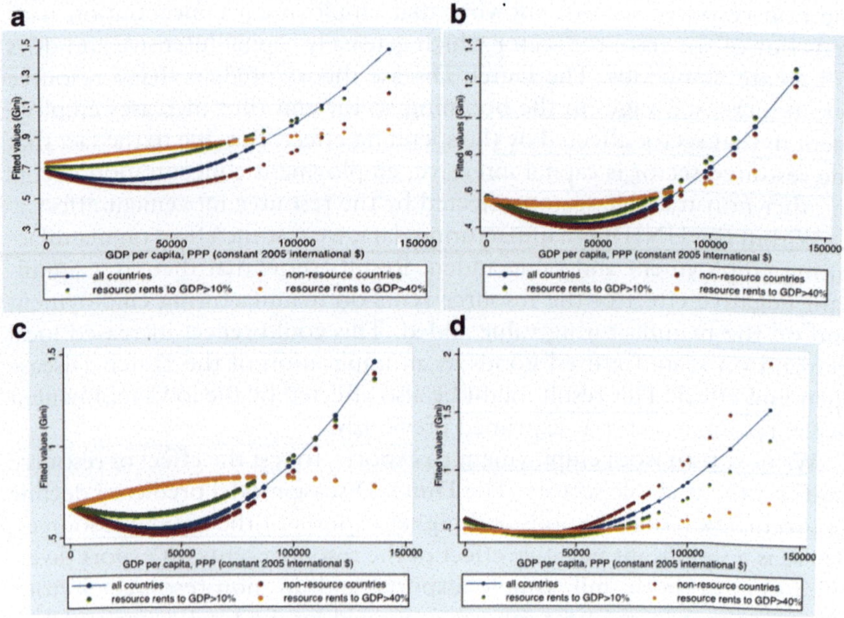

Fig. 2.3 Gini indices against GDP per capita and the share of resource rents. (**a**) Exports. (**b**) UNIDO manufacturing employment. (**c**) UNIDO manufacturing value added. (**d**) ILO sectoral employment

Oil and Gas Rents

The results show an insignificant effect in employment, either ILO overall employment or UNIDO manufacturing employment. However, there is a highly significant concentration in exports mainly affected by oil and gas exports. There is also a significant concentration in manufacturing value added; this concentration is found to be mostly within sectors that are highly related to oil and gas but classified individually in the UNIDO dataset (such as (9) coke, refined petroleum products, nuclear fuels; (10) chemicals and chemical product; (12) non-metallic mineral products; (13) basic metals) or sectors that produce locally consumed goods and fall within the non-tradable as they do not show up in exports (such as (1) food and beverages and (6) wood products (UNIDO 2012)), equally as suggested by the Dutch Disease model.

Forestry

The effect of forest rents on diversification is different than oil and gas. As explained earlier, the sustainability and commodity price heterogeneity might have the biggest role in this variance. Results show a significant positive effect of forest rents on overall sectoral employment diversification and exports. These results are also noted by Bhattacharyya and Collier (2014). Manufacturing employment and value added are significantly concentrated; this concentration mostly falls within sectors that are highly related to forestry and agriculture but classified individually in the UNIDO dataset (such as (1) food and beverages or (4) wearing apparel or (5) leather and footwear, or (6) wood products (UNIDO 2012)).

Heterogeneity Across Countries

Resource-rich countries differ in their dependence on natural resource rents, and other features are likely to influence the effect of resources, such as level of development and region. In this section, we test how this heterogeneity affects diversification.

Level of Development

We start by testing the diversification across developed and developing countries. Results show diversification coefficients in developed countries are barely affected by resource rents. There is a slightly significant negative effect on diversification in exports and value added, but no significant negative effect in employment either in full sample (ILO) or manufacturing (UNIDO). A possible explanation for this is that developed countries have a well-established manufacturing sector that would get affected in terms of exports share, but not in terms of manufacturing employment share as the resource sector is capital intensive and would not attract employment. Meanwhile, in developing countries, resource rents have a higher significant negative effect on export diversification, where exports get highly concentrated. Moreover, the results show a significantly negative effect on employment diversification in both sectoral and manufacturing employment. These findings show that manufactures are also exposed to get crowded out by resources, with a higher possibility in developing countries where manufacturing sectors are not highly developed, with less income and lower institutional quality, than developed countries.

Regions

We finally test the heterogeneity across regions, mainly by continents, in addition to the Middle East and North Africa (MENA) region. Across regions, significant diversification only happens in the MENA region, while employment in Asia, Europe and the Americas gets concentrated. However, results for manufacturing employment are different. Manufacturing employment gets more diversified in Africa with a high significant positive effect and more concentrated in the Americas. Asia, MENA and Europe manufacturing sectors have insignificant coefficients affected by resource rents. This might be explained by the fact that there are many resource countries located in the MENA region, and the resource effect is very high despite the small number of observations. Many of these countries have had resource rents (mainly oil and gas) for a long time before 1950, but most of them did not develop resilient manufacturing sectors and therefore we can see that manufacturing employment is insignificant. We find that sectoral employment in the MENA region is diversified between government jobs, a number of services sectors and other non-tradable sectors (such as (5) construction, or (6) wholesale, retail trade, restaurants and hotels, or (7) transport, storage and communication, or (8) financing, insurance, real estate and business services, or (9) community, social services and personal services). The value added figures are mostly matching the employment ones. When testing the effect of resource rents on exports, results indicate a high significant negative effect on export diversification. Across all regions tested, exports tend to get concentrated within the resource sector affected by resource rents, except for Asia, where exports get diversified slightly significantly.

A Brief on Economic Diversification in the GCC

Half of the world's oil production comes from the Middle East countries and particularly from the Gulf Cooperation Council (GCC), where economies are highly concentrated despite the efforts and advice to diversify and counter the high hydrocarbon dependency. The Gulf Cooperation Council countries include the Kingdom of Saudi Arabia, the state of Kuwait, the Kingdom of Bahrain, the United Arab Emirates (UAE), the Sultanate of Oman and the state of Qatar. These countries are part of the highest resource-dependent countries in the world. Our data shows that the share of resource rents to GDP in the GCC has ranged between 70 percent and almost 100 percent between 1975 and 2012 (depending on country-year data availability). Fossil fuels, mainly oil, are the main resources produced in the GCC region. Taking into consideration the high volatility that oil prices have been through in the last three decades, we can notice the long-term sustainability struggle and limited diversification this region has gone—and still going—through.

However, the countries vary in terms of diversification and resource dependency progress across the last three decades. The literature shows that the only GCC country that has gone through a relatively successful attempt of diversification is the UAE. According to Flamos et al. (2013), the UAE has been noted in the literature several times as a successful diversification example and in lowering the country's high dependency on oil exports and revenues. The UAE has managed to lower its resource rent to GDP share from 66 percent in 1979, when the first oil peak occurred, to less than 31 percent in 2007, the second oil peak. This occurred mainly due to the relative improvement in non-oil sectors as a result of Dubai's efforts toward economic diversification, particularly into tourism, finance and transport, serving as a regional trading hub.

Gelb (2011) has also noted Dubai's experience as one of the very few examples of developing countries that have built diversified economies from initial conditions of strong concentration in mineral sectors, in addition to Malaysia, Thailand, Chile, Indonesia and Sri Lanka. All these countries have diversified toward manufacturing, while Chile diversified its resource base to include new and more sophisticated products. According to Gelb, Dubai's strategy was to attract investments to invest in infrastructure, real property and a range of services, in addition to establishing a free zone to further build export capacity. And despite Dubai's high dependency on expatriate labor and skills, it managed to offer some lessons for other countries considering diversifying their economies through a massive free zone or similar policies. In order to do that, Dubai provided incentives to attract foreign direct investments and major multinational companies. These incentives included an efficient bureaucracy with little corruption, a regime of no taxes and low tariffs to attract international companies, a free market economy with low restrictions on movement of funds and transactions, high-tech infrastructure to sustain electronic-based system and e-government, public support and easy quick processes to issue visas to businessmen and visitors, allowing foreigners to own property in free zone areas and investing heavily in security. Very open trade and labor policy, a very low tax regime and a pegged exchange rate to the US dollar have made Dubai a relatively stable and low-cost base for business. Dubai nationals will still enjoy rent-based income, mostly from land and property rents and statutory participation in businesses usually run by expatriates.

Gelb (2011) summarizes the success factors from the mentioned examples in four main points: first, the importance of avoiding wild swings in the real exchange rate and periods of high overvaluations; second, the need to reduce costs for the non-resource sectors; third, the efforts to supplement market incentives; and, finally, the importance of openness to foreign investors, skills and new markets. In addition, Gelb concludes with some valuable policy recommendations in order to achieve a diversified economy, as sometimes good policies are not enough to reach that, like what happened in Botswana. Gelb's recommendations include first, the need to get some economy-wide "horizontal" basics right—good macroeconomic management is very critical; second, to build other types of capital to complement natural resource wealth; third, measures to bring down the costs of production in the new traded sectors; fourth, maintain flexibility, especially in dealing with foreign direct investments.

Looking into our data, we find that GCC countries are highly concentrated in exports, in employment and in value added. Concentration in exports is mainly driven by hydrocarbon fuels. But concentration in employment does not fall in oil sectors, as it is known to be capital intensive and does not hire a significant amount of labor. Despite its narrowness, we find that sectoral employment in the GCC region is diversified between government jobs, a number of service sectors and other non-tradable sectors. In more details, the UNIDO manufacturing data shows concentration in the manufacturing sectors as well, and that concentration mainly falls within two main categories:

- Sectors that are highly correlated with oil production, not necessarily extraction but related to the oil industry, such as "coke, refined petroleum products, nuclear fuels", or "chemicals and chemical products", or "non-metallic mineral products", or "basic metals".
- Sectors that produce locally consumed goods and fall within the non-tradable categories, but classified as part of the manufacturing, such as "food and beverages" or "wearing apparel" (UNIDO 2012).
- There is also a significant concentration in manufacturing value added, this concentration is found to be mostly within sectors that

are highly related to oil and gas but classified individually in the UNIDO dataset, or sectors that produce locally consumed goods and fall within the non-tradables as they do not show up in exports.

However, we do not see that the Dutch Disease model is applied in the GCC region, as GCC countries have had resource rents (mainly oil and gas) for a long time before 1950 (when the resource rent data began), but most of them did not develop resilient manufacturing sectors afterwards, and therefore, we can see that manufacturing employment is insignificant to the resource rent effect. The Dutch Disease effect, as described earlier, happens to economies with solid manufacturing sectors which gets affected negatively by the resource rents.

Conclusion

This chapter examines the effect of resource rents on diversification in exports, sectoral employment, manufacturing employment and value added. The resource rents in general have a significant negative effect on diversification; various levels of diversification occur in different economic sectors. The higher the resource rent share in a country's GDP, the less likely this country would go through the U-shaped path noted by Imbs and Wacziarg (2003). Alternatively, concentration increases rapidly through the development path.

However, there were some heterogeneous features among different country and natural resource groups. We find that there is a different effect between renewable and non-renewable natural resources on diversification. Non-renewable resources—examined by oil and gas—do not have significant effects on employment diversification, but they decrease export diversification, while renewable resources tend to increase export diversification and sectoral employment. We also look into different country groups; the effect of natural resources varies between developed and developing countries where manufacturing sectors are also diverse. Resource rents are likely to have a higher impact on diversification within developing countries, especially in employment where diversification gets decreased, but not affected in developed countries. However, in both country groups, resource rents decrease export diversification, indicating that manufacturing share in exports is affected in both groups, even when the manufacturing employment was not affected in the developed countries. Moreover, export diversification in all regions is significantly decreased. Manufacturing diversification is significantly decreased in the Americas and to a lesser extent in Asia, not affected in Europe and MENA but increased in Africa.

These results imply the Dutch Disease mechanism and are useful to policymakers in resource-rich countries who should be aware of how their labor market and exports are likely to be affected by the resource rents. Therefore, it would be very useful to test the institutional quality's impact on diversification, especially after having heterogeneous results between country groups.

Appendix: Data and Additional Tables and Figures

Employment Data

Sectoral employment data are from the International Labor Office and United Nations Industrial Development Organization (UNIDO 2012). ILO data covers 127 countries, while UNIDO covers 125 countries. The ILO data includes all economic activities at the 1-digit level between 1969 and 2008. Sectoral shares are in percentages. The unbalanced panel has 2369 observations (country-year). The ILO dataset reports employment in different classifications: some countries use the ISIC revision 2, others moved to ISIC revisions 3 and 4 in recent years, and some are using their own national classification. Employment data in the more disaggregated ISICrev3 and ISICrev4 were aggregated to ISICrev2, following Imbs and Wacziarg (2003), Timmer and Vries (2007) and McMillan and Rodrik (2011). If a country reports two revisions, the lower one is used. Official estimates are preferred over labor surveys. Data not following ISIC conventions are dropped. Table 2.1 shows the concordance between ISICrev3 and ISICrev2.

ILO data sometimes have sudden big changes in numbers in certain sectors, as countries sometimes change their calculation methods even if the same classification/revision is used. This is taken into consideration in this study, by dropping the observations that report these sudden changes making the panel more harmonized.

Our alternative data source is UNIDO, which covers manufacturing activities only at the 3-digit level of disaggregation (the main 23 industrial sectors) between 1963 and 2010 (INDSTAT2). (INDSTAT4 disaggregates

Table 2.1 Classifications between ISICrev2 and ISICrev3[a]

ISICrev2	*ISICrev3*
1. Agriculture, hunting, forestry and fishing	A. Agriculture, hunting and forestry B. Fishing
6. Wholesale and retail trade and restaurants and hotels	G. Wholesale and retail trade; repair of motor vehicles, motorcycles and personal and household goods H. Hotels and restaurants
8. Financing, insurance, real estate and business services	J. Financial intermediation K. Real estate, renting and business activities
9. Community, social and personal services	L. Public administration and defense; compulsory social security M. Education N. Health and social work O. Other community, social and personal service activities P. Households with employed persons

[a]McMillan and Rodrik (2011) and Timmer and Vries (2007)

to 4-digit level but only goes back to 1985.) The UNIDO dataset is consistent over the years and did not need adjustment. The unbalanced panel has 3564 employment observations (country-year).

Value Added and Labor Productivity

The UNIDO dataset also provides information on value added per sector, offering an additional measure of sector size and productivity in industrial employment. The value-added dataset covers almost the same period as the employment dataset, although some countries do not report the two sets equally. The unbalanced panel has 3465 value added observations (country-year).

Exports Data

Exports data are from the World Integrated Trade Solution (WITS), which is a collaboration between the World Bank and the United Nations Conference of Trade and Development. The export data covers 133 countries. Data is selected in SITC 1-digit aggregation containing the main ten trade sectors. Values are reported in constant US$1000 with base year

Table 2.2 Main differences between the chosen concentration measures

Index	*Distance concept*	*Decomposable?*	*Independence of input scale and population size?*	*Range in interval [0, 1]?*
Gini	Depends on rank ordering	No	Yes	Yes
Theil	Proportional	Yes	Yes	No
HHI	Absolute differences	Yes	No: decreases with population	Yes: but min > 0

Source: Cowell (2011)

2000. The unbalanced panel has 4575 observations (country-year). The WITS data values are consistent over the years and did not need any adjustment.

Diversification Indicators

Computing of these measures is done through Stata.[1]

We calculate diversity for all sectors and for all non-resource sectors. Specifically, in the ILO data, we exclude "mining and quarrying", and in the WITS exports data, we exclude "crude material, inedible, except fuels", "mineral fuels, lubricants and related materials" and "commodities not classified according to kind". The UNIDO data does not cover resource sectors at all.

Table 2.3 shows summary statistics for the diversification measures used in this study. Table 2.4 reports correlation between these measures, which is high. Figure 2.4 shows the historical performance of the diversification using the Gini index in all sectors examined.

Natural Resources Data

Several natural resources are used in this study: oil, gas, nickel, tin, copper, gold, iron, forest, coal, bauxite, silver, lead and phosphate. Resource rents are from the World Bank Wealth of Nations dataset and cover the period 1970–2008. Aggregate resource rent is calculated as the sum of all reported resources. The World Bank calculates resource rents as: Rents = Unit rent × production

Table 2.3 Summary statistics of sectoral concentration indices

Variable	*Obs.*	*Mean*	*Standard deviation (overall)*	*Standard deviation (between countries)*	*Standard deviation (within countries)*	*Min.*	*Max.*
ILO employment variables (all sectors)							
Gini	2369	0.5028	0.0787	0.0919	0.0374	0.2540	0.8329
Theil index	2369	0.4971	0.2230	0.2464	0.1360	0.1044	2.5860
HHI	2369	0.2273	0.0753	0.1004	0.0348	0.1562	0.9999
ILO employment variables (non-resource sectors)							
Gini	2369	0.4524	0.0877	0.1023	0.0413	0.2540	0.8132
Theil index	2369	0.4002	0.2094	0.2409	0.1175	0.1044	2.0630
HHI	2368	0.2307	0.0751	0.1011	0.0337	0.1590	0.8136
WITS export diversification variables (all sectors)							
Gini	4577	0.6531	0.1286	0.1168	0.0652	0.3132	0.9
Theil index	4576	0.9828	0.8018	0.6537	0.4968	0.1731	23.025
HHI	4554	0.3683	0.2059	0.1904	0.0950	0.1327	1
WITS export diversification variables (non-resource sectors)							
Gini	4575	0.6243	0.1139	0.0997	0.0658	0.3077	0.8888
Theil index	4574	0.8708	0.9329	0.6555	0.6931	0.1631	19.775
HHI	4558	0.3440	0.1590	0.1388	0.0901	0.1435	1
UNIDO manufacturing employment variables (employment)							
Gini	3564	0.5087	0.1086	0.1109	0.0435	0.2886	0.8823
Theil index	3564	0.5313	0.3302	0.4064	0.1397	0.1482	3.0334
HHI	3558	0.1345	0.0850	0.1016	0.0280	0.0612	0.8742
UNIDO manufacturing employment variables (value added)							
Gini	3465	0.6189	0.1151	0.1108	0.0470	0.3696	0.9321
Theil index	3465	1.1910	1.2741	1.164	0.7014	0.2352	18.045
HHI	2473	0.1370	0.0788	0.0791	0.0348	0	0.6234

(*continued*)

Table 2.3 (continued)

Variable	*Obs.*	*Mean*	*Standard deviation (overall)*	*Standard deviation (between countries)*	*Standard deviation (within countries)*	*Min.*	*Max.*
Independent variables							
Resource rents per capita	8202	3.04e + 08	1.72e + 09	1.35e + 09	1.18e + 09	0	3.92e + 10
GDP per capita	8160	10138.92	50980.34	18753.4	47841.88	132.825	4095673

Note: ILO data covers the years 1969–2008 (1-digit), the WITS data covers the years 1962–2012 (1-digit), and the UNIDO data covers the years 1963–2010 (3-digit). Resource rents per capita is calculated from resource rents (World Bank) and population (PWT 8.0). The main index used in this paper is Gini; however, the other indices are also used and report similar results, as the next table shows high correlation

Table 2.4 Correlation matrices of sectoral concentration indices

	Gini	*Theil index*	*HHI*
ILO employment variables (all sectors)			
Gini	1.000		
Theil index	0.897	1.000	
HHI	0.906	0.853	1.000
ILO employment variables (non-resource sectors)			
Gini	1.000		
Theil index	0.932	1.000	
HHI	0.926	0.917	1.000
WITS export\ diversification variables (all sectors)			
Gini	1.000		
Theil index	0.741	1.000	
HHI	0.897	0.802	1.000
WITS export diversification variables (non-resource sectors)			
Gini	1.000		
Theil index	0.677	1.000	
HHI	0.894	0.745	1.000
UNIDO manufacturing employment variables (employment figures)			
Gini	1.000		
Theil index	0.906	1.000	
HHI	0.727	0.803	1.000
UNIDO manufacturing employment variables (value added)			
Gini	1.000		
Theil index	0.678	1.000	
HHI	0.863	0.781	1.000

Unit rent = unit price − unit cost
All rents are reported in current US dollars.

The measure for resource rents used in this study is the log of resource rents per capita. Resource rents are available for a wide panel of countries for a long period of time, allowing testing long-term effects on diversification and minimizing the risk of sample selection bias. Normalization by population size, taken from the Penn World Tables, avoids a bias toward large countries. Several resources are aggregated, using data constructed using the same methodology, allowing us to examine the effect of different resource rents on diversification at the same time. This measure has been used by several recent studies (Ross 2006; Bhattacharyya and Collier 2011).

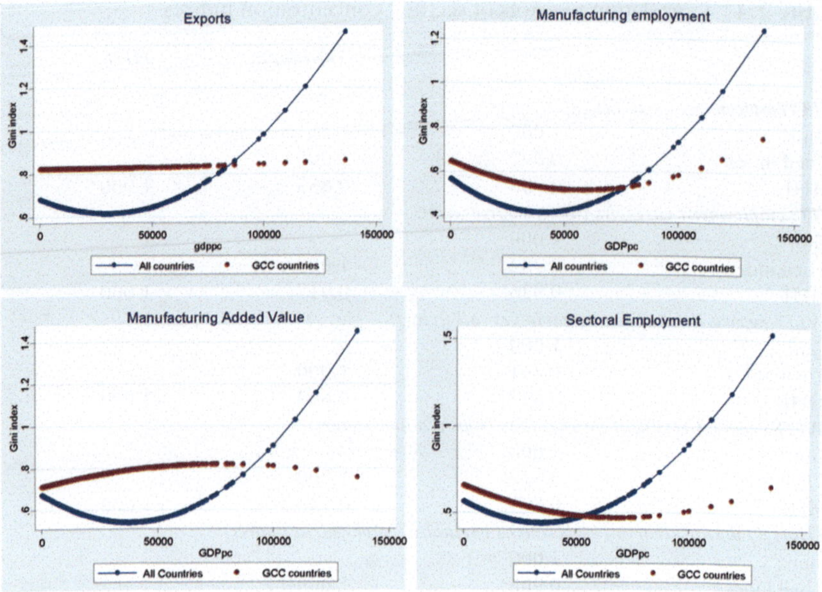

Fig. 2.4 Gini indices against GDP per capita and the share of resource rents in the GCC countries. Note: Data sources: ILO (2012), WITS (2013) and UNIDO (2012). The graphs show that diversification path takes a U-shaped curve in all countries as shown previously by Imbs and Wacziarg (2003). The red line represents the diversification path in the GCC countries along the development measured by growth in GDP per capita. The graphs show a different trend in the GCC countries, as concentration begins high and remains high despite income increases, especially in the case of exports. The UNIDO manufacturing employment and value added data show a high concentration as well, but the ILO sectoral employment data is not quite specific due to the small number of available figures

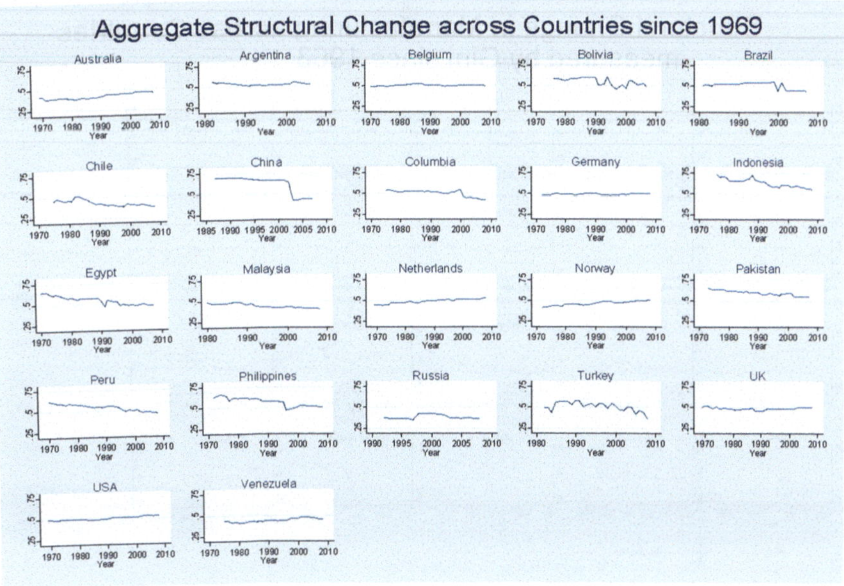

Fig. 2.5 Diversification in selected countries. Note: Aggregate structural change (or internal diversification) here is measured by Gini coefficient for the inequality of sector shares in employment. Higher Gini implies diversification concentration and vice versa. Aggregate implies that the figure includes both resource and non-resource sectors. The data is sourced from ILO

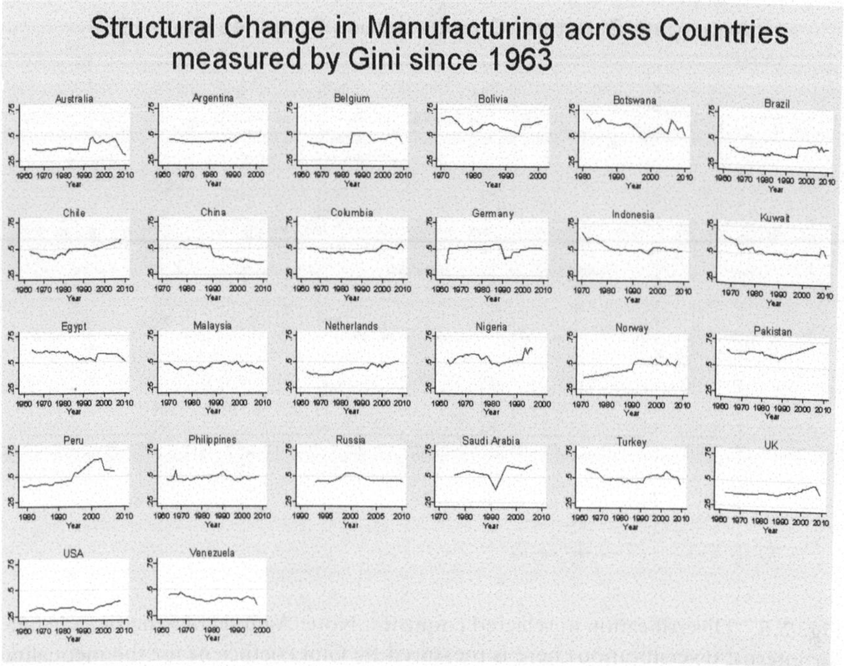

Structural change (or internal diversification) within manufacturing here is measured by Gini coefficient for the inequality of sector shares in employment. Higher Gini implies concentration and vice versa. The data is sourced from UNIDO

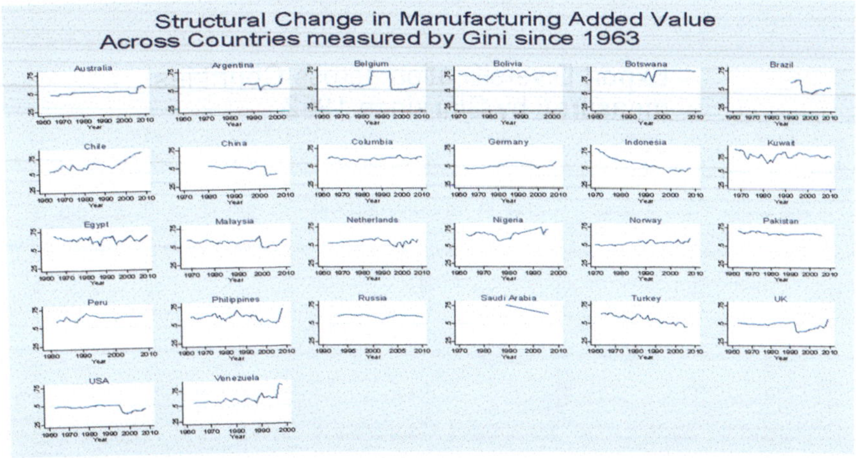

Structural change (or internal diversification) in manufacturing here is measured by Gini coefficient for the inequality of sector shares in value added. Higher Gini implies concentration and vice versa. The data is sourced from UNIDO

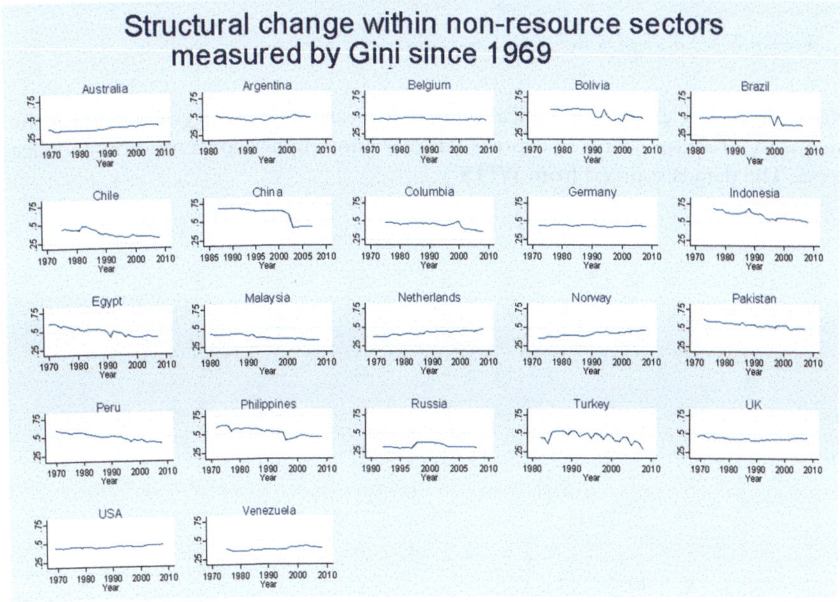

Structural change (or internal diversification) within non-resource sectors here is measured by Gini coefficient for the inequality of sector shares in employment. Higher Gini implies concentration and vice versa. The data is sourced from ILO

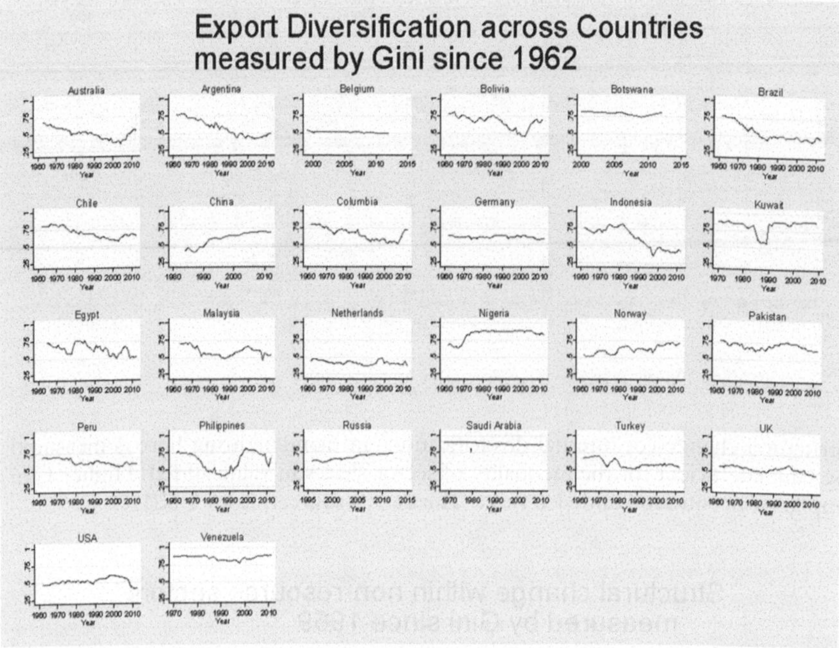

Note: Aggregate export diversification here is measured by Gini coefficient for the inequality of sector shares in exports. Higher Gini implies concentration and vice versa. The data is sourced from WITS

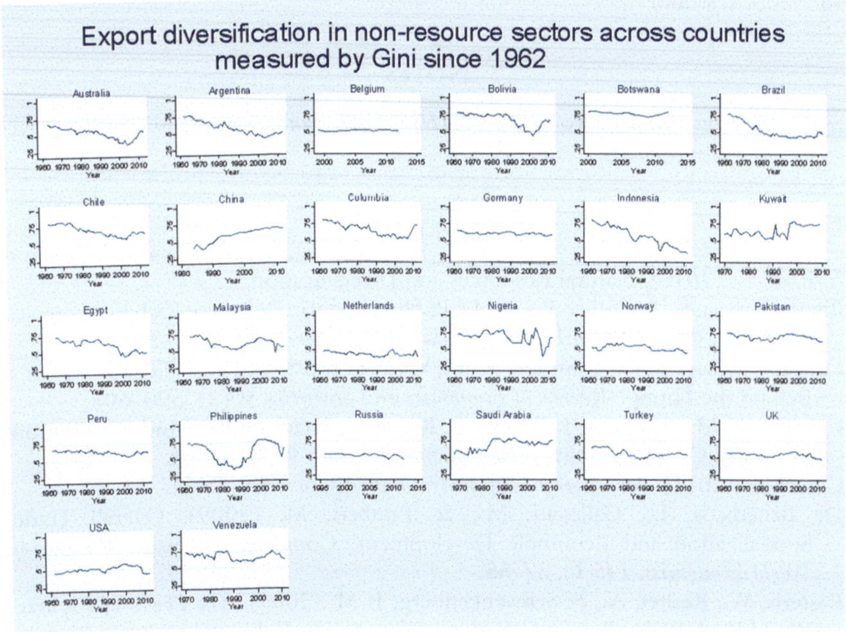

Note: Export diversification in the non-resource sector here is measured by Gini coefficient for the inequality of sector shares in exports. Higher Gini implies concentration and vice versa. The data is sourced from WITS

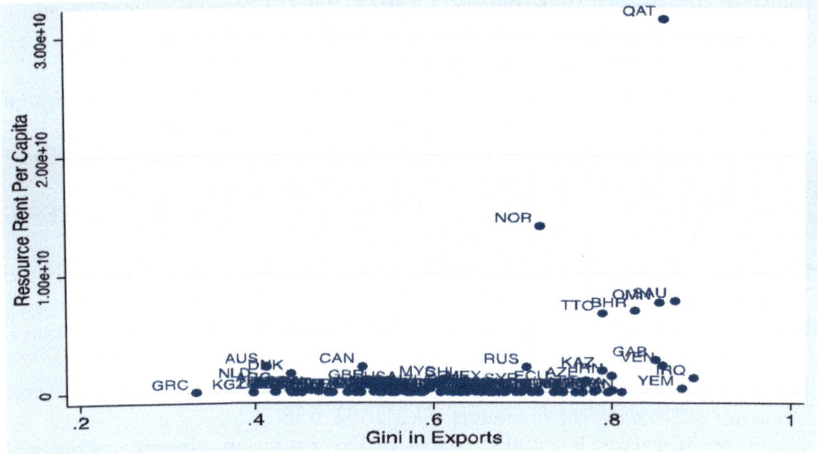

Fig. 2.6 Export diversification and resource rents per capita across countries. Note: Countries with higher resource rents per capita also have the highest concentration (Gini) in exports

Notes

1. Azevedo, João Pedro (2007) *AINEQUAL: Stata module to compute measures of inequality.*

References

Alsharif, N. (2015). Natural Resources and Diversification.

Bhattacharyya, S., & Collier, P. (2014). Public Capital in Resource Rich Economies: Is There a Curse? *Oxford Economic Papers-New Series, 66*(1), 1–24.

Cadot, O., Carrère, C., & Strauss-Kahn, V. (2011). Export Diversification: What's Behind the Hump? *Review of Economics and Statistics, 93*(2), 590–605.

Corden, W. M., & Neary, J. P. (1982). Booming Sector and De-Industrialisation in a Small Open Economy. *The Economic Journal, 92*, 825–848.

Cowell, F. (2011). *Measuring Inequality*: Oxford University Press.

De Benedictis, L., Gallegati, M., & Tamberi, M. (2009). Overall Trade Specialization and Economic Development: Countries Diversify. *Review of World Economics, 145*(1), 37–55.

Easterly, W., Reshef, A., & Schwenkenberg, J. M. (2009). *The Power of Exports.* World Bank Policy Research Working Paper Series, Vol.

Elbadawi, I., & Gelb, A. (2010). *Oil, Economic Diversification and Development in the Arab World.* Paper presented at the Economic Research Forum Policy Research Report.

Esanov, A. (2012). *Economic Diversification: Dynamics, Determinants and Policy Implications.* Revenue Watch Institute.

Flamos, A., Roupas, C. V., & Psarras, J. (2013). GCC Economies Diversification: Still a Myth? *Energy Sources, Part B: Economics, Planning, and Policy, 8*(4), 360–368. doi:10.1080/15567240903515000.

Gelb, A. (2011). Economic Diversification in Resource Rich Countries. In *Beyond the Curse: Policies to Harness the Power of Natural Resources* (pp. 55–80).

Gelb, A., & Grasmann, S. (2010). *How Should Oil Exporters Spend Their Rents?* Center for Global Development Working Paper No 221.

Gylfason, T. (2011). *Natural Resource Endowment: A Mixed Blessing?* CESifo Working Paper: Resources and Environment Economics No 3353.

Harding, T., & Venables, A. J. (2013). The Implications of Natural Resource Exports for Non-resource Trade.

Harding, T., & Venables, A. (2016). The Implications of Natural Resource Exports for Nonresource Trade. *IMF Economic Review, 64*(2), 268–302.

Hausmann, R., & Rodrik, D. (2003). Economic Development as Self-Discovery. *Journal of Development Economics, 72*(2), 603–633.

Imbs, J., & Wacziarg, R. (2003). Stages of Diversification. *American Economic Review, 93*, 63–86.

International Labour Office. (2012). *Yearbook of Labour Statistics*. Geneva: International Labour Office Press.

Ismail, K., & Arezki, R. (2010). *Boom-Bust Cycle, Asymmetrical Fiscal Response and the Dutch Disease*. International Monetary Fund.

Koren, M., & Tenreyro, S. (2007). Volatility and Development. *The Quarterly Journal of Economics*, 243–287.

Krugman, P. (1987). The Narrow Moving Band, the Dutch Disease, and the Competitive Consequences of Mrs. Thatcher: Notes on Trade in the Presence of Dynamic Scale Economies. *Journal of Development Economics, 27*(1), 41–55.

Lederman, D., & Maloney, W. F. (2003). *Trade Structure and Growth*. World Bank Policy Research Working Paper No 3025.

McMillan, M. S., & Rodrik, D. (2011). Globalization, Structural Change and Productivity Growth: National Bureau of Economic Research.

Moore, W., & Walkes, C. (2010). Does Industrial Concentration Impact on the Relationship Between Policies and Volatility? *International Review of Applied Economics, 24*(2), 179–202.

Papageorgiou, C., & Spatafora, M. N. (2012). *Economic Diversification in LICs: Stylized Facts and Macroeconomic Implications*. International Monetary Fund.

Ross, M. L. (2001). Does Oil Hinder Democracy? *World Politics, 53*(03), 325–361.

Sachs, J. D., & Warner, A. M. (1995). Natural Resource Abundance and Economic Growth: National Bureau of Economic Research.

Sachs, J. D., & Warner, A. M. (2001). The Curse of Natural Resources. *European Economic Review, 45*(4), 827–838.

Sala-i-Martin, X., & Subramanian, A. (2003). Addressing the Natural Resource Curse: An Illustration from Nigeria: National Bureau of Economic Research.

Stokey, N. L. (1988). Learning by Doing and the Introduction of New Goods. *The Journal of Political Economy, 96*, 701–717.

Tornell, A., & Lane, P. R. (1999). The Voracity Effect. *American Economic Review, 89*, 22–46.

United Nations Industrial Development Organization. (2012). *Database on Industrial Statistics*. Vienna: United Nations Industrial Development Organization.

van der Ploeg, F., & Venables, A. J. (2012). Natural Resource Wealth: The Challenge of Managing a Windfall. *Annual Review of Economics*, 4, 4, 315-+.

WITS. (2013). *United Nations COMTRADE Database*. World Integrated Trade Solution.

CHAPTER 3

Oil Resources and Diversification in a Small Open Economy: The Case of Oman

Said Al Saqri

Introduction

For more than 45 years, growth and income generation in Oman has been driven mainly by the oil sector. Oman gross domestic product (GDP) grew at an annual rate of about 6 per cent in 1969–2013, rising from US$5882 million in 1969 to US$45,304 million in 2013 (at constant 2005 prices), and per capita income grew at 2 per cent a year, rising from US$5882 to US$12,472, during the same period.

Despite the volatility nature of the oil income and the uncertainty surrounding the level and size of oil resources, the economy continues to grow. In fact, the government expected that oil production would start to decline by 1977. During the preparation of the first Five-Year Development Plan (1976–1980), policymakers, expected that by 1977, oil production would decline gradually and that by 1987, Oman would have used most of its oil resources, and therefore, it is important to diversify the source of income away from oil by investing in other sectors of

S. Al Saqri (✉)
Oman Economic Association, Muscat, Oman

A. Mishrif, Y. Al Balushi (eds.), *Economic Diversification in the Gulf Region, Volume II*, The Political Economy of the Middle East,
DOI 10.1007/978-981-10-5786-1_3

the economy such as manufacturing, services, agriculture, and fisheries (Development Council 1976, p. 14).

During the fifth Five-Year Development Plan (1996–2000), a vision for Oman's economic future was prepared. The vision was called *Oman Economic Vision: Oman 2020*. The vision was seen as an important step for Oman's future in order to evaluate past policies that focused on developing the basic infrastructure to induce diversification away from oil resources extraction activities and examine non-oil sector output dependence on government expenditure. In addition, the vision was seen as an important way to steer efforts and energies towards a more diversified productive base.

The Vision stated four major goals to be achieved by 2020: first, to diversify the sources of income away from oil dependence and attain sustainable development; second, to balance government expenditures and revenues; third, to develop human resource through education and health provision and maintaining the current standard of living and double the per capita income by 2020; fourth, to develop the private sector so that it leads economic growth.

This chapter aims to examine the diversification efforts in Oman away from oil dependence and the impact of oil income on output. It is our hope that the chapter will be an important contribution to the discussion of how Oman can diversify its sources of income away from oil income dependence.

Literature Review

What is economic diversification? How to measure economic diversification? Literature that investigates the role of natural resources in economic growth and development differs in defining what diversification is and the way diversification should be measured. The Development Council in Oman defines diversification as the ability to depend less on oil income and increase the output of other sectors of the economy. The Development Council stated, "Since oil is the main source of Oman's national income, the decline of oil revenues will inevitably be reflected in reductions in the gross national product unless measures are taken in the Development Plan to increase the value added in other sectors of the economy" (1976, p. 14).

Some researchers define diversification as the independence of an economy from revenues originating from export income. For example, Luke (1983), examining the role of oil companies in the economic development of the Arab OPEC countries, defined independence to mean economic industrialisation and independence of resource producers from industrial countries. Luke argued that, although the economies of the Arab OPEC countries experienced economic growth and increased standard of living because of increased export revenues, they have not experienced any significant economic diversification in the form of technological transfer and industrialization.

Other researchers define economic diversification from the point view of the percentage contribution of natural resource activities to GDP, share of natural resource exports to total exports, and the share of natural resource revenue to total government revenue. Hence, the higher the share contribution of natural resources in the economy's GDP, export share, and government income, the less diversified the economy is, while lower ratios suggest a more diversified economy. Askari (1990) used the share size of natural resources exports to GDP, ratio of natural resource exports to total exports, and the ratio of natural resource revenue to total revenue to measure the level of the economic diversification of the Saudi economy. Sachs and Warner (1995) used a similar method, by suggesting that resource dependent economies as those with a high value of resource-based exports to GDP, and hence the higher the ratio, the less diversified the economy is.

Following the poor economic growth of several resource-rich economies since the 1980s, researchers have also been defining diversification to mean strong economic performance, and that poor economic performance and GDP growth is an indication of reliance on natural resources and lack of a healthy productive base. For example, Limi (2006) argued that Botswana's strong GDP growth of 7.8 per cent during the years 1980–2006 is evidence of the country's success in diversifying its economy and decreasing its dependence on natural resources. Besides strong economic performance, Rosser (2004) used the share of non-natural resource exports, government revenues from non-natural resources, poverty reduction, and human development index indicators to show how Indonesia has successfully diversified its sources of income and reduced its dependence on natural resources.

Al-Saqri and Abdullahi (2010) investigated the inter-sectoral linkages between the oil and non-oil sectors in Oman and argued that the economy is not diversified because of the strong interdependency to natural resource activities, and the non-resource sectors have weak or poor linkages in the economy. Therefore, in their opinion, strong sectoral interdependency to natural resource activities implies poor diversification in the part of the economy.

In summary, diversification means less dependence on natural resource activities, and natural resources play a minor role in economic output and export income. In addition, diversification means strong economic growth. Notwithstanding, an important aspect of diversification is sustainability or the ability to sustain the levels of income and economic growth in the absence of natural resource. This lack of a self-sustaining productive base threatens the economies of resource-dependent nations when income falls or when resources are exhausted. We believe that the method of estimating the size of natural resource income or the linkage between the resource and the non-resource sectors does not answer satisfactorily an important dimension of diversification and that is, can the economy sustain its level of income and economic growth in the absence of natural resource income?

Similar to Al-Saqri (2010) and Al-Saqri and Abdullahi (2012), we suggest an alternative method of estimating diversification or independence from natural resource income and hence the ability of the economy to sustain its level of income and growth by investigating the sources of economic growth in the economy. Understanding factor inputs contributing to output growth will show how well diversified the productive sector of the economy is. If GDP growth has been mainly the result of employing more labour and capital resulting from oil income, then reduced oil income could have a negative impact on output growth. In such a case, it would be difficult to employ more labour and increase capital stock, so growth could stagnate and the whole question of sustaining income levels and GDP growth would be in peril.

However, if growth has been mainly the function of technological progress, then the absence of oil income would have less impact on GDP growth. Growth led by TFP may suggest increasing efficiency in the use of factor inputs and indicate that output is much more diversified and the economy is less dependent on oil income and that government's Five-Year Development Plans are successful, and the 45 years of oil investment are bearing fruits and becoming productive yet not dependent on oil sector activities. This can be achieved by investigating factor inputs and their contribution to GDP growth.

Objectives of the Study

The overall objective of this chapter is to examine Oman efforts to diversify its economy utilizing oil income. The chapter will try to answer the following major questiones: What are the factors contributing to GDP growth? What is the role of technology in the oil and non-oil sector growth? Can the economy sustain its income level and GDP growth in the absence of oil income? This will be done by estimating the total factor productivity of the Omani economy (TFP) of the oil sector and the non-oil sector. This is very important for several reasons. First, such analysis is important to understand the contributing factors to GDP growth and how they have changed throughout the past 45 years of the oil era. Second, it shows the role of technology in the oil and non-oil sector growth and how efficient economic agents have been in using factor inputs for the oil sector and the non-oil sector. Third, TFP analysis shows if non-oil growth in Oman was simply an accumulation of capital and labour, or whether it was also the result of technological progress. Fourth, a positive TFP development for the non-oil sector would also suggest that the productive structure could sustain GDP growth in the eventual exhaustion of oil resources.

In our opinion, this investigation is also relevant to the recent oil price fall since mid-2014 and its implication on the economic performance of GCC countries that could experience negative growth and large fiscal and current account deficits as a result of the recent oil price drops. Finally, yet importantly, although researchers have recognized the importance of oil resources in the growth of oil-dependent countries, there is little specific discussion on the indirect dependency, and the question of sustainability is, by and large, ignored most of the time by researchers.

Data and Methodology

The time series data used in this chapter was taken from several sets of data. The research used data gathered from World Bank's World Development Indicators, Oman's Statistical Year Books, and Penn World Tables. The time series covers 1969–2013. GDP data was deflated to constant 2005 prices. Gross capital stock was estimated from the Penn World Tables (Mark 8.0). Labour data were sourced from the Oman Statistical Year Books and Penn World Tables (Mark 8.0).

We divided the economy into oil and non-oil sector and estimated capital, labour, and technology coefficients, using the standard Cobb–Douglas (1928) production function $Y_t = A_t F(K_t L_t)$, where Y, K, L are output (GDP), capital, and labour, respectively, and A is the technology variable. First, we ran the log linear production function to estimate labour and capital coefficients and time trend (t) that captures technological change in Oman for the period 1969–2013. We then calculated the actual shares of capital and labour to income to estimate the sources of GDP growth in the economy. We did that by first specifying the marginal product and estimated capital and labour shares to output, and then measuring labour and capital inputs. Finally, we estimated TFP using the log linear neoclassical production function and solved for TFP.

Estimation of Variables

Capital, Labour Contribution to GDP

First, we used the following regression to estimate the relationship between GDP (dependent variable) and capital and labour variables (independent variables):

$$LnGDP_t = \beta_1 LnK_t + \beta_2 LnL_t + \beta_3 t + \varepsilon_t \tag{3.1}$$

We report three regression results: GDP Eq. (3.2), oil GDP Eq. (3.3), and non-oil GDP Eq. (3.3) and Table 3.1a–c, respectively. All explanatory variables are statistically significant. Furthermore, the cumulative sum (CUSUM) diagnostic tests and cumulative sum of squares (CUSUMsq) tests of parameter stability indicate that our model is stable and correctly specified.

GDP

$$\begin{aligned} LGDP_t = {} & \underset{(0.10)}{0.76LnK_t} + \underset{(0.17)}{0.44LnL_t} - \underset{(0.00)}{0.02t}, \text{ser} = 0.11, \text{R}^2 = 0.98 \end{aligned} \tag{3.2}$$

Oil GDP

$$\begin{aligned} LoGDP_t = {} & \underset{(0.01)}{0.06LoK_t} + \underset{(0.01)}{0.01LoL_t} - \underset{(0.09)}{0.00t}, \text{ser} = 0.00, \text{R}^2 = 0.98 \end{aligned} \tag{3.3}$$

Table 3.1 (**a**) GDP and factor inputs, 1969–2013. (**b**) Oil GDP and factor inputs, 1969–2013. (**c**) Non-oil GDP and factor inputs, 1969–2013

Variable	*Coefficient*	*Std. error*	*t-Statistics*	*Prob.*
(**a**) GDP and factor inputs, 1969–2013				
LK	0.761145	0.095474	7.972272	0.0000
LLABOR	0.438925	0.173377	2.531627	0.0154
@TREND	−0.024359	0.003728	−6.534764	0.0000
AR(1)	0.582851	0.134835	4.322711	0.0001
R-squared	0.984605			
Adjusted R-squared	0.983451			
S.E. of regression	0.111964			
Sum squared resid	0.501436			
Durbin-Watson stat	1.969745			
(**b**) Oil GDP and factor inputs, 1969–2013				
LOK	0.061479	0.006292	9.771682	0.0000
LOLBR	0.005680	0.014506	0.391568	0.6975
@TREND	−0.002544	0.092929	−0.027378	0.9783
AR(1)	0.999709	0.055225	18.10261	0.0000
R-squared	0.978291			
Adjusted R-squared	0.976663			
S.E. of regression	0.005233			
Sum squared resid	0.001096			
Durbin-Watson stat	1.861810			
(**c**) Non-oil GDP and factor inputs, 1969–2013				
LNOK	0.606905	0.103000	5.892291	0.0000
LNOLBR	0.698243	0.183559	3.803908	0.0005
@TREND	−0.019913	0.004679	−4.256346	0.0001
AR(1)	0.693056	0.135711	5.106840	0.0000
R-squared	0.990893			
Adjusted R-squared	0.990210			
S.E. of regression	0.096899			
Sum squared resid	0.375575			
Durbin-Watson stat	1.976873			

Non-oil GDP

$$\underset{}{LnoGDP_t} = \underset{(0.10)}{0.61LnoK_t} + \underset{(0.18)}{0.70LnoL_t} - \underset{(0.00)}{0.02t}, \text{ser} = 0.10, \mathrm{R}^2 = 0.99 \tag{3.4}$$

The results of three regressions show different things. The overall output of the economy in regression (3.2) indicates that capital and labour exhibit increasing returns to scale, suggesting a “catch-up growth” scenario, where capital and labour accumulation drove growth while trend t was negative; the results are similar to the findings of Al-Saqri and Abdullahi (2012). The regression suggests that 1 per cent change in capital results in 0.76 per cent in GDP and that 1 per cent change in labour results in 0.44 per cent in GDP. This result emphasizes the view that growth in Oman is a function of capital accumulation and labour employment rather than innovation and efficient utilization of resources. In addition, the sum of coefficients of capital and labour was more than 1, suggesting an increase in returns to economies of scale.

As for regression (3.3), the results show that 1 per cent change in capital results in 0.06 per cent in oil GDP and that 1 per cent change in labour results in 0.01 per cent in oil GDP, and although the probability results for oil labour variable and the trend are not significant, the t-statistics is significant and the overall model is significant. This result suggests several things. First, capital and labour play a minor role in oil GDP output. Second, the sector is capital-intensive; hence a 1 per cent change in labour results in just 0.01 per cent in oil GDP. Last but not least, this method of estimating oil GDP may be not the best since it is influenced heavily by oil price change.

Non-oil GDP results (in regression (3.4)) show that 1 per cent change in capital results in 0.60 per cent change in non-oil GDP, and 1 per cent change in labour results in 0.70 per cent change in non-oil GDP. This shows that non-oil GDP is influenced by capital and labour change. In addition, such a close association emphasizes regression (3.2) results—that is, output growth in Oman is the result of increasing capital and labour rather than innovation and efficient utilization of resources. In other words, non-oil GDP growth is dependent on capital and labour variables, and these two variables are dependent, in return, on oil income.

Capital, Labour, and TFP Coefficients: Calculating Actual Coefficients

Using the Cobb–Douglas production function and following Mankiw (2002), we first specify the marginal product of labour and capital, respectively, as:

$$MPL = (1-\alpha)Y / L \tag{3.5}$$

$$MPK = \alpha Y / K \tag{3.6}$$

where *Y, K, L* are output, capital, and labour, respectively.

Equation (3.5) states that the marginal product of labour (MPL) is proportional to output per worker, and Eq. (3.6) states that the marginal product of capital (MPK) is proportional to output per unit of capital. We calculated capital and labour shares to output, or $MPL \times L$, in Oman for 1969–2014.

Figure 3.1 shows the ratio of labour to total income in Oman over the period 1969–2013. On average, the labour share of output is about 0.3, and using constant returns to scale (CRT), capital's share of output, therefore, should be 0.7. This result is close to the regression result we obtained earlier in Eq. (3.2).

Second, we specified the Cobb–Douglas production function as follows:

$$Y_t = A_t F(K_t L_t) \tag{3.7}$$

where *Y, K, L* are output (GDP), capital, and labour, respectively, and A is the TFP. Differentiating the production function with respect to time and decomposing the model to estimate the growth rates of the production function into sources of growth, we obtain the following:

$$\frac{\dot{Y}}{Y} = \frac{\dot{A}}{A} + \frac{mpkK}{Y}\frac{\dot{K}}{K} + \frac{mplL}{L}\frac{\dot{L}}{L} \tag{3.8}$$

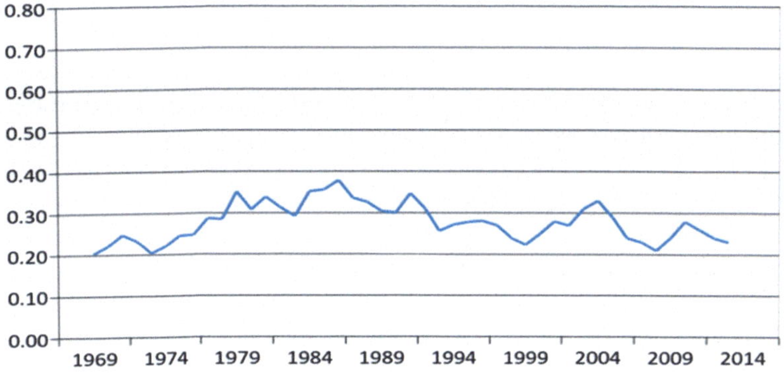

Fig. 3.1 Ratio of labour income to total income, 1969–2013. Source: Oman Statistical Year Book and Penn World Tables (Mark 8.0)

where *mpk* and *mpl* are the marginal product of capital and labour, respectively, under the assumption of competitive factor markets, constant returns to scale, and technological progress. Then, $mpkK/Y$ and $mplL/Y$ are the shares of compensation to capital (αk) and labour (αl) in total output, respectively.

Assuming constant returns to scale, the growth rate of the economic output is decomposed into TFP growth and the weighted sum of the growth of capital and labour. This can be expressed as:

$$\frac{\dot{Y}}{Y} = \frac{\dot{A}}{A} + \alpha \frac{\dot{K}}{K} + (1 - \alpha)\frac{\dot{L}}{L} \tag{3.9}$$

Rearranging Eq. (3.9) and solving for TFP, we obtained the following:

$$TFP = \frac{\dot{A}}{A} = \frac{\dot{Y}}{Y} + \alpha \frac{\dot{K}}{K} + (1 - \alpha)\frac{\dot{L}}{L} \tag{3.10}$$

Measures of Factor Inputs (Labour)

There are three methods used to estimate labour input. The first method uses the number of hours worked, and the second method uses the number of workers in an economy; see Aiyar and Dalgaard (2005). The third method, also called human capital, uses either the first or the second method adjusted to the number of schooling years completed by the population. This latter method is used because of the positive impact of education on worker quality and/or efficiency (Maudos et al. 1999). For this exercise, we used time series data on the number of people working in Oman.

Measures of Factor Inputs (Capital)

There are two main methods of estimating capital stock, a "direct method" from stock survey results, or an "indirect method" using yearly investment data from the national accounts. The indirect method of estimating capital stock in turn uses two alternative methods. The first method is called the benchmark-year method, and it estimates capital stock by direct observation, through surveys, for a benchmark-year. The second indirect method uses a discounted accumulated value of historical investments up to a benchmark-year, and it is called the perpetual inventory method (Albala-Bertrand 2001). We use the perpetual inventory method to calculate Oman's capital stock. Following Khan (2005) and Ahmed and Suardi (2007), the method is as follows:

$$K_t = (1-\delta)K_{t-1} + I_t \tag{3.11}$$

where K is the capital stock, I is the value of investment, and δ is the rate of depreciation.

The series of capital stock from an initial $K(0)$ is the initial capital stock plus the weighted sum of past investments, adjusted for depreciation. This can be expressed as:

$$K_t = (1-\delta)^i K(0) + \sum_{i=0}^{t-1} I_{t-i}(1-\delta)^i \tag{3.12}$$

The initial capital stock is estimated as follows:

$$K_0 = \frac{I_0}{(g+\delta)} \tag{3.13}$$

where g is GDP growth. The depreciation rate is subjective, and researchers use a rate between 4 per cent and 10 per cent. We have chosen an average of 7 per cent.

The neoclassical growth model shows that GDP will grow by the accumulation of labour and capital until the marginal return to capital is equal to the marginal return on labour. However, to achieve sustainable growth, technology, knowledge, and skills must be increased. More specifically, the TFP contribution to GDP, also known in the literature as "Solow residual," must increase and lead GDP growth. Using the production function to estimate Oman's TFP, we use the log linear function of the production function and solve for TFP as follows:

$$LnTFP_t = LnY_t - (\alpha)LnK_t - (1-\alpha)LnL_t \tag{3.14}$$

TFP Test Results

Following the specification of Eq. (3.14), the results show that, on average, the capital contribution to GDP growth in the period 1970–2013 was 161 per cent and that of labour was 29 per cent, but that the TFP contribution to output growth was –91 per cent (see Table 3.2a). In addition, the results show that, on average, the capital contribution to oil GDP growth in the period 1970–2013 was 76.68 per cent and that of labour was 23.16 per cent; thus, the TFP contribution to output growth was +00.16 per cent (see Table 3.2b). Furthermore, the results show that, on average, the capital contribution to non-oil GDP growth in the period 1970–2013 was 89 per cent and that of labour was 18 per cent, but that the TFP contribution to output growth was –6 per cent (see Table 3.2c).

Our results (in Table 3.2a and Fig. 3.2) are similar to Al-Saqri and Abdullahi (2012). According to them, Oman had –65 per cent. Moreover, Makdisi et al. (2000)found similar results for the Middle East and North Africa (MENA) region. According to those authors, with the exception of Egypt, Morocco, Tunisia, and Turkey, all MENA countries included in their sample had negative TFP growth. Elhiraika and Hamad (2001) also found that the TFP of the United Arab Emirates (UAE) was negative. Nevertheless, we decomposed the GDP of Oman to oil GDP and non-oil GDP. TFP results for non-oil GDP suggest that non-oil GDP growth for Oman has just been mainly a function of capital and labour accumulation. However, TFP results for oil GDP show evidence of efficient use of factor

Table 3.2 (**a**) GDP growth and the production function, 1970–2013. (**b**) Oil GDP growth and the production function, 1970–2013. (**c**) Non-oil GDP growth and the production function, 1970–2013

	ΔlnY	ΔlnK	ΔlnL	$\alpha\Delta lnK$	$(1-\alpha)\Delta lnL$	$\Delta lnTFP$
(**a**) GDP growth and production function, 1970–2013						
Average	0.06	0.14	0.05	0.09	0.02	−0.05
Factor input contribution to growth				*161*	*29*	*−91*
(**b**) Oil GDP growth and production function, 1970–2013						
Average	0.09	0.10	0.06	0.067	0.020	0.000
Factor input contribution to growth				*77*	*23*	*16*
(**c**) Non-oil GDP growth and production function, 1970–2013						
Average	0.10	0.13	0.05	0.09	0.02	−0.01
Factor input contribution to growth				*89*	*18*	*−6*

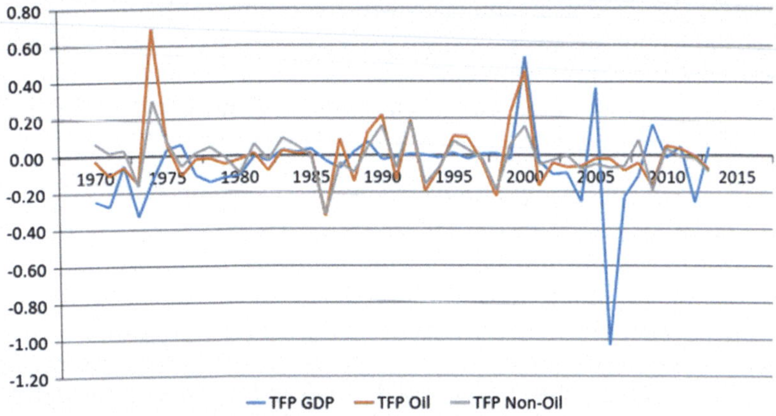

Fig. 3.2 TFP trend, 1970–2013

inputs and that oil GDP growth for Oman has not just been mainly a function of capital and labour accumulation but also technological progress.

Conclusions and Implications

This chapter investigated Oman economic diversification and tried to assess how sustainable income and GDP growth by asking three major questions:

1. What are the factors contributing to GDP growth?
2. What is the role of technology in the oil sector and non-oil sector growth?
3. Can the economy sustain its income level and GDP growth in the absence of oil income?

The overall results suggest that GDP growth is driven mainly by capital accumulation and labour employment rather than by innovation and efficient utilization of resources. The initial regression (regression (3.2)) estimation indicated that 1 per cent change in capital results in 0.76 per cent in GDP, and that 1 per cent change in labour results in 0.44 per cent in GDP. Moreover, although capital and labour play a minor role in oil GDP output (in regression (3.3)), non-oil GDP (in regression (3.4)) results emphasize the view that output growth has been mainly the function of capital and labour variables.

Secondly, the results from our analysis of factor inputs contributing to GDP growth show that TFP contribution to growth in the period 1970–2013 was –91 per cent for GDP and –6 per cent for non-oil GDP (see Table 3.2a and 3.2c). Notwithstanding, the TFP contribution to output growth for oil GDP was +00.16 per cent (see Table 3.2b). This result for oil GDP gives evidence of efficient use of factor inputs and that oil GDP growth has not just been mainly a function of capital and labour accumulation but also technological progress.

In conclusion, Oman needs to have a long-term strategy that will drive and sustain economic growth beyond oil. To sustain growth technology, knowledge and skills must be increased. This can be achieved through better education and training. In addition, policymakers must look into structural reforms, including policy and institutional reforms that will liberalize trade, encourage foreign investment, and make the business environment more transparent and business friendly. The trade policy might be geared towards encouraging the import of capital goods instead of consumer goods that would not add value to output.

References

Ahmed, A. D., & Suardi, S. (2007). Sources of Economic Growth and Technology Transfer in Sub-Saharan Africa. *South African Journal of Economics, 75*(2), 159–178.

Aiyar, S., & Dalgaard, C.-J. (2005). *Total Factor Productivity Revisited: A Dual Approach to Development Accounting*. Washington, DC: International Monetary Fund.

Albala-Bertrand, J. M. (2001). *A Benchmark Estimate for the Capital Stock: An Optimal Consistency Method*. Working Papers 434. London: University of London.

AlSaqri, S. (2010). *Petroleum Resources, Linkages and Development: The Case of Oman*. Centre for Strategic Economic Studies, Faculties of Business and Law. Melbourne, Victoria University.

ALSaqri, A. S., & Abdullahi, A. (2012). Natural Resource Depletion, Productivity and Optimal Fiscal Strategy: Lessons from a Small Oil-Exporting Economy. *The IUP Journal of Applied Economics, 6*, 56–80.

ALSaqri, A. S., & Abdullahi, A. (2010). Mineral and Non-Mineral Sector Interdependency: Empirical Evidence from Oman. *IUP Journal of Applied Economics, 9*, 14–33.

Askari, H. (1990). *Saudi Arabia's Economy: Oil and the Search for Economic Development*. Greenwich: JAI Press LTD.

Cobb, C. W., & Douglas, P. H. (1928). A Theory of Production. *American Economic Review, 18*, 139–165.

Development Council. (1976). The Five-Year Development Plan (1976–1980).

Elhiraika, A. B., & Hamed, A. H. (2001). *Explaining Growth in an Oil Dependent Economy: The Case of the United Arab Emirates*. Explaining Growth, Rio deJaneiro.

Khan, S. U. (2005). Macro Determinants of Total Factor Productivity in Pakistan. *SBR Research Bulletin, 2*.

Limi, A. (2006). *Did Botswana Escape from the Resource Curse?* IMF Working Paper WP/06/138. International Monetary Fund, Washington, DC.

Luke, T. W. (1983). Dependent Development and the Arab OPEC States. *The Journal of Politics, 45*(4), 979–1003.

Makdisi, S., Fattah, Z., & Limam, I. (2000). *Determinants of Growth in the MENA Countries*. Oxford: Centre for the Study of African Economies, Oxford University.

Mankiw, N. G. (2002). *Macroeconomics*. New York: Worth Publishers.

Maudos, J., Pastor, J., & Serrano, L. (1999). Total Factor Productivity Measurement and Human Capital in OECD Countries. *Economic Letters, 63*(1), 39–44.

Rosser, A. (2004). *Why Did Indonesia Overcome the Resource Curse?* Brighton: Institute of Development Studies.

Sachs, J. D., & Warner, A. M. (1995). *Natural Resource Abundance and Economic Growth*. Cambridge: National Bureau of Economic Research.

CHAPTER 4

Policy Implications of the UAE's Economic Diversification Strategy: Prioritizing National Objectives

Sterling Jensen

Introduction

The public interest is an essential aspect of political theory. States and political leaders use the public interest to justify their actions. In the debate about public interests, political theory has long debated the relationship between ends and means. This debate is summed up in the question, "do the ends justify the means?" While political ends have been the main model of contemporary political philosophy, means have also become an important part of modern political theory. Political theory suggests that political leaders make policies intending to use their means to advance either their own or the public interest largely based on a social contract the state or ruler has with its people. However, since a state or ruler's means are limited, states must prioritize which interests and goals are more important to pursue. This prioritization is shaped by the state or ruler's assumptions about threats, challenges and opportunities to public interests emanating from their environment. States then devise measurable national objectives in order to protect and advance the national interest concerned. In international relations theory, a state's public

S. Jensen (✉)
National Defense College, Abu Dhabi, UAE

A. Mishrif, Y. Al Balushi (eds.), *Economic Diversification in the Gulf Region, Volume II*, The Political Economy of the Middle East,
DOI 10.1007/978-981-10-5786-1_4

interests, ends or national objectives are the basis of political and strategic analysis. Correctly understanding what a state is trying to achieve, or which national interests it is pursuing, is a principle factor for interpreting a state's policies and behavior. In the context of the end–means question in political theory and national interests in international relations, this chapter examines the policy implications of the United Arab Emirates' economic diversification strategy, which it has adopted since the 1980s and deemed a strategic priority. The chapter starts with a layout of the domestic and international context in which the diversification strategy has evolved, then links the strategy and its policies to the UAE's national interests. Finally the chapter analyzes the implications of six of the most prominent economic diversification policies on the UAE's other national objectives.

Domestic and International Context

In the late 1970s, the UAE, starting with Dubai, began in earnest to diversify its economy away from the oil sector. Rapid and unpredictable fluctuations in oil prices, as well as prospects of depleting oil reserves, were a destabilizing factor for not only government budgets but also the economies of respective emirates which relied on oil revenues. The UAE introduced policies to encourage private investment and domestic productivity, largely policies that initially directed investment to the construction and real estate sectors, but then to transportation, communication and manufacturing (Elhiraika and Hamed 2006). In fact, the share of UAE oil revenue to GDP fell nominally from 70 percent in 1970 to 40 percent in the 1990s (Hoauas and Heshmati 2014). Today, the UAE claims oil revenue only makes up 30 percent of the UAE economy. While a large portion of the non-oil investment has come from public investment in infrastructure and construction, there have been decreasing marginal rates of capital return on these investments, which supports an argument that UAE efforts to diversify the economy have not increased total factor productivity (Hoauas and Heshmati 2014). Leading factors to low productivity are reliance on low-skilled labor, a social contract that provides Emirati nationals an abundance of high-paying public sector jobs, high government subsidies and the "kafala" sponsorship policy (Haouas and Soto 2012). Despite economic inefficiencies caused by a social contract that provides Emiratis economic benefits and security in exchange for political loyalty, the main justification for large public investments in infrastructure is that they would attract domestic and foreign investment. In a way, the UAE's economic diversification plan is a "if you build it, they will come" strategy. In essence, a large part of the UAE's economic diversification strategy has been building a world-class infrastructure to attract the type of investment needed to develop a diversified economy with a vibrant private sector.

In 2010, the UAE introduced Vision 2021, which included a strategy and policy objectives to achieve economic diversification through building a knowledge-based economy. Two years before Vision 2021, Abu Dhabi released its Economic Vision 2030, which is Abu Dhabi's economic strategy to achieve a knowledge-based economy. As the UAE's economy is highly dependent on energy exports (even though nominally energy exports only constitute approximately 30 percent of GDP), in particular Abu Dhabi, which funds nearly 65 percent of the UAE federal budget, economic diversity and sustainability is of strategic importance (UAE Ministry of Economy 2015). Along this point, in February 2015 Crown Prince of Abu Dhabi, Sheikh Mohammed Bin Zayed, said at a national governance conference that the UAE is working toward the day Emiratis can celebrate, rather than mourn, the last barrel of oil is shipped from UAE shores (The National 2015b). This goal is ambitious, and it will require implementing sound policies by prioritizing national objectives and ensuring that competing policies do not hamper implementation.

UAE's National Interests and Strategic Goals

Vision 2021 establishes seven strategic priorities to advance UAE national interests, which are (1) a cohesive society and preserved identity, (2) a first-rate education system, (3) world-class healthcare, (4) a competitive knowledge economy, (5) safe public and fair judiciary, (6) a sustainable environment and infrastructure, and (7) a strong global standing (UAE Government 2010). Effective statecraft requires governments to prioritize their interests in order to achieve them (Deibel 2007). It is not enough to say that an interest is important. All interests are important, but states are limited in their resources and capabilities to pursue all their interests at the same time with the same level of commitment. Effective states or governments assess their environment for challenges, threats and opportunities to their interests and prioritize which national objective they believe they can successfully achieve at a given time (Deibel 2007). However, the process of prioritizing an interest over others does not mean the state will achieve it. States must not only prioritize their interests, but also ensure they have the required resources or a plan to obtain the resources necessary to achieve an objective that advances the targeted national interest. For example, the UAE identified in a follow-up "UAE Government Strategy 2011–2013" target sectors and strategic enablers to guide economic policy to achieving Vision 2021, which are building skilled human capital, providing customer-centric service, having efficient financial management, good governance, dynamic government networks, an effective legislative process and integrated policy-making and effective government communication. While these identified enablers may indeed be essential for the UAE to successfully diversify its economy, to be effective, policy goals must be translated into actionable and measurable objectives that the state uses to guide resourcing and management. The state must also recognize that resources and efforts to increase economic diversification might come at the expense of pursuing other national objectives deemed as important. It is not necessarily risky for a state to not prioritize its national interests; however, it can be significantly risky for a state to not prioritize its national objectives. Therefore, it is important to put the UAE national objective of economic diversification in the context of the UAE's top national priorities.

A national objective is something more measurable than a national interest (which is more an ambition), and effective objectives are ones that are clearly achievable. If states set objectives that are not achievable or too ambitious, they risk wasting resources in pursuit of a goal they might never accomplish. Also, if a state claims it has two or more national objectives with equal priority, yet those national objectives compete for resources or work at cross purposes, then a state also risks adopting inefficient courses of action. For example, the UAE has a national interest to retain its identity, but it also has a national interest in economic prosperity. These two national interests, which are not inherently contradictory, can work at cross purposes when they are translated into ministerial policies that must be implemented. The policy objective of Emiratization with an aim to retain Emirati identity and the policy objective to build a diversified-knowledge-based economy with an aim to further economic prosperity often come in conflict with each other. These two policy objectives often use conflicting sub-policies, operations or tactics to achieve those objectives. Dubai's efforts to successfully host Expo 2020 illustrate this point. In order to prepare for Expo 2020—a means Dubai and the UAE federal government decided was an opportunity to achieve national objectives of building the UAE national brand, attracting foreign investment and boosting the tourism industry—the UAE has relied on low-skilled labor in the construction sector. Adopting these economic policies to prepare for Expo 2020 comes into conflict with an Emiratization goal of decreasing the role for foreign workers and increasing the role of Emiratis, as well as an economic diversification sub-policy of decreasing the role of low-skilled laborers in the workforce.

Another example of how a policy can serve one national interest, but undermine another, is the kafala sponsorship policy, which influences the labor market. Some argue that while the kafala policy in the UAE serves the multiple purposes including helping control labor mobility, providing locals a means of alternative income through patronage and sponsorship, and retaining political control over foreign laborer (Al-Noaimi and Omelaniuk 2013), it also decreases labor productivity, burdens social services and costs the government extra money in infrastructure (Haouas and Soto 2012). It also exposes the country to potential human rights violations that in an integrated world can damage a national's branding efforts (Al-Noaimi and Omelaniuk 2013). Countries often have to balance between pursuing different interests at the same time and making trade-offs in the present in order to advance other interests in the future.

If Emiratization and economic diversification goals cannot be implemented as complements, then the state will have to decide which goal is more urgent and important to advance so those two goals do not contradict each other. A policy to require companies to hire Emiratis might undermine economic diversification efforts, whereas hiring foreign labor to achieve economic diversification might undermine Emiratization efforts. While attempts to base economic diversification on an Emiratization policy might be ideal, it is also difficult to implement given Emirati perceptions of acceptable work and the small size of the Emirati labor market compared to labor market demand (Forstenlechner et al. 2012). It appears the UAE is currently prioritizing its economic diversification strategy over Emiratization because the state continues to not meet Emiratization quotas, likely due to a desire to finish ambitious economic projects (Salama 2013). The reasoning for this prioritization would be that the basis of the UAE's future state power will need to rely on a more sustainable economy and human capital capabilities during volatile fluctuations in oil prices (UAE Government 2015).

Meanwhile, some would argue the UAE government must also maintain its social contract of providing economically rewarding jobs to

Emiratis and lessen their economic burdens in exchange for political loyalty (Forstenlechner and Rutledge 2010). It seems Emirati leadership is transitioning from maintaining a social contract, which tends to provide Emiratis high-paying public sector jobs, into developing a social contract, which challenges Emiratis to improve and diversify their skill sets in order to become more productive in the private sector. The government has an interest in having a more efficient bureaucracy and providing Emiratis incentives to join the private sector. Reports of at least 90 percent of Emiratis working in or reliant on the public sector illustrates, though, that it is a challenge for leadership to balance political and economic realities. Government leaders will need to encourage Emiratis to be more productive and less dependent on the public sector without tarnishing their loyalty to the UAE's unique political system. Thus, the 2021 target is to have 5 percent of the private sector be employed by Emiratis (it is currently 1 percent) according to the UAE Government (2015).

When economic prosperity becomes more of a priority than preserving cultural values, there are voices that strengthen the argument that the UAE is losing its identity in the pursuit of wealth and that cultural identity needs to be the driver of the UAE's success rather than economic prosperity being the sustainer of cultural identity. They argue that Arabic is not the lingua franca in an Arab country and that incentives to learn English far outweigh the incentives to learn Arabic. Educators in the Emirates have complained that the new generation of Emirati students is neither strong in Arabic nor English and that, without being rooted in their native language, their sense of Emirati identity will weaken (Raddawi and Meslem 2015).

It is not uncommon to read articles in local UAE newspapers or hear Arab visitors to the UAE talk about coming to the UAE and not being able to communicate with people due to the lack of Arabic speakers in the service industries. One argument for preserving cultural identity while balancing the need for foreign workers is to gradually replace South Asian laborers for temporary Arab workers from places such as Syria, Yemen, Iraq, Egypt and North Africa (Forstenlechner and Rutledge 2011). This could keep low-skilled wages low and also promote and preserve the Arabic language and culture in the UAE. This policy change, though, brings with it other political and social risks (Forstenlechner and Rutledge 2011). It may be easier for the UAE to dismiss South Asian workers in a time of crisis than Arab laborers who would be more difficult to expel from the country if they claim they are unable to return to their home countries. This could make the UAE vulnerable to the Jordanian and Lebanese phenomenon of having more multigenerational, non-citizen Arabs permanently settled in its nation. These difficult policy trade-offs are at the core of the challenges the UAE faces when attempting to implement its economic diversification strategy. An overview of the main polices the UAE is pursuing to achieve economic diversification provides insight into possible policy trade-offs or conflicts to each one.

Economic Diversification Policies

There are three main sectors impacted by the UAE's economic diversification policies: first those connected to trade and manufacturing sectors; second, the financial and services industries sectors; and third, those connected to developing the private sector and Emiratization.

***Trade and manufacturing sectors*:** In the last 5 years, the UAE has increased trade liberalization. According to Young (2014), while the transport and communications sectors did not rebound after the 2009 crisis (likely due to not implementing the latest technology and continued reliance on manual labor), the UAE's heavy investments in shipping ports and airports will likely reverse that trend. The World Economic Forum's 2012 Trade Enabling Index ranked the UAE's transport infrastructure as the first in the Gulf, which will likely enable the UAE to become the entry point for a significant amount of goods reaching the GCC. However, if the UAE does not improve productivity in its labor market, it will not be able to completely benefit from the gains from more trade.

The UAE's competitive advantages for trade are location, infrastructure, low-cost access to energy, capital and free trade zones. The UAE has used its two major shipping ports and international airports in Dubai and Abu Dhabi to leverage its trade position. Two-thirds of the world's major cities are at maximum an 8-hour flight from the UAE (Robehmed 2014). Also, according to the US Energy Information Agency (2012), nearly 35 percent of the world's seaborne energy passes through the Strait of Hormuz per day (17 million bpd). The UAE's diversification strategy is heavily invested in its trade position and gives the country the infrastructure needed to reap benefits from these competitive advantages.

More than a fourth of the UAE's trade occurs in the free zones, and this number is growing (UAE Federal Customs Authority 2014). There are trade-offs, though, with the reliance on free zones to open trade. It becomes more difficult to help develop domestic small and medium enterprises (SMEs) when it is easier for international companies with more intellectual property, access to productive and high-skilled labor to dominate markets being based in the free zone rather than in the areas that need most economic development.

As an oil exporter, the manufacturing sector has relied on oil-intensive industries such as aluminum, petrochemicals and now micro-chips. Manufacturing has also relied on low-skilled labor rather than technology and efficiency for its growth strategy. It has also relied on subsidized energy. Figures are that 5.5 percent of the UAE's GDP goes to energy subsidies. This is not sustainable. In January 2015, Abu Dhabi reduced energy subsidies and for the first time charged citizens for water consumption, though at a marginal rate.

The UAE is one of the largest consumers of energy per capita in the world. This high energy consumption is not a sustainable trend. Resources then, especially manufacturing that requires low-skill laborers, increases public expenditures, energy and scarce natural resources such as water. These factors contribute to the UAE's low total factor productivity and are not setting the UAE up for a sustainable, knowledge-based economy.

An example of the recent acquisition of Global Foundries illustrates the UAE's challenges in its economic diversification strategy. Global Foundries is the second largest semiconductor foundry in the world. In October 2014, IBM paid Global Foundries US$1.5 billion to take its unprofitable microchip unit (Bloomberg News 2014). In return for taking the microchip unit, Global Foundries will service IBM's microchips for the next 10 years in exchange for access to IBM's intellectual property (Bloomberg News 2014). The UAE is interested in getting into the semiconductor business because this is a knowledge-based industry that could potentially serve multiple objectives in the economic diversification strategy. The challenge with the semiconductor business is that it is driven by very rapid change. Innovation must be at the forefront of any serious attempt to be a leader in the semiconductor industry. Silicon Valley in California is renowned for this cutthroat atmosphere, which uses its high-tech ecosystem, married with first-class universities, to innovate and develop the industry. Without that ecosystem, the UAE will be at a disadvantage. If the UAE is unable to build a sustainable IT sector and ecosystem in the UAE, it might end up funding a foreign company's development and employees without much in return.

Both the trade sector and manufacturing industry are directly related to the development of the UAE's defense industry. Most GCC countries are interested in building domestic defense industries due to their reliance on weapons purchases from the West and East as well as their large spending on security-related projects. GCC defense spending accounts for 83 percent of the total Middle East. In 2014, the MENA region spent US$140 billion in 2014, which was a 30 percent increase from 2011 (IHS 2014). At nearly US$20 billion in defense spending per year, the UAE is the 15th largest defense spender and fourth largest defense importer in the world (Bouyamourn 2015). Chairman of the Abu Dhabi Department of Economic Development, Ali Majid al-Mansoori, said that the UAE's defense industry is the cornerstone of the country's economic diversification strategy (Bouyamourn 2015). Countries that want to build a defense industry need to know exactly what interests they are trying to advance by doing it. Generally governments have two main objectives in developing a domestic defense industry: economic diversification and national security. Since defense spending is a large part of a government's budget, many countries do it because they want an indigenous capability to train, equip and supply their own security forces while stimulating their own economy. This is the basic principle behind an import substitution industrialization policy that many developing countries have tried to use to build domestic industries. Being able to support domestic armed forces helps support local industrial and manufacturing companies, decreases the need for foreign currency to import defense requirements, and helps governments gain domestic legitimacy by providing more local jobs. A successful domestic defense industry can also provide an opportunity for countries to diversify their economy and increase exports.

The UAE's defense industry has evolved in the last 20 years to now focus on high-tech, small-scale defense manufacturing and servicing. The reason for this strategy is that low-tech, labor-intensive industries are not in harmony with the intended direction of the UAE's indigenous workforce and industrial base. The UAE has an interest in reducing its reliance on low-skill labor-intensive industries. By focusing on low-scale, high-tech products such as unmanned aerial systems, defense electronics, cyber warfare, night-vision systems and military communications, the UAE could link its large investments in the industrial and ICT sectors to its defense industry (George 2013; Sophia 2014).

One of the vital components of developing a defense industry is the industrial and manufacturing base of the country. With a small population and limited human capital and industrial base, the UAE has to carefully choose which industries it can adapt to its defense needs and pursue economies of scale to be a competitive producer of defense products. High-tech defense capabilities require large R&D investments and technology transfer. They also require cutthroat innovation to remain competitive. The UAE's current high-tech, small-scale strategy relies on joint ventures with foreign firms and contractual requirements that ensure technology transfer and high-skill labor to the UAE (Carvalho and Kasolowsky 2013). The key will be how to convince cutting-edge international defense companies to partner with the UAE in joint ventures when many of these companies guard their intellectual property. One way to do this is to offer funding for future joint R&D projects in which the UAE plays a partner role in developing the new technology.

The new Emirates Defense Industry Company's Chairman, Sheikh Homaid al-Shimmari, admitted at the IDEX conference in 2015 that success of the UAE's defense industry strategy relies on Emiratis being interested to gain the skills necessary to support the high-tech requirements. The UAE cannot rely on foreign labor to build a sustainable defense industry. Without Emiratis investing their own human capital into the industry, the UAE cannot achieve its goal. This presents a challenge that other small countries have faced when trying to build a defense industry: competition with the private sector for high-skilled labor. Building the private sector industry and building a defense industry require different business models and skill sets. While the private and public sector can feed off of each other and cooperate in joint projects, countries with larger labor pools and industrial bases are able to cross-pollinate ideas easier as there is a larger market of human capital to choose from. However, with a very limited presence of UAE nationals in the private sector, the UAE will have to ensure that its defense industry does not hemorrhage the human capital needed to develop the private sector (Blom et al. 2013). The government will have to prioritize the orientation of its defense industry policy so that it complements private sector development and not hinder it. If the government seeks more economic diversity through its defense industry, as it has stated in the past, then it will need to adopt a business model that relies on competition, innovation and free-market capitalism. It will need to specialize in niche markets to gain and maintain a competitive advantage. Despite its small population, the UAE can specialize in certain areas that can make it a formidable competitor in the global defense industry. But it will have to incentivize Emiratis to work in the defense sector without jeopardizing the private sector, and it will have to maintain its competitive edge against countries in the region wanting to build their own defense industries.

The UAE is already making strides in the maintenance, repair and overhaul sector, but the next step will be to determine how the UAE's private and public sector efforts can complement each other rather than compete for resources in developing its low-scale, high-tech defense industry. The UAE could also coordinate more with Saudi Arabia, Egypt, Jordan and other Arab countries developing defense industries to benefit from their respective strengths. Joint ventures between Arab allies rather than just with Western and Eastern allies would set the stage for future cooperation and coordination in establishing a regional defense industry that benefits from the strengths of each member. The GCC is already in talks about decreasing trade barriers and increasing economic integration. The defense industry could be an important part of future trade between GCC countries.

***Financial sector and services industry*:** The main arguments about weaknesses in the UAE's financial markets are that they are heavily concentrated in construction and real estate, deleveraged in SMEs, abundant in non-performing loans and weak in domestic capital markets (Young 2014; Hertog 2015). Another criticism is that the UAE's non-oil sector companies are still heavily reliant on subsidized oil and capital coming in the country through oil (El Anshasy and Katsaiti 2013). Without the oil, many of these companies would not be profitable and therefore are not sustainable without significant oil-backed financing. While foreign direct investment (FDI) is nearly 2.5 percent of GPD, public sector investment is also the main driver of investment (UAE Ministry of Economy 2014). Government spending feeds the UAE economy and relies on procyclical fiscal policies. When oil prices are high, there is an increase in public spending; whereas when oil prices are low, there is a decrease in spending. Some analysts argue that more countercyclical fiscal policies would be more conducive to developing a sustainable economy (El Anshasy and Katsaiti 2013).

The UAE has strong monetary stability, largely due to its currency's peg to the US dollar. While the UAE has to rein in inflation without monetary flexibility, its fiscal policy options are the main government tool it can use to stimulate and slow down the economy. When oil prices are high, ambitious government projects are introduced. The influx of government spending stimulates the economy, but increases inflationary pressures. If the government were to cut spending during periods of high growth, it could better balance inflationary pressures, and then during periods of low growth, it can use fiscal policy to increase public spending to stimulate the economy. This is a more sound policy. The question is what is keeping the UAE from adopting this type of approach. Commitments to ambitious projects such as Abu Dhabi Ports, Expo 2020 and expansion of the Dubai and Abu Dhabi airports are examples as to why the government has not been adopting countercyclical fiscal policies. Abu Dhabi and Dubai are trying to build the infrastructure needed to support more private sector growth. These long-term projects require significant public spending, and it makes more financial sense to fund these ambitious projects when funds are readily available rather than seeking out international loans or securing funding through a domestic bond market. The higher priority to complete these projects is prolonging organic economic growth through increases in efficiency and innovation. Recognition that innovation has been lacking in the UAE's economy prompted UAE leadership to call 2015 the year of innovation. This might be a great motivational goal, but it does not appear that companies are sufficiently incentivized to innovate when they are so heavily subsidized.

The financial sector is a fundamental part of building a sustainable economy. Yet it has been a challenge for the UAE to help SMEs receive the finance needed to grow. Due to the difficulty of finding financial services from banks, Emirati SMEs turn to receiving grants from non-profit organizations such as the Khalifa Fund for development assistance (The National 2015a). One argument, which is prevalent in development literature is that SMEs need more business management skills before being able to truly become efficient innovators. Competition, innovation and growth need to drive economic growth more than just finance. One way for the government to foster effective competition and innovation would be to cut certain subsidies and government funding to large private sector companies operating locally. Deregulation and the sale of government assets gradually would push Emiratis to the private sector, but would likely be a significant cost to Emirati stakeholders important to maintaining the current social contract.

Imbalances in the UAE's financial sector have implications for the development of the UAE's service industry; the development of this industry is vital to the viability of the UAE's economic diversification strategy. The UAE's non-oil sector currently relies heavily on the low-skill labor-intensive real estate, construction and manufacturing sector. As previously discussed, this business model is not sustainable. The new objective is to achieve economic sustainability and diversification through a knowledge-based economy. Economic diversification will need to overcome a few significant challenges. First the UAE will need to attract high-skill laborers and companies willing to undertake research and development (R&D) in the UAE rather than doing it abroad and selling the intellectual property to the UAE. Second, the UAE will need to maintain a competitive advantage in the services industries, which requires continual innovation.

One of the services industries the UAE has invested heavily in for diversification is the tourism sector. The UAE has already started linking its tourism sector to its trade policies. The large expenditures to build the transport sector, mainly airports, were to not only enable an increase of trade but also facilitate an increase in tourism. The UAE assumes regional turmoil in the Levant, Iraq, Yemen, Egypt and North Africa will encourage potential tourists to visit the UAE. In the last ten years, the UAE's tourism sector has averaged 18.8 percent of total GDP. This is much more than the 12.7 percent average seen in other GCC countries (Young 2014). While Dubai started investing in tourism before the other emirates, the others have followed suit, especially Abu Dhabi, which has significantly increased investment in the tourism sector. Abu Dhabi has invested in film production and luxury and leisure tourism with attractions such as the Emirates Palace, Ferrari World and the Yas Marina Formula One track. A recent illustration of Abu Dhabi's investment in the film industry is the *Furious 7* blockbuster that was partially filmed in Abu Dhabi and featured in the film, which became one of the highest grossing films in history. The same is true for the December 2015 release of *Star Wars VII: The Force Awakens*, which was partially filmed in Abu Dhabi. Abu Dhabi is investing in the film industry on the assumption that such international exposure will enhance the emirate's brand as a high-tech and luxurious, modern Gulf country that retains its identity. Moreover, producing high-budget films in Abu Dhabi also stimulates its local economy and provides opportunities for Emiratis in the film industry to gain valuable experience and connections.

As mentioned previously, Dubai's heavy investment in hosting Expo 2020, which is an historic opportunity for not only the emirate but the country as a whole to increase capacity in its services sectors, comes with significant costs and risks. First, with low labor productivity and a private sector relying on real estate and construction, preparations for Expo 2020 could undermine the growth of the SME sector. Banks are much more willing to loan money to the more reliable construction and real estate sectors, rather loaning to more risky SMEs. To address this problem, the UAE government recently passed a law saying SMEs should make up more of a bank's loans. However, this law will be difficult to enforce because many banks do not have an incentive to comply during a period of perceived economic slowdown.

Private sector reform and Emiratization: The lack of financial depth, the difficulty of SMEs to get financing and a limited service industry are linked to challenges in private sector reform. Due to the significant lack of human capital capabilities compared to the labor market requirements needed to not only maintain growth but increase it, emirates have adopted a growth model of funding large multimillion-dollar manufacturing and services companies with the intention of them being anchors to help increase local human capital capabilities for future SME growth. In many developing countries, SMEs are the drivers of economic growth and diversification (Stallings and Studart 2006). The grassroots approach to innovation and growth works easier in countries with large labor pools. If the UAE were to focus on developing SMEs for more short-term gains at the expense of the "going big" approach (such as with UAE government-owned Mubadala or merchant family-owned Emaar), there would likely be less capital invested because SMEs would not be able to effectively absorb the billions of dollars required to build the infrastructure needed to attract foreign investment. Additionally, other than the oil and construction sectors, the UAE lacks the local-national human capital required to develop these other industries. The UAE has a strong consumption-based market, such as grocery markets, retail and vehicles, but there are not many high-tech or biotech SMEs led by Emiratis. Building industries based on the UAE's competitive advantage (low-cost access to energy, labor and capital), such as foundries and chip manufacturing, needs large-scale investment in order to be able to be competitive in an international market. The UAE is betting that by developing these anchor companies, such as Mubadala, the UAE's competitive advantages can be leveraged effectively to create the human capital needed to drive future SMEs. However, if Emiratis do not gain the human capital and interest necessary to maintain a local ecosystem of SMEs in strategic sectors for a knowledge-based economy, then the state-owned enterprise "anchor" strategy will likely fail.

Ultimately, the UAE's private sector reform is constrained by two competing national objectives. First is to create acceptable jobs for Emiratis. Second is to maintain a competitive advantage in the international market for its products. A measure of the reforms' success will be the mix of UAE exports. As the UAE is oriented toward a free-market economy, it must produce products at a lower marginal cost than its competitors to remain competitive. In order to create acceptable jobs for Emiratis and remain price competitive, the UAE will have to subsidize the salaries of Emiratis working in the private sector, as companies could easily get high-skilled labor for a cheaper price by hiring imported labor. Thus, without the subsidies in the short term, the UAE companies can't remain price competitive. However, this approach also has its drawbacks, as salary "top-ups" have been used in countries such as Kuwait, but are yet to show promising results in improving private sector development.

Another effort to stimulate the private sector are free zones. Free zones are one of the UAE's main business attractions. International companies with interests in operating in the Middle East choose to make headquarters in the UAE free zones to pay fewer taxes. While this is a good incentive to bring in foreign investment to support economic diversification, it too has significant trade-offs. Since the established social contract is that the government will provide jobs, social services and protection in exchange for political loyalty, the government, which relies heavily on oil revenues to fund government expenditures and subsidies, will also eventually have to diversify its sources of income. At low oil prices, the trajectory of government spending is not sustainable. While the Dubai government has started to diversify its sources of income, the rest of the emirates, especially Abu Dhabi, will likely have to cut more subsidies and introduce taxes to have a more sustainable fiscal policy (Haouas and Soto 2012). Yet there are two major trade-offs to introducing more taxes. First, a corporate or value-added tax (VAT) might decrease foreign direct investment (FDI) and a VAT tax may decrease consumption, thus undermining the intended goal to diversify the economy through more FDI and more consumption. Second is the challenge of taxation without representation. Taxes will have to be highly discriminatory as to not encourage local Emiratis or established residents/companies to seek more political representation, especially in the case of an income tax. A taxation scheme might work in the short term; however, there may be longer-term implications that could expose the government to unintended challenges.

One of the largest challenges to private sector reform is getting Emiratis to be part of it. Many private companies do not hire locals due to lack of sufficient qualifications, not accepting working hours schedules and high salary expectations (Nazzal 2014). Private companies in the free zones are not required to hire Emiratis, so many do not. Many of those companies outside of the free zones hire locals as a means to do business in the country. Of those Emiratis exclusively working in the private sector, many work for the large merchant-family-owned businesses such as Emaar and the Al-Futtaim Group, or in the banking and insurance sectors, because these sectors are deemed more suitable by UAE nationals. Private sector managers would argue that UAE nationals are not incentivized to become more productive because they assume they can be promoted more based on social connections than on merit. On the other hand, Emiratis often express discontent with the private sector because they feel companies are not vested in the professional development of their Emirati employees (Badr 2015). If a company invested in the Emirati's professional development rather than focusing on developing the non-nationals, then more Emiratis would be more incentivized to stay in the private sector rather than exploiting any chance to receive a public sector job (Ryan 2014).

Superficially, there are many Emiratis who participate in the private sector as token joint owners in companies outside of the free zones. UAE law stipulates that at least 51 percent of ownership of registered businesses in the UAE must be joint-owned by Emirati citizens. Even casual conversations with non-Emirati business owners will reveal that many Emirati joint owners are merely owners in name. As long as the Emirati sponsor receives his or her share of the profits, which can be seen as a local sponsorship tax, the business can usually operate without significant Emirati oversight. In practice, many Emiratis are members of boards of companies seeking to operate in the UAE, which can provide significant supplemental income to already inflated government wages. Reforming the ownership law to allow more foreign ownership in the companies would decrease prices, increase incentives to operate outside of the free zones, and possibly help make private companies more competitive internationally, but the cost would be less supplemental income and oversight for local nationals who are token partners in the private sector.

But even Emirati business leaders have voiced concern over Emirati willingness to work in the private sector when more lucrative public sector jobs requiring fewer qualifications are available. The private sector jobs require more training and expertise to be productive than the public sector jobs. An Emirati would have to do more to receive equal pay in the private sector. Currently, the most likely incentives driving Emiratis to work exclusively in the private sector are patriotism, lack of public sector jobs, lack of social connections to get a decent public sector job, or, in very few cases, higher salaries in the public sector because the local national is highly skilled, motivated and qualified. The lack of Emiratis in the private sector is a known problem. They must sacrifice at least short-term financial gain and a less demanding work schedule in order to work in the private sector.

One researcher says that the UAE's overreliance on public sector jobs causes structural inefficiencies that perpetuate the lack of Emiratization in the private sector (Hertog 2015). The argument is that the overwhelming desire by Emiratis to obtain a government job translates into more social science and humanities degrees rather than in business and the hard sciences, which are needed to have a sustainable-knowledge-based economy. With more Emiratis interested in getting the easiest higher education possible in order to qualify for government jobs, higher education is inadvertently undermining sustainable private sector development. What is required is an incentives scheme to encourage more Emiratis to complete and excel in math and hard sciences, which the government has begun with the development of technical high schools such as the Institute of Applied Technology (IAT). The gap between the private sector and education is not new, and the UAE government has undoubtedly acknowledged it and is trying to address it. Abu Dhabi alone has invested billions to establish internationally recognized and accredited higher education programs in the emirate, not only to raise the profile of the UAE and attract international talent but more importantly to provide local Emirati students the opportunity to get a first-class higher education without having to go abroad to get it. The Masdar Institute of Science and Technology, the New York University (NYU) Abu Dhabi campus, and the new National Defense College (NDC) are good examples of this approach, but it is yet to be seen if UAE nationals will actually attend these colleges in large numbers and apply their education to the workforce. The Masdar Institute has partnered with MIT, and the NDC has partnered with the US National Defense University. These are capital-intensive undertakings and are a risk because if local Emiratis are not sufficiently incentivized to acquire the skill sets necessary to enable their presence in the private sector and increase public sector efficiency, then the result might be heavily subsidizing non-local higher education and building an array of Potemkin education villages.

Perhaps the future viability of the UAE's private sector and successful implementation of Emiratization relies on the future employment preferences of current primary and elementary aged students. It may be too difficult to change the professional trajectory of middle school and university students. However, if there is more push to encourage Emiratis to specialize in the STEM disciplines (science, technology, engineering and math), then they could be able to be the ones driving future SME development. This is the reasoning behind new curriculum reforms introduced by the Abu Dhabi Education Council in the summer of 2016 (Pennington 2016).

One of the other challenges to Emiratization is logistical. There is a pool of only 300,000 Emirati laborers in a market with up to five million laborers in the country. In the 11 identified sectors targeted in the Vision 2021 and Abu Dhabi Vision 2030, Emiratis alone cannot saturate these sectors even if they forsook public sector jobs in significant numbers. Additionally, there is competition among these sectors to attract Emirati talent and there is no clear prioritization of where Emiratis should be working in the private sector; therefore, the limited human capital might be misallocated. One possible solution could be a policy that prioritizes strategic sectors and provides incentives to Emiratis to work in these sectors.

While there are social implications to relying on temporary foreign workers, there are also many benefits. By having temporary workers from different ethnic and cultural backgrounds who will work at lower costs and can be easily dismissed, the UAE can prevent the establishment of unions and other collective agreements that could significantly increase labor costs without necessarily improving productivity. Innovation in developed countries can be bogged down by labor unions that use their human capital as leverage to extract concessions from employers, though improved worker conditions can be an incentive for innovation and higher productivity.

UAE policies to liberate trade and develop the manufacturing sector, while having a limited financial sector and services industries, can cause constraints on UAE efforts to develop the private sector and incentivize more Emiratis to be more productive in the economic diversification strategy. Designing economic and social policies that are more in harmony with each other, rather than in tension, would help lessen the negative effects some of these policies can have on each other. Orchestrating this harmony at a strategic level and following through will be the UAE's greatest challenge in achieving its economic diversification goals.

Conclusion and Lessons Learned

Where the UAE is today from where it was in the 1970s or 1980s or even 2000s is remarkable. However, there are still many challenges facing the UAE due to policies adopted to achieve economic diversification. As the Ruler of Dubai, Sheikh Mohammed bin Rashid, has stated, while vision is vital for success, it cannot make it happen by itself (Al-Maktoum 2012). Success requires a collective effort and critical thinking about the trade-offs needed to achieve this vision and connecting it to the UAE's overall national interests, so policies do not work at cross purposes.

In addition to labor productivity, one of the UAE's main challenges in economic diversification is leveraging its purchasing power to have well-balanced and sustainable industries. Economic sustainability requires the UAE to adopt a value-added business model. The government may be able to easily start businesses, but business continuity will rely on its ability to add value to products and services without sacrificing other more important national interests. Ultimately, the experiment in economic diversification relies on the Emiratis themselves. It is in the interest of many international companies to keep the UAE dependent on foreign expertise and productivity. However, it will only be by incentivizing Emiratis to develop marketable qualifications and entering into the private sector that the UAE's economic sustainability strategy will work in the long term. The UAE will always have foreign labor to assist in its economic development, but a shift to more high-skilled labor with more Emiratis in the private sector will give Emiratis more control over and sustainability in their economic future.

Institutionally, the UAE remains personality- and tribal-based rather than institutionally-based. While business and public sector leaders frequently change positions, change in company leadership is not creating continuity in institutional culture. New ministers and directors often bring with them new priorities and institutional cultures. The current proactice of relying on personality and family connections decreases productivity and efficiency and can make it more difficult to formulate and implement strategic policy.

Emirati leaders often say they aspire to achieve the success of Singapore. However, there are clear differences in the Singapore and Emirati approaches to economic diversification in that Emiratis have relied on foreign workers to realize their goals, while the Singapore government enabled its citizens to be the main drivers of innovation and economic development. Singapore's strong emphasis on education and private sector development has been a major driver of its remarkably fast developmental success. By adopting an economic diversification strategy which relies on foreign labor, the UAE has been able to provide a high standard of living to its citizens, but it has also hemorrhaged a lot of its wealth to remittances and incentivized Emiratis to avoid working in the private sector. Unless the UAE is willing and able to increase the nationalization of high-skill foreign laborers in key markets, the current trajectory of UAE growth might mean more of the same: demographic changes leading to social pressures that widen the deepen the tension between economic prosperity and preservation of culture and identity.

The UAE's economic diversification strategy is an example of how a small country has embarked on an ambitious path in an area of the world suffering from crisis after crisis. Its development has been driven by vision and natural resources, yet there have been trade-offs to this strategy. Policies derived from an objective to diversify the economy have possibly undermined other national objectives, such as Emiratization. However, this ends-means relationship is not new. Successful states and political leaders prioritize their national interests based on the challenges, threats and opportunities they perceive in their domestic and international environments. The question is if the UAE will make the sacrifices needed to ensure this trajectory is sustainable without significantly undermining other vital national interests.

References

Al-Maktoum, H. H. S. M. B. R. (2012). *My Vision: Challenges in the Race for Excellence*. Dubai: Motivate Publishing, Chapter 2: The Vision.

Al-Noaimi, A. R., & Omelaniuk, I. (Eds.). (2013). *Labor Mobility: An Enabler for Sustainable Development*. Abu Dhabi: The Emirates Center for Strategic Studies and Research.

Badr, A. (2015, August 9). *Developing Leadership Skills Among Emirati Nationals*. Abu Dhabi: The National.

Blom, M., Castellacci, F., & Fevolden, A. M. (2013). *The Trade-off Between Innovation and Defense Industrial Policy: A Simulation Model Analysis of the Norwegian Defense Industry* (pp. 1579–1592). Amsterdam: Technological Forecasting & Social Change/Elsevier 80.

Bloomberg News. (2014, October 19). *IBM Agrees to Pay Global Foundries 1.5 Billion to Take Chip Unit*. New York: Bloomberg.

Bouyamourn, A. (2015, February 26). *Idex 2015: UAE Defense Industry Helps to Diversify the Economy*. Abu Dhabi: The National.

Carvalho, S., & Kasolowsky, R. (2013, February 19). *UAE Leads Gulf Arab Push to Build Up Domestic Defense Industry*. London: Reuters.

Deibel, T. L. (2007). *Foreign Affairs Strategy: Logic for American Statecraft*. Cambridge: Cambridge University Press.

El Anshasy, A., & Katsaiti, M.-S. (2013). Natural Resources and Fiscal Performance: Does Good Governance Matter? *Journal of Macroeconomics, 37*, 285–298.

Elhiraika, A. B., & Hamed, A. H. (2006). Explaining Growth in the Oil-Dependent Economy: The Case of the United Arab Emirates. In J. Nugent & H. Pesaran (Eds.), *Explaining Growth in the Middle East* (pp. 359–383). Syracuse, NY: North Holland/Elsevier.

Forstenlechner, I., Madi, M. T., Selim, H. M., & Rutledge, E. J. (2012). Emiratisation: Determining the Factors that Influence the Recruitment Decisions of Employers in the UAE. *The International Journal of Human Resource Management, 23*(2).

Forstenlechner, I., & Rutledge, E. (2010, Summer). Unemployment in the Gulf: Time to Update the 'Social Contract,'. *Middle East Policy, XVII*.

Forstenlechner, I., & Rutledge, E. J. (2011, Winter). The GCC's Demographic Imbalance: Perceptions, Realities and Policy Options. *Middle East Policy, XVIII*(4).

George, J. (2013, November 29). *UAE to Be a Global Tech Hub*. Abu Dhabi: Emirates 24/7.

Haouas, I., & Soto, R. (2012). *Has the UAE Escaped the Oil Curse?* Instituto de economia, Pontificia Universidad Catolica de Chile, Documento de trabajo n. 412. Santiago, Chile: ISSN.

Hertog, S. (2015, May 11). LSE Alumni Presentation at the Ritz Carlton. Dubai.

Hoauas, I., & Heshmati, A. (2014). *Can the UAE Avoid the Oil Curse by Economic Diversification?* IZA Discussion Paper No 8003. Bonn, Germany: IZA, p. 5.

IHS Global Defense Budget Report. (2014, December). Englewood, CO: Jane's.

Nazzal, N. (2014, April 22). *Working Hours a Challenge for Emiratisation*. Dubai: Gulf News.

Pennington, R. (2016, August 29). *Sweeping Reforms in UAE Schools Overhaul*. Abu Dhabi: The National.

Raddawi, R., & Meslem, D. (2015, December). Loss of Arabic in the UAE: Is Bilingual Education the Solution? Bahrain: International Journal of Bilingual & Multilingual Teachers of English. ISSN 2210-1829.

Robehmed, N. (2014, June 4). *How Dubai Became One of the Most Important Aviation Hubs in the World*. New York: Forbes.

Ryan, J. (2014, September 7). *Unique Challenges Facing Emiratisation in the Private Sector*. Abu Dhabi: The National.

Salama, S. (2013, December 3). *Emiratisation Quotas Won't Work, Warns Academic*. Dubai: Gulf News.

Sophia, M. (2014, March 30). *UAE's IT Spending to Top $4.6bn in 2014*. Dubai: Gulf Business.

Stallings, B., & Studart, R. (2006). *Finance for Development: Latin America in Comparative Perspective*. Washington, DC: Brookings Institution Press.

The National. (2015a, January 8). *New Khalifa Fund Initiative to Support UAE SMEs*. Abu Dhabi: The National.

The National. (2015b, February 10). *Sheikh Mohammad Bin Zayed's Inspirational Speech for a Post-oil UAE*. Abu Dhabi: The National.

UAE Federal Customs Authority. (2014, December 21). *Free Zones Trade Bulletin, 21st Issue*. Abu Dhabi: UAE Government.

UAE Government. (2010). *UAE Government Strategy 2011–2013*. Abu Dhabi: UAE Government. Retrieved December 23, 2015, from https://www.moca.gov.ae/?wpfb_dl=4

UAE Ministry of Economy. (2014). *Annual Economic Report 2013*. Dubai: UAE Ministry of Economy.

UAE Ministry of Economy. (2015). *Trade, Economy and Investment Report*. Foreign Trade Division, Foreign Trade Policy Department. Dubai: UAE Ministry of Economy. (2nd Quarter 2015).

US Energy Information Agency. (2012, September 5). *Strait of Hormuz Is Chokepoint for 20% of World's Oil*. Washington, DC: US Energy Information Agency.

Young, K. (2014). *Political Economy of Energy, Finance and Security in the UAE* (p. 43). London: Palgrave.

CHAPTER 5

Dubai's Model of Economic Diversification

Ashraf Mishrif and Harun Kapetanovic

Introduction

Dubai has made significant progress in its economic development since the early twenty-first century. Analysts attribute much of Dubai's economic success story to its unique business environment that is very attractive to businesses, shoppers and more recently to academics and researchers. What makes Dubai unique is the scale of its economic activities, the efficiency of business and financial services and tourism facilities. This is apparent in its ambitious plans to become the main trading hub in the Gulf region, and turn some of its major companies and facilities in airline, aviation, ports, logistics, construction, real estate and finance into world-class services providers (Nyarko 2010). In contrast with Abu Dhabi, where oil contributes approximately 90 per cent of the UAE's oil revenues and annual production and explains much of its economic development, Dubai has very little oil reserves and its oil contribution to GDP has declined from 5.48 per cent in 2000 to only 1.4 per cent in 2013. As a result, Dubai has little to do with the rentier state model of economic development. Despite the uniqueness of this case, little attention has yet been paid to this success story in the heart of the oil-rich GCC countries. Only a handful of scholarly works cover this development approach such as those

A. Mishrif (✉) • H. Kapetanovic
King's College London, London, UK

A. Mishrif, Y. Al Balushi (eds.), *Economic Diversification in the Gulf Region, Volume II*, The Political Economy of the Middle East,
DOI 10.1007/978-981-10-5786-1_5

written by Al-Sayegh (1998), Davidson (2007a, b), Hvidt (2009) and Schiliro (2013), at the time when GCC countries are seeking innovative approaches to diversify their economies.

This study argues that part of the success of Dubai's economic development is owed to its small, open and well-integrated economy into the global economic and financial system. The city-state may have received substantial financial support of its oil-rich sister city, Abu Dhabi, during the 2008–2009 global financial crisis; hence, oil is still an important factor in its long-term sustainable development. What is crucial here to stress is the misperception that oil is the driving force for Dubai's economic development. Indeed, Dubai is centrally positioned in a region that is well endowed with hydrocarbon resources, and this may have allowed many to believe that its economic prosperity, almost by default, is ascribed to abundant oil revenues. Perhaps that is the reason why the Dubai model has not received due attention from the academic community despite apparent economic and business success. While much of literature on the GCC economies focuses on the availability and role of natural resources in economic development, the rentier state theory offers little to explain Dubai's development drivers, motivations and outcomes. We also argue that the rentier state theory is somewhat deterministic, and its pejorative nature may have, in fact, inadvertently contributed to inadequate research of Dubai's economic model. Moreover, the posturing connotation of Dubai with the rentier state theory has obscured many strengths of its development paradigm; hence, the limitations and various lessons of Dubai's economic model are not examined well enough.

In this chapter, we attempt to show that Dubai has successfully diversified away its economy from the natural resource dependence, with oil revenues contributing less than 1.5 per cent of the GDP. We are not intending here to investigate how Dubai has diversified its main economic sectors. The aim is to identify and examine the drivers of Dubai's economic development, highlighting salient features and economic structures that enabled this development model to yield a highly diversified economy. We show that the success of Dubai is not accidental and hence it is important to understand the merits of its developmental approach and its relevance to regional economies. However, we find that in-depth comprehensive analysis of Dubai's economic trajectory is a daunting task for several reasons: (1) official data is scarce and not very reliable; (2) the boundaries between local vs. federal policies are often blurred, as Dubai is a city with great autonomy within the UAE; (3) the size of Dubai's economy is not significant globally as compared, for example, with Singapore or Hong Kong to attract attention of researchers; and (4) the impact of regional factors such as oil and access to liquidity are often overemphasized. We acknowledge that the role of oil is undeniably an important factor in shaping the economies of Dubai and other GCC countries, but in the case of Dubai, oil plays the role of a catalyst as opposed to being a hindrance, as resource curse theory may suggest. Hence, we start with the discussion on whether the rentier state theory is applicable to Dubai in the first place. This is followed by analysing the key elements of Dubai's economic development model. In section three, we assess the strength of the model by examining its capacity of coping with the debt crisis in the aftermath of the 2008 global financial crisis.

Rentier State Theory and Dubai

Some literature considers Dubai's model within the context of the rentier state theory and neo-patrimonialism. Originally, Mahdavy (1970) attempted to highlight economic challenges faced by the oil-exporting countries and suggested ways to address such problems. Closely related to the rentier state theory is the theory of the resource curse, which similarly looks into poor economic performance of resource-rich economies. Resource curse theory attributes an 'anomaly' economy or an economy with adverse socio-economic consequences to the fact that a substantial portion of national revenue is derived from the oil and energy-related income. Gray (2011) defines the rentier state theory as a state-society relationship, in which the state generates a large portion of income from rents or externally derived payments, typically that of oil and gas. This theory considers the state autonomous from society. It assumes that states do not need to impose any taxation as long as they distribute rent income to society. In turn, the state does not need to have any development strategy.

In fact, Ruthledge (2014) considers these two theories as two elements of the same paradigm. In this particularly critical account of the rentier state and resource curse theories, she points out that rentier state theory has become more deterministic (and pejorative) in nature in the late 1980s onwards. More importantly is that the state is used in a broader meaning to include the institutions of government, commercial entities and the citizens as a whole. Gray (2011) discusses rentier state theory in a context of economic achievements firstly in Dubai, but also in Abu Dhabi and Qatar, and concludes that these states do not fit in the original framework of this theory. Notably, it seems that there is increasing recognition that not only Dubai, but also other GCC states deserve more attention in understanding their developmental model and the specific role of oil revenues. El Katiri (2014) aptly describes the strong economic-welfare function as a distinguishing feature of GCC economies in relation to other resource-rich states. She defines the type of state in the GCC, as a Guardian State—a state in which benevolent state elites aim to maximize social welfare supported by the state autonomy in decision-making. The relatively small population sizes, geographical position and inherited governance mechanisms such as tribal societies are some of the key factors of the apparent divergence from the expected outcomes of the classic rentier state theory.

These are important learning developments. Assuming that such a state as Dubai exhibits all the features of the rentier state theory and primarily autonomous from the society, it would be difficult to envisage how such an economy would be able to make such a progressive economic advancements in essentially an environment without abundant natural resources. As we shall explain below, the Government of Dubai has traditionally played a key role in economic development, not only in policy-making and regulation but also in making direct investments in private enterprises. Pradhan (2009) refers to this sort of state investment as *a best case of the success of state-led capitalism*.

The theory of a 'Guardian State' makes important contributions in explaining development models relevant to GCC economies. It recognizes the resource-led nature of a development model similar to the rentier state theory, but it also highlights its strong socio-economic welfare objective function. This is how the term 'guardian state' developed. However, the success of guardian states to promote economic growth has never been free of some negative externalities, which are often associated with resource wealth and include a high propensity for waste and systemic dilution of market incentives. As a result, sustainability of economic growth is thereby a key challenge in guardian state economies.

Characteristics and Components of Dubai's Development Model

One of the main characteristics of Dubai's economy is being small, open and well integrated into global economic and financial systems. Free movements of factors of production, including capital and labour, as well as of goods and services are a cornerstone of its development strategy. Dubai pursues a regime that is consistent with liberal economic policies and does not impose restrictions on capital inflows and outflows or taxes on capital or labour, except foreign banks and oil companies that are reliable to paying 10 per cent corporate tax. A diverse corporate sector has developed, led by public sector companies such as Emirates Group, DP World, and comprising a myriad of global and international firms operating in virtually every sector of the economy.

Another key development in Dubai's economy is the rapid growth in real GDP in the past 15 years. According to Dubai Statistics Centre, Dubai's real GDP has almost tripled from AED 113 billion in year 2000 to AED 293 billion in 2010 and to AED 335 billion in 2014. Notably, this period includes the negative effects of the 2008/2009 global financial crisis and Dubai's debt crisis, without which the growth could have been much more impressive. The negative effect of these crises is reflected in negative GDP growth rate of −2.5 per cent in 2009.

Historically, Dubai has played the role of a regional entrepôt. Bearing in mind the demographic diversity of Dubai's population throughout time as well as the nature of trade business meant that a broad range of economic, institutional, political and cultural factors have shaped the evolution of Dubai's economy. Hvidt (2009) supports this argument by arguing that Dubai's overall development process has to be seen in the broader context, implying a multi-causal explanation. Hvidt (2009) lists nine parameters that define Dubai's model: (1) government-led development (ruler-led); (2) fast decision-making and 'fast track' development; (3) flexible labour force; (4) bypass of industrialization—creation of a service economy; (5) internationalization of service provision; (6) creation of investment opportunities; (7) supply-generated demand (first mover); (8) market positioning via branding; and (9) development in cooperation with international partners.

Similarly, Nyarko (2010) discusses elements of UAE's development strategy, which may also broadly apply to Dubai. His main elements are defined as (1) a political system, which has resulted in the perception of stability and minimal political risk, encouraging investment; (2) oil; (3) development strategies that have resulted in a very dynamic business environment; (4) openness to foreign skills and management; and (5) labour policies that have enabled the immigration of vast numbers of foreign low-skilled workers. Along similar lines, Davidson (2009) argues Dubai's new post-oil economy benefits from its long history of trade, merchant immigration, re-export activity and its relative openness compared to its Arab peninsular neighbours. Indeed, Dubai's demographic circumstances, together with the geographic position it occupies, have underpinned and determined the nature of its development process.

It is certainly true that all of the above factors have played a significant role in shaping the development path and outcomes in Dubai's economy. Nevertheless, one could argue that some of these factors are more of an exogenous nature from Dubai's standpoint, given the limited control it has over them, while some others are actually direct result of a broader principle or a policy. For example, fast decision-making is the result of a specific role the Government of Dubai plays and its governance approach. Meanwhile, some policies are formulated at the federal level such as the labour policy, where Dubai has limited scope or control. One could also argue that Hvidt's bypass of industrialization and creation of investment opportunities can be more of an effect than a cause or driver of Dubai's model. Bypassing industrialization is a natural outcome for Dubai, having in mind rapid and recent accumulation of wealth, limited natural resources and a small domestic population. It is true, however, that bypassing industrialization has led to the development of a service-based economy and the governance mechanism as practiced today. Similarly, the creation of investment opportunities is a consequence of its development and governance approach. Thus, the challenge in defining Dubai's economic model lies in distinguishing between the sources of its development and the effects of its policies and strategies.

Dubai and the UAE Political and Economic Setting

To understand Dubai's development model, its path and strategy, one needs to distinguish between federal policies and Dubai's own development strategy. Dubai's economic autonomy is confined within a broader UAE economic framework, which includes macroeconomic policy, labour policy, regulatory frameworks for banking and financial industry, and foreign exchange regime, among other policies determined at the federal level. Federal policies are the result of a common and shared economic and political dynamics of the seven emirates. When it comes to policy formulation, Dubai has a strong influence but not decisive over the national or federal policies. In fact, federal policies are reflective of Dubai's economic circumstances, but Dubai often finds itself in the legal loopholes, especially when it has to manoeuvre around the legal pillars to implement its own policies. For instance, Davidson (2007b) highlights the case of the first residential house sales to expatriates and the creation of free zones, as a measure to circumvent the federal restrictions on property ownership by expatriates.

Although Dubai has to manoeuvre between what is federal and what is its own, evidence shows that its macroeconomic and regulatory structures are aligned with the federal system; hence the emirate is largely influenced and shaped by the common federal policies. This is apparent in key areas such as monetary policy, exchange rate policy, fiscal policy, including taxation, ownership policy and company law. For instance, Dubai follows the federal policy of pegging the UAE dirham to the US dollar, which implies that a local monetary policy must align with US monetary policy, as well as tracking the US interest rates regardless of the phase of its own economic cycle. Such policies do not necessarily serve the best interests of Dubai at all times, as the rigidity of monetary policy due to the dollar peg greatly contributed to the exacerbation of the business cycle in Dubai in late 2007/2008. As Dubai's economy was experiencing a broad expansion, the US economy was going through difficulties that led it to run an expansionary monetary policy such as a low interest rate policy, which in Dubai's case was unfavourable and a pro-cyclical measure. Despite such adverse effect, the federal system supported Dubai to overcome its debt crisis in 2008–2009. Dubai also benefits from the federal immigration and labour policy that are highly flexible and, along with other federal policies, are one of the key developmental pillars of Dubai economic model. Thus, UAE macroeconomic policies serve as a broader framework for Dubai's developmental strategy and facilitator for its unique approach to economic development. Figure 5.1 illustrates this and explains the key elements of Dubai development model, as explained below.

Government-Led Economic Development

In contrast to the rentier state theory, which assumes government's passive role in economic planning and development, the role of the Government of Dubai has been significantly large in the Emirate's economic development. This role is in line with the argument developed in the guardian state theory, which asserts that those states markedly differ from most other economies not only by its resource wealth but also by the 'guardian' role the government plays. Al-Sayegh (1998) argues that Dubai has a long tradition in a strong government role in economy, greater inter-

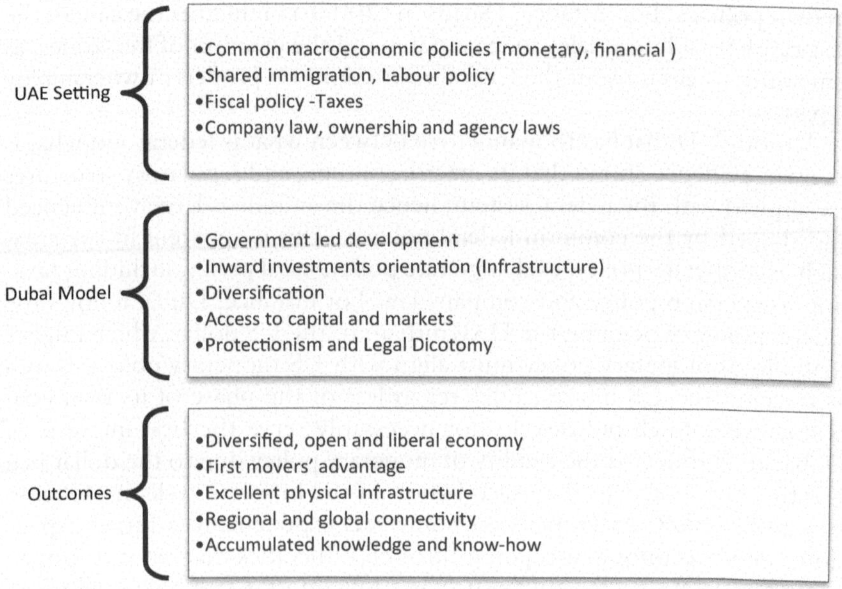

Fig. 5.1 Dubai economic development model. Source: Authors' own analysis

action with the business community and consolidated social contract with its citizens. Importantly, the relationship between the state and its citizens has not come about as a result of oil revenues and rents distribution but rather the vice versa. It is also important to note that the specific role played by the Government of Dubai is primarily inherited through centuries of old relationships between Dubai's rulers and its merchant community. El Katiri (2014), who highlights the pre-existing political and economic structures as a distinctive feature of the Guardian States, underlines this tradition. The pre-existing structures include the tribe as the central social unit in structuring socio-political life. The tribe is divided into families and headed by the tribal sheikh whose role as a guardian is to lead his family members and protect their socio-economic interests.

Developing on its tradition and existing structures, Dubai has developed idiosyncratic governance mechanisms and oriented its government towards a proactive state entrepreneurship and investment policies leading to greater diversification in all economic sectors. Hvidt (2009) attributes much of Dubai's exceptional growth levels in 2000–2007 to the quality of leadership and initiative of the Government, which are felt in the development and modernisation of public services, institutional frameworks, legislation, regulation and infrastructure, as well as the launch of strategic projects such as tourism ventures, the Internet and Media City, Health Care City, Logistic City and Dubai's International Financial Centre—all of them are developed, financed and run by the government. These initiatives have been the driving force behind the impressive development and the catalyst for private sector companies to follow the government lead and participate in the development process.

One can also argue that the institutional structure and centralization of decision-making has enabled the government to easily control and efficiently run its key economic organizations. In addition to the local government represented in the Dubai Municipality and its affiliated authorities that are responsible for the day-to-day running of the city-state, the newly created Executive Office is the place, where the ruler manages all economic activities and new developments such as mega projects, SOEs, FDI, free zones, ports, investment banks and specialized cities. The ruler has also placed his most trusted men in charge of the Dubai Holding, Dubai World, The Department of Economic Development, Dubai Municipality and Emaar. Hvidt (2009) argues that 'although this is not a democratic ideal, this kind of centralisation allows for fast decision-making and significant coordination of development activities and investments'.

Dubai's Governance Model and the Role of Merchants

Given its unique governance approach, Dubai's model is a deviant case of economic development. The peculiarity of this case reflects the nature of the relationship between the ruling family and the merchant community, when Dubai was an entrepôt in the Gulf and derived its prosperity from trade and commerce. Al Sayegh (1998) argues that Dubai's merchants have played an important role in shaping Dubai's economic and political development. Scarce resources and trade meant that merchants and rulers needed to work together to secure their livelihood. Partnerships, genuine creativity and innovation were utilized to create businesses and develop channels to support all kinds of economic activities. Dubai's natural harbour, strategic location and thriving merchant community maintained it as entrepôt for many decades. Contrary to expectations, the merchants' influence did not slow down with the advent of oil; rather it has taken advantage of the new wealth to continue its influence and contribution to the development process until today. Indeed, the government and the merchants share the responsibility for developing and contributing social aspects of their society. Social development has never been confined to strictly government affairs, as merchants have taken on additional roles as service suppliers, urban planners, culture mediators and internationalists who represent the Gulf throughout the world.

Interestingly, on many occasions the ruler's income was not as high as that of the pearl merchants. In fact, there were many times when the ruler resorted to the merchants for financial assistance. Financial dependency of the ruler on the merchant community and vice versa implied the need to focus on business development. In addition, it allowed merchants to have an upper hand or at least equal influence with the ruler in matters affecting their lives. Since the early twentieth century, rulers used to appoint merchants to his Majlis (advisory board); majlis was constituted as a consultative body and has effectively become a de facto government led by the ruler and composed of merchants. The relationship between the ruler and Dubai's merchants remains until today. In fact it became even more complex given the legacy of old relationships. The critical juncture took place in the early twentieth century when the ruler of Dubai persuaded the business community of the Persian city-state Lingah to relocate to Dubai. It instituted the strong private sector and pro-business development path which has characterized Dubai ever since.

As a result, Dubai's achievements are remarkable and noteworthy not only in terms of its economic performance but also in how that performance was achieved. The cosmopolitan nature of Dubai's merchants has added an important dimension in the fabric and nature of the business conduct and its economic structure. Given limited natural resource endowments, the small size of the local labour force, the complex political surrounding and challenging global economic environment, this governance model has proved to be particularly resilient.

One cannot underestimate the achievements of Dubai in this complex environment in terms of social cohesion, safety and a high standard of living. It is clear that Dubai's economic and social aspects are often inseparable as religion and culture shape Dubai's decision-making process through its own management and governance styles. Therefore, combining economic and social achievements of Dubai's model in a complex environment with many exogenous economic and social factors points out that its success is intrinsically driven.

State Entrepreneurship

An important characteristic of Dubai's government engagement in the economy is entrepreneurship. The role of state-guided entrepreneurship cannot be overemphasized as many SOEs are effectively competing in international markets. Shome (2009) argues that state entrepreneurship, as in the case of Singapore, is crucial for small, transitional economies to achieve global competitiveness. Dubai shares a similar orientation, where the state entrepreneurship model seems to be working efficiently. Unfortunately, entrepreneurship in Dubai has not received much attention in academic literature, and hence sharing the general scarcity in research indicates that this aspect of Dubai has largely been overlooked (Nasra and Dacin 2009). In fact, in the period from 1990 to 2006, there was no single article focusing on the examination of entrepreneurship in the Middle East as a whole; only in 2015 that Sherbiny and Hatem produced a historical account of the relationship between state and entrepreneurs in Egypt since 1805. Again, a plausible explanation to this phenomenon could be the perception of the GCC economies as rentier economies and hence not deserving the attention of the research community.

Nevertheless, our examination of the Dubai experience acknowledges the growing role of the state in entrepreneurial activities. This case underscores a contrasting vision to what rentier state theory posits—that the state is deriving rents from the revenues on the account of natural resources and redistributes them within the economy with the objective of keeping the regime in power. The Government of Dubai has undertaken investments and created businesses with private sector management orientation. Such companies, often so-called government related entities (GREs) including Emirates Group, Emaar, Nakheel and Dubal have been used as main investments and development vehicles. It is not uncommon to find the definition of GREs as '100 per cent government owned, private sector company', a definition that reflects both ownership and the intended governance style of Dubai's GREs. While being publicly owned, the GREs' management and governance orientation are that of private sector entities. Hence, the Government of Dubai has a multiplicity of roles to play. Whether it acts as a policy maker, regulator or investor, the default objective is business expansion and economic development.

Another key driver of successful state entrepreneurship is the interplay between the various public and private sector actors in the development process. Hvidt (2007) argues that there is apparent absence or lack of formal institutions and channels to link the public and private sector companies; this absence of formal institutions has been compensated for by the Majlis, the liberal economic policies and the multiple role of leadership through which the distinction between the public and the private sector gets blurred, as many private businesses are often absorbed into the governance structure. As many members of the ruling family are engaged in private investments, one could argue that strong ties between the public and the private sector exist in practical policy formulation and implementation. The close public-private partnership can also be noticed in the division of work and labour, where the government officials focus on the design and formulation of policies and projects while outsourcing to some private companies the task of providing useful intelligence and feasibility studies, and to some others the possibility of decentralising the implementation of policies and projects. Hvidt (2007) adds that this form of engagement shows the extent to which the government has been instrumental in creating many economic actors through the establishment of both public and semi-private companies.

On a final note, one could argue that the development of the entrepreneurial sector in Dubai has largely depended on the role played by the state through public policies, regulation, public spending, public services and corporate leadership. The governance model has contributed to creating well-managed, profitable SOEs in Dubai, thus contradicting the commonly accepted views on inefficiency of SOEs and poor quality of public sector in rentier economies due to large bureaucracies. Hertog (2010) argues that the source of SOEs' success is the profit-driven and market-oriented management 'that is autonomous in its daily operations, hence insulated against political and bureaucratic predation, and that receives clear incentives from a strictly limited, coherent set of high-level principles in the political regime'. This success is enabled firstly by the absence of a populist-mobilization history of economic development, and second, a substantially decisional autonomy of the regime leadership from interest groups within state and society.

Inward Investments and Development Orientation

The attraction and facilitation of foreign direct investment has topped Dubai economic agenda for many years. FDI is instrumental in national capital formation in countries such as Dubai that is suffering from scarcity of natural resources. FDI does not only compensate for the lack of domestic capital resources, but it is also vital for employment generation and transfer of technology and knowledge. Dubai has been an attractive destination to global FDI inflows. This is owed primarily to its high levels of integration in the global economy and the relatively liberal, friendly business environment. Dubai has also invested heavily in its infrastructure, including roads, ports and industrial and free zones such as Jebel Ali Free Zone, while streamlining its administrative procedures and reducing the cost and time of doing business. It has also improved its legal and regulatory frameworks, allowing full foreign ownership of properties and business premises in certain business services and professions such as accountancy and legal services.

While the improvement in infrastructure has been a key factor in attracting inward FDI, the rise in FDI capital flows has simultaneously financed major infrastructure projects essential for the city's economic development, particularly in areas such as ports, roads, bridges, power generations, water desalination, schools, hospitals, construction and real estate. One can only praise the long-term strategic plan that began with the 1950s, with the dredging of the Creek in 1955 and the development of Port Rashid in 1972—to the more recent Al Maktoum International Airport and a vast network of highways as well as a strong global connectivity that places Dubai as a top-class city worldwide. All these investments in infrastructure-related industries have not only created jobs and business opportunities but they have also fuelled Dubai's exponential economic growth and facilitated its economic diversification.

Trade and the manufacturing sector have also played an important role in the development of Dubai. Trade is one of the traditional pillars of the economy and has been a window through which the city-state has achieved its tremendous openness to the regional and global economies, even though it has also amplified its economic exposure to international economic and trade cycles. Unlike other GCC countries with strong oil revenues, Dubai has not shifted from *production-state to allocation-state,* thereby creating a vibrant and dynamic economy. Given the tremendous income from oil exports in the 'allocation state', the population assumes a role of passive recipient of services and benefits and as such, the state and the private sector are far less dependent on each other than in the production-state. This is why Dubai's economic sustainability essentially depends on its ability to maintain a production state orientation and avert conversion into allocation-state.

One can also argue that Dubai's inward investment orientation is reflected in infrastructure investments and development, creation of GREs across industries, and establishment and promotion of a pro-business environment. Dubai actively participates in competitive local and international markets, while creating new state assets in various forms, shapes and industries. This, in turn, creates new business and ample investment opportunities for local and foreign private sectors, thereby sending a positive signal to foreign investors and global markets (Hertog 2010). Dubai's economic development path highlights the positive effects of diversification via commitment to development that resulted out of a series of policies of inward investments, diversification, openness and liberal economic policies that coupled with pragmatic leadership, and all of them have resulted in a rather unique economic model.

Unhindered Access to Capital and Labour Markets

As Dubai is not endowed with abundant natural resources and consequently does not have abundant liquidity, access to international capital and banking markets is one of the critical factors that have contributed to accelerated growth and development of the Emirate. Dubai Government and GREs, while not being rated by international rating agencies, have successfully raised funds in international capital markets using conventional and Islamic instruments. GREs financed their growth using a combination of equity and debt. Nonetheless, a negative aspect in this respect is that access to international capital markets precipitated Dubai's Debt Crisis in late 2008.

Similarly, the ability to attract and maintain a necessary foreign workforce is yet another factor of Dubai's economic model. The economic success of Dubai is underpinned by the growth of its population, which is essentially driven by the influx of expatriate workers and their families. Almost 90 per cent of the population is composed of non-nationals, representing close to 95 per cent of the total workforce. The strong population growth has induced increased demand for real estate, retail, tourism and services. In turn, a flexible immigration policy as per the federal law, a highly efficient government apparatus and the availability of business and job opportunities support population growth.

Dubai's development has been driven by labour-intensive sectors that have seen the largest inflows of low-skilled non-national labour. Data shows sharp increases in labour inflows in labour-intensive sectors such as construction, real estate and services. However, large labour inflows have been accompanied by declining labour productivity. Economic growth in the UAE has been outpaced by labour force growth in recent years, leading to declines in labour productivity per capita. Figure 5.2

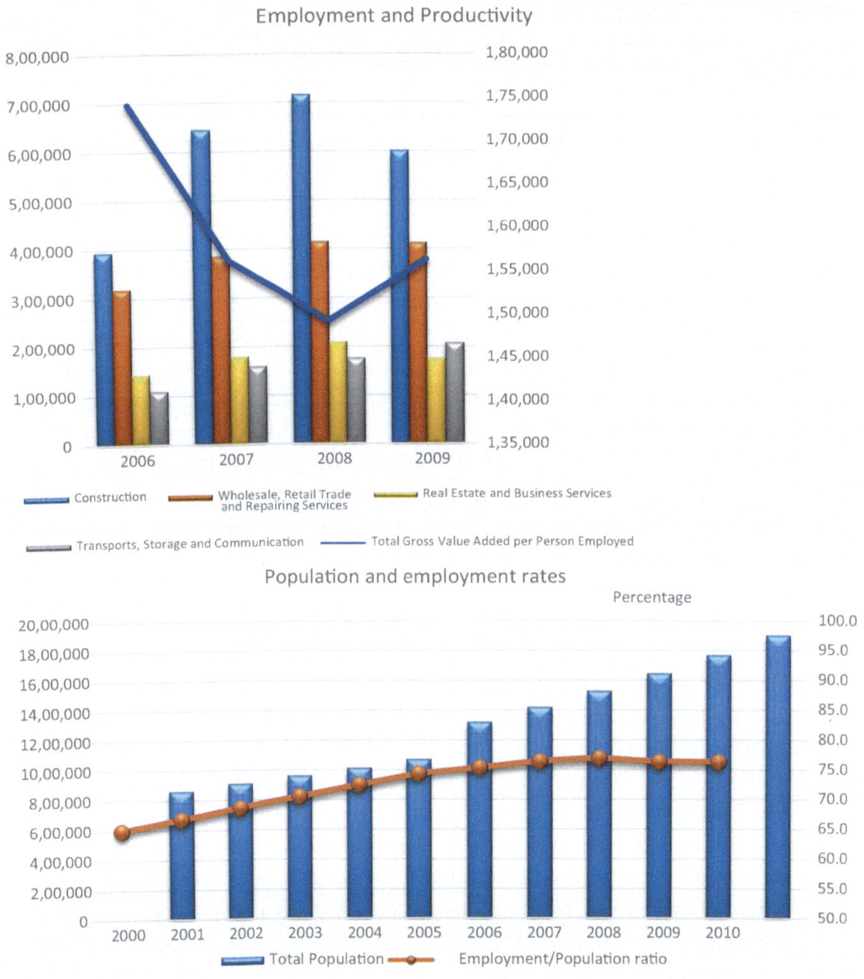

Fig. 5.2 Relationship between employment and productivity (2006–2009) and population (2000–2010). Source: Dubai Statistics Centre

shows that labour force growth was substantial, in particular, prior to the recent crisis—reaching over 10 per cent annually from 2006 to 2008. It also exhibits a declining labour productivity that is a negative spillover effect, as argued by the guardian state theory. Yet, another important reflection of the guardian state is the large proportion of the national workforce employed in the public sector. The public sector is an attractive employer due to various rent streams and contacts, generous retirement packages, job security, favourable working hours and good prospects of promotion with time. Dubai is no exception to this productivity anomaly. This is worsened by the inability of the private sector to match the public sector's high reservation wage (El Katiri 2014). In addition, employment subsidies in the private sector coupled with the nationals' employment quotas, further exacerbate a rent-seeking incentive system as a source of economic benefit. Hence, public sector employment policies contribute negatively to labour productivity resulting essentially in wastage of resources.

To improve future sustainability of the existing economic approach, the Government of Dubai seeks to promote a gradual move towards a knowledge-based economy and an economic policy moving towards encouraging capital investment and promoting growth in higher value-added sectors. The ability to attract and increasingly retain qualified human capital is essential in ensuring that these shifts occur.

Protectionism and Legal Dichotomy

Dubai's demographic structure with a small local population is in stark contrast to the size of its economy and the number of foreign workers and businesses. In addition to labour market incentives, subsidies and quotas, the federal government has developed schemes to protect the economic interest of the local population mainly by mandating Emirati ownership of at least 51 per cent of any business established in Dubai. Exempted from this rule are certain activities such as professional jobs of accountants, lawyers etc. who are allowed to set up 100 per cent foreign-owned businesses. Ownership limitations also extend to property and asset ownership.

Given the limited attractiveness of such restrictive policies to prospective foreign investors, a number of free zones have sprung throughout Dubai. Currently, there are 22 distinct zones targeting different industry clusters and client bases. Hence, Dubai confines liberal economic policies in terms of property and business ownership and business conduct within the special economic free zones. The ever-growing economy has necessitated the creation of a new institutional framework in the form of specialized free zones. This has allowed Dubai to create and manage international and national legitimacy by way of decoupling new economic structures from traditional national institutions. As such, Dubai has effectively been able to become an attractive destination for international investors while keeping its political stability within the Middle East (Nasra and Dacin 2009). A case in point is that of the Dubai International Financial Centre (DIFC), a federal free zone focusing on provision of financial services. Strong and Himber (2009) argue that the legal autonomy of the DIFC is a scalable strategy suitable for global free-market reforms. While the DIFC has its separate Common Law based legislation within the free zone including its own courts, this legal system exists in parallel to Dubai and federal legislation.

Outside the free zones, the Company Law of the UAE requires only locals to own property and businesses and provides some protection mechanisms, perhaps as a reflection of the rentier orientation in which the state is effectively covering social costs and economic welfare benefits.

Economic Diversification Strategy

Dubai's economic development strategy has gone through various phases. The first phase is to shift its dependence away from oil revenues. Oil revenues played an important role in Dubai's quest for development in the early post-discovery years, but this effect has been recently indirect, through the higher liquidity that Abu Dhabi and other GCC oil exporters have injected in Dubai's economy (Nyarko 2010). In fact, Dubai's oil contribution to GDP is now insignificant, accounting for 1.4 per cent in 2013. Contrary to other oil-rich exporting countries that experienced slower economic development due to natural resource endowments, Dubai has not suffered from the Dutch disease phenomenon because of its capacity to take advantage of available regional liquidity to jumpstart economic transformation and achieve diversification.

The second phase of diversification is closely linked to inward investment and development orientation strategy that focuses primarily on developing and investing into enabling sectors such as infrastructure and communications. In fact, the success of this long-term policy of developing and investing into enabling sectors has allowed the development of other dynamic and striving economic sectors such as financial services, tourism and manufacturing. Without this deliberate strategy to develop and diversify the economy away from oil, the resource curse theory would apply.

The third phase of development and diversification is enabling Dubai to develop a competitive edge resulting in a diversified, open and liberal economy. Dubai was the first in the region to open up to foreign capital and labour in a significant way and consequently gained large benefits from the first movers' advantage. The creation of economic clusters and free zones have gained critical mass and allowed for the introduction of economies of scale, which turned the city-state into a regional and global hub for many international companies and multinational corporations.

The fourth phase of diversification is the move towards the creation of a knowledge-based economy. Dubai's model has not only been closely watched and emulated by Abu Dhabi and other small GCC countries such as Qatar, but it has become an exemplary model of capitalising on the already excellent physical infrastructure to develop a first class regional and global connectivity. Attracting and retaining a skilled workforce has also resulted in the accumulation of knowledge and know-how, which pave the ground for less labour-intensive economic development. However, many challenges such as educational development and sufficient investment in research and development have yet to overcome.

Dubai Debt Crisis: How Sustainable Is Dubai's Development Model?

One can hardly make a fair and sound judgement on the sustainability of the Dubai development model without analysing the most stressful test that the city-state has ever experienced: Dubai debt crisis in 2009. This crisis exposed major structural weaknesses in the way the financial and real estate markets operated in the pre-global financial crisis of 2008. In the 2000s, Dubai had experienced an extraordinary growth across most economic sectors. Local credit markets were at the highest levels similar to those of real estate and stock markets, where speculation was the norm rather than the exception. It was also noted that IPO listings were hundreds of times oversubscribed, executives were paid seven-figure bounces and GREs were acquiring high-profile international trophy assets.

Hasan (2010) argues that debt crisis peaked at the government's announcement of US$59 billion debt-payment-standstill on November 26, 2009. Prior to the announcement, the global financial crisis was already in full swing and resulted in virtually shutting financial markets and loss of confidence across markets. Owing to its open economy with strong reliance on global trade flows and access to global financial markets, Dubai's economy experienced major disruptions in activity across sectors, while structural vulnerabilities were exposed. Among key weaknesses were pro-cyclical fiscal and monetary policies that exacerbated by the dirham's peg to the US dollar. Cevik (2011) provides empirical findings indicating how pro-cyclical fiscal policies prior to the crisis reinforced the financial sector cycle, exacerbated the economic upswing, thereby contributing to the build-up of macro financial vulnerabilities. However, for the purpose of this discussion and strictly speaking from Dubai's angle, fiscal and monetary pro-cyclical weaknesses are exogenous factors over which Dubai has limited control.

Nassehi (2013) explains Dubai/UAE open capital account policy as an instrument of a liberal environment for foreign capital, but also as a factor exacerbating Dubai's boom-bust cycle. Dubai's construction boom encouraged the influx of immigrant labour that was instrumental to Dubai's high economic growth. This boom was funded by a rapid increase in foreign borrowing—mainly short term. Foreign liabilities held by the banking sector rocketed from AED 35 billion in 2003 to AED 320 billion in 2007, representing 33 per cent of GDP in 2007. Chailloux and Hakura (2009) also attribute sharp increases in foreign deposits in the banking industry—which rose from AED 47 billion to AED 127 billion in 2007—to the expectations of a dirham revaluation, only to be reversed in mid-2008.

This has posed severe internal liquidity pressures in the economy. Ample liquidity in the banking sector meant cheap money that was lent mainly to GREs. Increased liquidity followed by increased credit and elevated inflation levels were not offset by tightening of monetary policy, given dollar peg restrictions. Contrary to desired monetary policy, the UAE had to follow a low interest rate regime as per US monetary policy which resulted in negative interest rates. Due to the absence of a domestic debt market and the Central Bank's inability to conduct sterilization, Dubai's boom cycle was heightened. Further, due to high domestic liquidity and ensuing increased credit levels in the financial system, Dubai's corporates—mainly GREs—have also raised short-term funds in international markets, banking and capital. According to the IMF, at its peak, external debt of the banks and the GREs amounted to 74 per cent of GDP.

Interestingly, Nassehi (2013) also relates the oil boom of the mid-2000s and the perceived implicit government guarantee for GREs' debt, to the debt overhang. The so-called crony capitalism led international banks to provide finance to GREs despite obvious moral hazard risks, which have contributed largely to pro-cyclical credit growth.

One of the prime lessons of Dubai's debt crisis is the realization of the inability of Dubai's financial markets to serve local development needs and the excessive reliance on short-term debt accumulated by the majority of Dubai's GREs. Clearly, not being able to refinance such debt has led Dubai into a spiral. Dubai's financial markets are primarily cantered on the banking industry, which was highly exposed to the real estate sector. According to the IMF estimates, commercial banks' exposure to the real estate amounted to 29 per cent of their total assets in 2010. This exposure took place not only via lending to developers but also through retail mortgage finance, construction finance, as well as personal loans that were contracted mainly to finance real estate acquisitions.

Following the debt crisis, Dubai took important steps to prevent the repetition of earlier mistakes by bringing about greater discipline in public spending, rationalizations and standardization across the real estate market, and greater efficiency in public services. Nevertheless, the risk of debt overhang still looms over Dubai, albeit at much more manageable levels. Since the beginning of 2011, Dubai's economy has rebounded and recorded growth, and this is expected to continue at a similar pace in the medium term. In spite of persisting global economic challenges and modest global growth, Dubai has shown resilience and a great capacity to bounce back—not withstanding its structural challenges, driven by traditional sectors such as trade, logistics and transportation, and tourism.

Concluding Remarks: Dubai's Unorthodox Approach to Diversification

We have systematically developed an understanding of Dubai's economy by examining its performance and structures to derive its development model. Given the uniqueness of Dubai's economic path and achievements, Dubai's economic story has not been adequately researched. While Dubai's economic performance is analysed in isolation from its historical, cultural and religious background, we have shown that the success of

Dubai is not incidental. In fact, it is the result of policies instituted by the founding fathers of the Emirate in the early 1900s.

In contrast to prevalent views on various inefficiencies associated with resource rich economies as framed in the rentier state theory, Dubai's model of development rests on the (1) government leadership with specific governance and state entrepreneurship models, (2) inward investment orientation, (3) unhindered access to capital and labour markets, (4) protectionism and legal dichotomy and (5) policy of systematic diversification.

This model seems to better differentiate between causes and effects of Dubai's economic development approach than some models previously put forward. Other models found in a limited literature do not offer a coherent and internally consistent model that provides a framework to capture various drivers at play. Therefore, these models fail to provide clear explanations of Dubai's developmental path. Rather, such models seem to point to Dubai's success as a haphazard set of developmental priorities that emerged as an answer to opportunistic circumstances.

Economic development and diversification have been facilitated by leadership commitment to development and access to labour and capital markets, among others. However, a debt crisis in 2008–2009 reveals many structural weaknesses. An important lesson was the realization of Dubai's pro-cyclical macroeconomic policies, structural weaknesses in the real estate market, shallow and underdeveloped financial markets, weaknesses in public spending policy and inadequate support for private sector development.

References

Al-Sayegh, F. (1998). Merchants' Role in a Changing Society: The Case of Dubai, 1900–90. *Middle Eastern Studies*, 34, 87–102.

Cevik, S. (2011). *Policy Coordination in Fiscal Federalism: Drawing Lessons from the Dubai Debt Crisis*. IMF Working Paper.

Chailloux, A., & Hakura, D. (2009). *Systemic Liquidity Management in the U.A.E.: Issues and Options*. Working Paper. IMF.

Davidson, C. (2007a). Arab Nationalism and British Opposition in Dubai, 1920–66. *Middle Eastern Studies, 43*, 879–892.

Davidson, C. (2007b). The Emirates of Abu Dhabi and Dubai: Contrasting Roles in the International System. *Asian Affairs, 38*, 33–48.

Davidson, C. (2008a). *Dubai—The Vulnerability of Success*. New York: Columbia University Press.

Davidson, C. (2009). Dubai: Foreclosure of a Dream. *Middle East Report, 251*, 8–13.

El-Katiri, L. (2014). The Guardian State and Its Economic Development Model. *The Journal of Development Studies, 50*, 22–34.

Gray, M. (2011). *A Theory of "Late Rentierism" in the Arab States of the Gulf*. Occasional Paper No 7. Center for International and Regional Studies, Georgetown University School of Foreign Service in Qatar.

Hasan, Z. (2010). Dubai Financial Crisis: Causes, Bailout and After—A Case Study. *Munich Personal RePEc Archive*.

Hertog, S. (2010). Defying the Resource Curse: Explaining Successful State-Owned Enterprises in Rentier States. *World Politics, 62*(2), 261–301.

Hvidt, M. (2007). Public-Private Toes and Their Contribution to Development: The Case of Dubai. *Middle Eastern Studies, 43*(4), 557–577.

Hvidt, M. (2009). The Dubai Model: An Outline of Key Components of the Development Process in Dubai. *International Journal of Middle East Studies* (Center for Contemporary Middle Eastern Studies, University of Southern Denmark), 397–418.

Mahdavy, H. (1970). The Patterns and Problems of Economic Development in Rentier States: The Case of Iran. In *Studies in Economic History of the Middle East from the Rise of Islam to Present Day*, by M.A. Cook, 428-467. London: Oxford University Press.

Nasra, R., & Dacin, T. (2009). Institutional Arrangements and International Entrepreneurship: The State as Institutional Entrepreneur. *Entrepreneurship Theory and Practice, 34*, 583–609.

Nassehi, R. (2013). Haunted by Capital Inflows: How "Hot Money" from Abroad Fuelled UAE's Financial Crisis. *International Journal of Sustainable Human Development, 1*, 76–83.

Nyarko, Y. (2010). *The United Arab Emirates: Some Lessons in Economic Development*. Working Paper: World Institute for Development Economics Research No 2010, 11.

Pradhan, S. (2009). *The UAE's Economic Policy and the Current Global Meltdown: An Appraisal*. Working Paper Series. Dubai: Gulf Research Centre, Dubai School of Government.

Rutledge, E. (2014). The Rentier State/Resource Curse Narrative and the State of the Arabian Gulf. *Munich Personal RePEc Archive*.

Schiliro, D. (2013). Diversification and Development of the UAE's Economy. *Munich Personal RePEc Archive*.

Sherbiny, N., & Hatem, O. (2015). *State and Entrepreneurs in Egypt: Economic Development Since 1805*. Hampshire, UK: Palgrave Macmillan.

Shome, A. (2009). Singapore's State Guided Entrepreneurship: A Model for Transitional Economies. *New Zealand Journal of Asian Studies, 11*, 318–336.

Strong, M., & Himber, R. (2009). The Legal Autonomy of the Dubai International Financial Centre: A Scalable Strategy for Global Free-Market Reforms. *Institute of Economic Affairs, 29*, 36–41.

CHAPTER 6

Diversification and Specialisation in the Gulf's Digitised Creative Sectors

Náder Alyani

Introduction

In this chapter, we explore the need to integrate sectoral learning and skills development into sectoral policies, particularly in priority sectors that have a significant potential to contribute to economic diversification (and where appropriate, develop a simultaneous move towards specialisation). We first provide a circumscribed review of the creative sector as a potential employment-creating sector, specifically in the digitised creative segment in Iran, Saudi Arabia, and United Arab Emirates. Whilst acknowledging the previous work on the education and training systems and the increased entrepreneurship education efforts in these countries (and a brief glance at the long-standing macro debate on *resource-curse* and/or *resource-blessing*), we focus on the learning and upskilling required for innovating in the nascent creative sub-sectors. We pay particular attention, based on our previous empirical undertakings, to sub-sectors such as digital commerce (e.g. start-ups and new technology-based firms); digital marketing and advertising (e.g. mobile value-added services—VAS); media and entertainment

N. Alyani (✉)
College of Business Administration, Prince Mohammad Bin Fahd University (PMU), Khobar, Saudi Arabia

LLAKES Centre, UCL IOE, University College London, London, UK

A. Mishrif, Y. Al Balushi (eds.), *Economic Diversification in the Gulf Region, Volume II*, The Political Economy of the Middle East,
DOI 10.1007/978-981-10-5786-1_6

(e.g. television and film, and gaming); and fashion. Our geographical focus, in terms of assessing policies and policy risk, remains on the city-level context of Abu Dhabi and Dubai, Khobar (with a glance at Jeddah), and Tehran.

Secondly, exploring the in-situ learning episodes within a conceptual model, created via primary and secondary data sources, we point to the prominent use of skill webs as means of in-project upskilling and a resource for development of interprofessional learning and judgement capability, which forms a core ingredient for innovation. Lastly, the final section briefly points to recent policy vistas and concludes.

In policy terms and derived from economic geography, we remain mindful of the 'promising-practices' trends from London and Seoul (with United Kingdom and recently Republic of Korea viewed as the leading proponents of the *Creative Economy* policies for sustainable growth). Additionally, we acknowledge the broader policy tension between diversification and specialisation, concluding that at different stages of economic development, and within different sectors-in-progress of a national economy, both strategies may need to be cyclically operationalised and evaluated (cf. UNIDO 2012).

New Sectors and Employment in the Gulf

We start by briefly considering digitalisation within our context, with a glance at Iran, Saudi Arabia, and United Arab Emirates: Digitisation is a global phenomenon and industrial pattern that is revolutionising how companies and service providers, such as private firms and the State, interact and transact with their customers and service users. The creative sector in the Gulf is profoundly affected by this changing wave, including the broad diversification issues (Cherif and Hasanov 2014; Hvidt 2013; IMF Survey 2014; see also, Hvidt 2015) and in the absence of research and sectoral statistics, this chapter explores the meso-level and micro-level factors.

For the sake of clarity, the historically steeped and geographically established term of *Persian Gulf* (originating from the early Greeks) and the newer term of *Arabian Gulf* (based on Pan-Arabism ideology of 1960s) are the full official terms currently used, respectively, in Iran and Gulf Cooperation Council (GCC) States (e.g. KSA and UAE), to refer to the same waterway and region.

As the Gulf region countries differ significantly in their stages within the sectoral evolution, our focus in this chapter is on possible education and training, human capital management, and infrastructure (physical and social) policies that is required for reaching the full potential of the sector.

By bridging the skills gap and creating sectoral skill webs, the burgeoning sector can then offer employers, employees and the State viable and sustainable pathways to growth.

Sectoral learning is an important cornerstone of our argument. The importance of sectoral learning in the overall economic development has recently been covered in detail, with reference to *catch-up* (Malerba and Nelson 2012) and in relation to the necessary structural change towards *economic growth* (Hausmann 2015; Hausmann et al. 2014). As an upfront caveat, we are cautious about the mainstream policy (*mis*)use of the notion of *human capital*, as actual practice and longitudinal data indicate a more complex picture (cf. Lauder 2014) than the one commonly portrayed by policy aspirations, plans and documents.

Our route within the chapter is as follows: the next section ('A Continuing Legacy of Mismatch in Education and Training') sets the contextual scene, in a brief and thus circumscribed manner, before moving in the following sub-section ('The Digitised Creative Sector in Brief') to look at the features of the digitised creative sector. Section 'Debates on Natural Resources as a Blessing or a Curse' bridges across a range of debates on resource blessing and/or curse and introduces the useful recent analytical concept of *Dutch knowledge disease*. Then the following sections ('Learning and Development in and for the Creative Sector' and 'Sectoral Upskilling for Interprofessional Learning and Judgement') deal with issues of enterprise-based processes of workplace learning and development, and rapidly zoom in on the issue of interprofessional judgement, including a brief conceptual discussion and an outline of our model. The last section ('Concluding Remarks: Digitised Creative Sector Upskilling') concludes by exploring implementation and policy realisation mechanisms as a core factor in policy and programme design (and re-design), highlighting that *sectoral catch-up* requires a unified approach of directions in upskilling schemes, delivered together with the private sector. Furthermore, we visit the necessity for continued reforms in the education as well as a coherent industrial policy and labour market policy/practice, particularly via *strategic incrementalism*, whilst pointing towards the new vistas in policy.

Policy-design and -implementation cycles typically take a number of years (e.g. 3 to 5 years) to materialise, during which period some of the core issues can change and dynamically evolve: foresight for managing *policy risk* is thus crucial to understand how the processes may play out, utilising evaluation analytics and potential impact assessments, so as to avoid unintended consequences on the outcome scenarios.

A Continuing Legacy of Mismatch in Education and Training

There is much written and broadcast in the journalistic realm, often with a geo-political twist, and an increasing volume in consultancy reports broadly about the Gulf region, yet relatively little robust material is directed at the specific economic and sustainable (and carefully coordinated *sequential*) development processes that are required. So, whilst the long-term policy aim of economic diversification is a near-constant priority rhetoric, little coherent and consistent attention has traditionally been paid to new sectors with the overhaul of an industrial policy, such as the creative sectors, in Islamic Republic of Iran (IRI), Kingdom of Saudi Arabia (KSA), and United Arab Emirates (UAE). That (often incidental) policy and practice oversight is however changing, with some attention to the tensions between the simultaneous need for diversification at the macro, and specialisation at micro level of economic sectors.

Within the recent years, Iran, KSA, and UAE—emerging as key regional actors by virtue of their geographic, demographic and market size, and geostrategic and economic reach—are actively seeking ways to secure their economy's future, looking East as well as West, and beyond their hydrocarbon assets: these include designing and formulating more cohesive and sufficiently implementable policies to build an ability for entrepreneurial innovation to drive their economies in line with international best practice (e.g. from IMF, OECD and G20), and in parallel, enhance their citizens' skills for competitiveness, in spite of chronic educational, skill, and employment challenges. The fluctuations in, and since mid-2014, the cyclical downward pressure on oil and commodity prices have prompted a renewed examination of interconnected policies to build an ability for innovation, so as to further develop and diversify economic sectors.

There is a robust body of interdisciplinary evidence accumulated over the last three decades indicating that innovation—and the skills to learn to, and continue to innovate—building upon workplace learning and commercial purpose of projects, enhanced by education and lifelong learning are of paramount importance in nations' economic development. This is increasingly being better understood and captured, beyond a policy buzzword and rhetoric, in a succession of recent development plans and national strategies of Iran, Saudi Arabia, and United Arab Emirates.

The genesis of this chapter is an ongoing research project on sectoral and enterprise-level processes on the linkages between innovation and human capital, and specifically on skill development (including discussions on the *crisis* of youth un-/employment issues, and in some cases, "*yester-years' youth*" of under 35, still struggling within the system), examining a number of globally emerging patterns. Whilst there are clearly many similarities with the global position both on employment, unemployment, underemployment and mismatching of skill issues, and an acknowledgement of the diversity and challenges of education (e.g. Higher Education and Technical Vocational Education and Training (TVET) systems globally), a few unique challenges are also identified, specific to the countries in our focus.

As an example, whilst it should be highlighted that, based on dedicated local and national level work in the last five years, assisted by UNESCO and UNEVOC, the renewed brand and image of the TVET systems in the three countries have been somewhat elevated; the legacy of the systems in the perception of many employers, parents and young people themselves, remains problematic. As a landmark World Bank report commented, within the region, TVET has traditionally been viewed as:

> the 'poor cousin' of the education family ... [and regionally, have been] relatively unsuccessful in linking training with employment ... [furthermore, as] TVET is usually the reserve of those who have not done well in compulsory education, many students do not have a firm grasp of the basic skills necessary to learn more challenging technical competencies ... [and thus, it] largely fails to put students on a clear pathway to further education and training options. (Galal 2008, p. 93)

Furthermore, three early caveats are worth front-loading here: Firstly, Iran, Saudi Arabia, and UAE, in the last decade and half, have witnessed a massive rise in both public and private provisions of their higher education, and as such, many university and polytechnic/further education college graduates now compete in the school-leavers' labour market and talent pool. Whether the quality of the expanded higher education sector has kept up with its quantity; whether the choice and specificity of courses of studies offered has been congruent with the needs of the labour market; and how far of a *decoupling* between education and economic growth now exists—are all open debates.

Robust and up-to-date data on the link between education and economic growth within the three countries is hard to pin down: a historical analysis (1960–2003) covering the far larger region, and aggregated data of Middle East and North Africa (MENA) points to a weak link (Galal 2008, Chap. 2).

Additionally, consider a recent empirically robust argument (using longitudinal and big-data tools) in development economics advocated by Harvard University's Centre for International Development, highlighting that:

> 'As is often the case, the experience of individual countries is more revealing than the averages. China started with less education than Tunisia, Mexico, Kenya or Iran in 1960, and had made less progress than them by 2010. And yet, in terms of economic growth, China blew all of them out of the water.' [...] (Hausmann, p. 22). Furthermore, '... there is more bad news for the "education, education, education" crowd: most of the skills that a labour force possesses were acquired on the job. What a society knows how to do is known mainly in its firms, not in its schools. At most modern firms, fewer than 15 percent of the positions are open for entry-level workers, meaning that employers demand something that the education system cannot—and is not expected—to provide.' (ibid.: 23)

Secondly, whilst there are existing surveys of the education and skill development systems including TVET and lifelong learning (LLL), both regionally (Galal 2008) and in the three countries (cf. UNESCO-UNEVOC 2014; for a recent commentary, see Baqadir et al. 2011), we have attempted to steer in a different, and in our view, potentially more generative direction. Thus, in this chapter it is not our intention to address 'macro' education and economy's links, reforms and policy implications but rather wish to open a preliminary dialogue and reflection by looking at new sectors and the associated changes in work arrangements (instead of the 'legacy' education and training systems, within existing sectors), based on the specific focus of our study. Our inquiry, therefore, starts from the changing nature of the *upstream* economy and work, rather than the *downstream* education and training systems.

Our third caveat, again based on the specific sectors under exploration—is to background the national systems and wherever possible foreground, and thus focus more on the local city-wide and regional ecosystems based on the enterprises in practice, specifically at Abu Dhabi and by natural sectoral extension—Dubai, UAE; Khobar (and a glance at Jeddah, for comparative purposes); KSA; and Tehran, Iran. Lastly, we do not claim finality on our current perspective for the four city regions, as our work on a sector-specific empirical level remains in-progress.

Condensing a range of *macro-meso-micro* level policy issues, we highlight that three overarching strategies are actively at play, whilst being contested, debated, and promoted at the national level of the three countries explored; these national strategies can be themed across three strands as:

- Diversification of the economy, including specialisation efforts in selected sectors and linking in with global value chains (GVCs)
- Technological 'catch-up' and development, and
- Labour market restructuring

These strands are highly interconnected and sensitive to market demands and perceptions. At times, stability needs to be re-injected (by the State) to retain the system's balance and avoid too blatant of 'market-failures'. A core notion, underlying these strands, is to build up the national capabilities and improve the prospects of national competitiveness. Equally, there is an increasingly visible policy acknowledgement, at all levels of the political echelons of the three countries, that new sectors which have the potential to generate new private sector jobs—and thus reduce and relieve the burden of unemployment, particularly in the 'educated young'—are in need of developmental assistance (in similar spirit to *infant industries* policies of previous decades), in an effort to build a sustainable job-creation pipeline. This is particularly intense where there is a demographic youth bulge. In short, whilst the state is still the key *enabler* and to a large extent, the *provider*, it cannot remain so indefinitely. Therefore, the role of the private sector and small and medium enterprises (SMEs) and within that—the fast-growing new technology-based firms (NTBFs) and their potential in offering a lion's share of future *decent jobs*—is under policy spotlight. Furthermore, whilst manufacturing has traditionally been viewed as the bastion of industrialisation (and thus, 'progress') in these countries, it is now the service sectors that act as the firm- and employment-creation engine, and offer a more secure mechanism to the potential of higher value-added growth path (potentially by linking to global value chain networks).

In line with international policy trends, innovation and entrepreneurship, and by extension educating for innovation and entrepreneurship, is starting to be consistently promoted and supported. In this policy domain within the region, a range of policy tools, instruments and metrics such as longitudinal data offered by World Bank's '*[Ease of] Doing Business*', the Global Entrepreneurship Monitor (GEM) project and related analysis, and World

Economic Forum's innovation and human capital indicators and *Global Innovation Index*, embedded within their annual *Global Competitiveness Report* are drawn upon both by comparative researchers and policy analysts.

In parallel and in line with global trends (UNCTAD 2008; Strategy&, PwC 2013), policies to enhance a move towards a *Creative Economy* and as part and parcel of that, vibrant digitised creative sectors are increasingly apparent on the three countries' *policy radars.*

Before ending this sub-section, a last point of information is called for. Whilst accurate and up-to-date sectoral data is hard to come by, general descriptive data such as national (and city-regional) economic and demographic trends are now readily available online from multiple sources (e.g. World Bank 2015); therefore we have not felt it necessary to list these explicitly. However, the following unique demographic patterns could be helpfully noted.

By the start of 2016, relatively *conservative estimates* indicate that demographics of our three countries in question are as follows. Kingdom of Saudi Arabia's population is around the 30 million mark, of which approximately 45 per cent will be female (and 55 per cent male; higher due to a large migrant labour force): The growth rate is stabilised at around 1.5 per cent per annum, with an approximate migrant (non-Saudi) population of 32 per cent. The population of United Arab Emirates is around the 10.5 million mark, of which approximately 31 per cent will be female (and 69 per cent male; much higher due to a significant unaccompanied male labour migrant percentage): the growth rate is stabilised at around 3 per cent (whilst bearing in mind that with a population of about 3.4 million in 2004, UAE saw double-digit demographic growth, primarily via migrant workers, between 2005 and 2010), and an approximate migrant (non-Emirati) residents of 85+ per cent. Lastly, Iran's population is likely to reach the 80 million mark, of which approximately 49.5 per cent is female (and 50.5 per cent male, including a small number of migrant labour, relative to the overall population): the growth rate is stabilised at 1.25 per cent and an approximate (non-Iranian) population of 2–2.5 per cent mainly composed of the majority Afghan migrant, and a smaller, Iraqi émigré communities. Whilst labour 'nationalisation' (meaning the full utilisation of local workforce) is not currently a particular challenge for Iran where regulations on using 'local content' is embedded into all international (and joint-venture) contracts, it has become a lingering policy challenge for UAE and KSA (referred to as *Emiratisation* and *Saudisation* of the labour force).

As to the city-regions within our focus, Tehran's city population is (probably under-reported at) around 8.4 million, with 12.6 million in the Tehran metropolitan area—marking it as Iran's most significant business hub and largest urban area, and the largest city in Western Asia. Whilst Abu Dhabi and Dubai in UAE, Khobar (including the *Dhahran-Khobar-Dammam* connected spatiality and satellite cities), and Jeddah in KSA may be somewhat smaller in terms of population—each of these city-regions are ambitiously and consistently endeavouring to place themselves as the sector-specific business hubs of their region.

Abu Dhabi, for example, leads the way in terms of sector-specific planning and infrastructural projects, and has increasingly placed greater emphasis on the creative sector such as focusing on Arabic-language digital media content (Financial Times 2014) and location for the creative sector (such as the setting for *Jakku* in the recent 'Star Wars: The Force Awakens'). Equally, although at early stages, Khobar and Jeddah (and Riyadh) are capacity-building for the sector based on niche markets and improving infrastructure, including practical assistance on national-level practice and policy borrowing, inter alia, from Republic of Korea (KDI 2012) and global consulting firms (McKinsey Global Institute 2015). This is couched within a background of significant economic and sectoral diversification policy aspirations within Saudi Arabia's future planning with Vision 2030 and National Transformation Programme 2020 in effect superseding the traditional five year development plan cycle (for a glance at industrial policy, see McKinsey Global Institute 2015).

Whilst the largest in terms of demographics, Tehran's industrial and sectoral policy outlook is somewhat more organic and 'bottom-up driven'. With the relative détente of geopolitical tensions with Western powers and international sanctions relief, and re-election of Iran's centrist and pragmatic presidential administration post Summer 2017 (notwithstanding Iran and Saudi Arabia's regional issues), this includes various emerging innovative service designs, enhanced by boundary-spanning interactions and sectoral expertise, and seed-financing with the technology diaspora communities via USA and EU, but also lumbered with significant infrastructure, (lack of) sectoral 'implementable policy' and skills provision challenges, as well as continuing macro-economic (ranging from stagflation to recessionary) concerns on achieving "non-inflationary and inclusive growth".

In the next sub-section, we briefly outline core features of the digitised creative sector in general, before turning our attention to our model based on previous research.

The Digitised Creative Sector in Brief

There is an increasing volume of diverse literature on the creative (and cultural) industries and sectors, including definitional differences in various countries: reviewing the field, which has also become firmly established as a global policy concept, is not our task here. Rather, we limit ourselves to noting the following: creative sectors build on widely accepted assumptions that investment and innovation in entrepreneurial 'creative' services can generate economic return and growth—both on a city/regional level and by extension—feed into national levels. The creative features refer to an economic sector in which creativity, human and social capital, combine with urbanised interconnected entrepreneuriality, rather than relying on purely physical assets of land, labour, and financial capital. As the field has grown and matured, a number of sectoral approaches have identified the digitised segment of the creative sector as a core area worthy of careful policy attention (see also, Bhargava and Al Kaabi 2014; Strategy&, PwC 2013). As of 2015 re-classifications, the sector includes sectoral categories such as 'film, video, and photography', 'music and the visual and performing arts', 'software, computer games and electronic publishing', as well as advertising, design, fashion, crafts and, museums and galleries.

It is worth pointing out however that the above classifications do not always hold strictly, as in the day-to-day practice of the sector, firms frame and attempt to solve business problems by cutting-across different sub-sector specialities. Consider, for example, a mobile application software development project, which is funded by a bank for the dual purpose of its advertising and branding, as well as enhanced service design (e.g. in creating multi-channel service delivery for interactions with the bank, collection of data-points and transactions with the client's account). Or a lifestyle website with instructional videos on Arabic cuisines and culinary, which markets niche fashion and kitchenware (craft) too—essentially acting as an advertising test-bed and gateway platform, including recommendation on music to cook, or to dine with. Convergence in technology and social trends therefore can create complex interdisciplinary and thus, interprofessional skill requirements for the project's back-office.

Added to the older discourses on creative industries and sectors, a more recent policy frame has turned towards endorsing a *creative economy* concept, as a potential pathway to growth and job-creation for specific regions and cities of the developing (and developed) economies. We therefore acknowledge that both the digitised creative sector activities, and the broader creative economy concept, despite their inherent ambiguities, have started to draw the attention and interest of the policy makers—both globally and in the Gulf region.

That said, a brief commentary on the terminology would be useful. Analysts point to the trend that other nomenclatures have—in various periods of the recent decades—been adopted for similar conceptions, such as the digital-/internet-economy, information-economy/-society and even bordering on knowledge economy terrains. Others have more recently provided a detailed analysis and critique of the associated learning challenges (Guile 2010). Additionally, the process of digitisation is now assumed to fulfil the requirements for a general purpose technology (GPT), which can then (potentially) contain far reaching economic and societal consequences, as it has rapidly so far spread, and continues to spread, 'universally through disparate aspects of production and consumption in the economy' (Handke and Towse 2013, p. 2).

Within our case countries, we find however that the concept of *learning economy* (Lundvall and Johnson 1994) offers more fidelity and nuances in highlighting the sectoral shift towards a creative economy. At the risk of a long quotation, a useful clarification is offered by Lundvall (1999, p. 32), as follows:

> 'Learning' is not an unfamiliar concept in economic theory, but it is normally given a quite specific and limited definition depending on the theoretical context. Often it refers to agents getting more accurate information about a given state of the world and normally it does not incorporate what is at the core of what non-economists mean by learning: the acquisition of skills and competencies. For the Austrian School, learning processes are closely tied to the market and to transactions (Hayek 1978). Arrow (1962) introduced learning-by-doing in analyses of economic growth and Rosenberg (1982) introduced learning-by-using in connection with the use and production of complex technological systems. The analysis of 'the learning economy' can be seen as a follow-up and extension of their analyses and of how knowledge and competence emerge in a process of learning-by-interacting, i.e. in an inter-play between firms or between individuals. (Lundvall 1988)

With the terminology attended to, we turn next to briefly outline, in broad terms, some of working features of the nascent creative sub-sectors. For our purposes, following a brief sectoral description, we retain our attention on digital marketing and advertising (e.g. mobile value-added services—VAS); media and entertainment (e.g. television and film, and gaming); and digital commerce (e.g. start-ups and new technology-based firms, which is currently riding on a wave of interest), and fashion, within our geographical focus.

At this moment in time, our empirical data based on previous work is a combination of primary (firm-based organisational ethnography) and secondary sources of document analysis for Tehran (Alyani 2017), and secondary sources, policy document analysis and desk research for Khobar (and Jeddah), Abu Dhabi, and Dubai (Bhargava and Al Kaabi 2014; for a policy context, also see Jamjoom 2012; Baqadir et al. 2011).

So as to ground our conceptual argument on interprofessional learning and judgement, we selectively draw on recent studies (Guile 2011a, b, 2012a, b) where the issue of interprofessional learning and judgement within the sector, inter alia, has been addressed. Building on those earlier conceptual work, we move on to provide an abridged outline of our model, based on a recent sectoral study of innovation and learning within the digitised creative sector (Alyani 2017). As we explore, by analysing and interpreting the in-situ learning episodes on a conceptual level, via primary and secondary data sources, we point to the prominent use of *skill webs* as means of in-project upskilling and a resource for development of inter-professional learning and judgement capability which forms a core ingredient for innovation.

Debates on Natural Resources as a Blessing or a Curse

Before moving away from this section, however, towards our micro- and meso-level analysis, a glance at the macro issue of natural resources are helpful. For the sake of brevity and flow, we provide an abridged outline; citations and reviews can be found elsewhere (Alyani 2017, 2018).

In searching for a way forward to economic development and growth, primarily amongst economists and business planning community focusing on the Gulf region (a significant proportion of whom highly value mathematical economics and econometrics, as a seemingly 'tangible and accurate' framing mechanism, despite its recent 2007–2008 global crisis failing models (2012, 2013)), there has been an ongoing debate on natural resources as a blessing or a curse. The debate which still creates much heat (yet little guiding light or policy insights) in Iran, and (increasingly, less so) in some of Saudi Arabia and UAE policy circles, originated from the international academic community and outside of the gulf region. In a highly abridged and abstracted format, we offer a summary as follows.

Development economics theory, traditionally, has looked closely at how developing economies may capitalise on their natural resources, as a developmental cornerstone. Soon after country specific studies and disaggregation of data became the norm, however, researchers started to pose not only the advantages but also the disadvantages of natural resource wealth, based on some (including correlational) evidence, which suggested that natural resources actually act more as a drag, rather than a facilitator of national growth. This led to the notion of natural resource 'curse', referring as a label to the proposition that high dependence on natural resource extraction and manipulation hinders economic growth, and, by extension, diversification.

A fair amount of the related debates and discussions have also linked with, and converged on a metaphorical 'syndrome', entitled the 'Dutch disease' (first coined by *The Economist* in late 1977 when historically reviewing the problems in the economy of Holland, upon discovering a large natural gas field in 1959). The idea of Dutch disease suggests that when there is an abundance of natural and easily tradable resource, foreign exchange earnings are bolstered which leads to the appreciation of the national currency in the exchange rates. This currency appreciation subsequently causes a 'crowding out' of the other economic activities in the open and tradable part of the economy, as well as highly accommodating and increasing public sector growth and non-trading activities.

Parallel to these factors, natural resource extraction and production are generally capital-intensive activities, broadly requiring high fixed costs, but may not (certainly with the technological advances in the current decade such as in shale oil extraction) lead to significant employment creation, based on high level of specialised and technological processes. Also, the price of natural resources, or commodities as far as the stock exchanges recognise them, are generally volatile, which means that a fiscal reliance on them bring with it an inevitable risk of severe macroeconomic fluctuations, with significant peaks and troughs in returns. These fluctuations may not only negatively affect growth performance but also the high volatility undermines any significant actual or policy support in long-term investment activities, primarily amongst which is economy-wide, sectoral, or private-sector led research and development (R&D).

However, as time has gone by, it has become increasingly obvious that whilst relevant, macroeconomic considerations do not portray the entire picture. A range of other factors around human and societal (accountability and governance) processes and systems seem to play an equally critical role. Abundant natural resources, which generally tend to accrue directly to the government, serve as an attractive lure for rent-seeking—that is seeking to gain privilege and a share of the assets and returns through political clout and connections rather than economic activity and achievements—and subsequently *rentier* arrangements in economies and states, a phrase coined during a conference at SOAS, University of London in 1970, and later refined by others.

There is now a rich and varied literature on both the natural resource 'curse' and 'blessing', and Dutch disease (and related terms such as 'Norwegian paradox', where low R&D and high economic performance are equally apparent), spanning several decades. The literature has broadly moved on, and many have pointed to the importance of micro- (and much more recently, meso-) level activities and highlight that the causal link (rather than correlational relationship) between resource abundance and growth remains highly contestable. An emerging line of research has evaluated a range of recent statistical studies, and is now concluding against the presence of a natural resource 'curse', particularly when it refers to oil and mineral wealth.

Studies on the experience of a number of other developed economies, such as Australia, Canada, Norway, Finland and Sweden (with reference to the latter two's pulp and paper industry as the source of important spillovers and spinoffs, benefiting their long-term growth potentials) is in line with the non-existence of a resource curse conclusion.

Others have moved the debate on by suggesting that better descriptive labels such as 'innovation and human capital poor' may in fact act as a more accurate conceptual frame (Smith 2007). Whatever label is used, however, it is clear that the circumstances described create a tendency towards weak incentives and motivation for R&D activities, entrepreneurial risk-taking, and upskilling required of technology start-ups for innovation activities.

Notwithstanding, following this brief synopsis, one could quite legitimately hold the opinion, developed out of recent rethinking in the field, that the regional economist and economic planning community's continuing interest in resources curse and blessing, and Dutch disease—within neat but ultimately irrelevant mathematical analysis, expressions and formulas (as *Greek-lettered* economics)—has become rather esoteric. The debate is certainly not producing any further guiding light in policy, and worse still, may lead to numerous cul-de-sacs on growth and generative sectoral policies. In short, the agenda and tools to deal with the underlying problems may well have moved on and as the problems are often not given, they need to be reframed and worked-up to, in their own space and time.

That said, we remain grateful for the insights that the debates in the community and the reviews of the extant literature has provided and would assert that it is not merely the Dutch disease and resource curse that continues to weigh down economic development in the Gulf, but the 'Dutch knowledge disease' in actual sectoral practices. 'Dutch knowledge disease', a term and phenomenon introduced recently by an innovation economist (Soete 2005) when reviewing the shift from traditional national industrial to innovation policies, has been summarised as 'a lack of knowledge renewal in both industrial and services sectors based on a dual phenomenon of "crowding out'. First, a crowding-out of basic research in the private sector, with, for instance many domestic champions having drastically, under international pressure, cut back their own privately funded fundamental research activities. And, secondly, a crowding out of more applied and market driven research in universities as a result of domestic competition putting a strong premium on academic, basic research" (Soete 2007, p. 282—Fn 10).

It is thus the more nuanced term of the 'Dutch knowledge disease' and its continuing challenges which is much more apparent in the sectoral context of this study.

The Upskilling of the Creative Sub-sectors

Learning and Development in and for the Creative Sector

In order to analyse and interpret the upskilling requirements and trends of the creative sub-sectors, and the nuanced role of learning and development within it, we draw on a recent research project strand. Building on both policy trends and empirical observations within the sector in the United Kingdom (Creative Industries UK 2014), Guile's nuanced commentary (2012b, p. 301) highlights that the creative sector is

> characterised by: (a) external labour markets (i.e. contract-based) where employment opportunities emerge as people participate in occupational networks; and (b) cultures and practices that require two forms of knowledge, namely, vocational practice (i.e., mix of knowledge, skill, and judgement) and social capital (i.e. knowledge of networks to secure contracts for employment).

We would now add that the latter point on social capital, and ***horizontal network participation*** may well also be required to adequately fulfil the vocational practice elements, especially when the professional is met by interprofessional challenges. Furthermore, we would draw a similarity to the 'two forms of knowledge' stated in the above quotation to the required *technological knowledge* in the act and process of innovating, viewed as 'at once a body of understanding and a body of practice' (Nelson 2000, pp. 66 & 72).

Guile's study drew on case studies of young people who were:

> 'attempting to develop the expertise, connections, and self-promotional skills to gain opportunities to work' and as a conclusion, suggested 'that policy makers should rebalance existing educational policies based on the acquisition of the higher level qualifications with policies that assist intermediary organizations (i.e., local bodies) to devise programmes that provide young people with opportunities to develop their vocational practice and social capital and to develop insights into how to deploy the latter entrepreneurially to secure contracts for their services.' (Guile 2012b, p. 302)

Moving further to a specific level of ***modus-operandi*** within the sector, i.e. working in projects and with an interprofessional team, recent research has also highlighted the simultaneous growth and challenges of interprofessional learning (Guile 2012a, pp. 84–86). Interdisciplinary research on learning including contributions from economic geography, placed projects and the features of project work, centre stage, as a new manifestation of workflow process management. This new workflow could also include pedagogic elements and processes.

Studies on projects, as an organising principle of workflow, depending on intra-company and inter-company arrangements, have highlighted different learning challenges. Commentating and analysing Grabher's study (2004), Guile (2012a, pp. 85–86) highlights a few issues, which we quote at length here, as it directly relates to our argument later, that:

> the primary challenge in the IT industry is to strike a balance between securing one-off ventures, which require bespoke solutions, and repeatable commissions where knowledge about software systems can be 'accumulated' and 'modularised' (i.e. codified) to assist staff to reuse extant knowledge and, in the process, keep costs down (Grabher 2004, 107). In contrast, [...] the primary challenge in the advertising industry as having a reputation for devising 'original campaigns' that reflect closely clients' preferences to

secure new accounts (ibid.). [...] IT project teams consist of different specialisms whereas advertising companies deploy staff to work on the 'client' (i.e. liaison) or the 'company' (i.e. creativity) side of advertising campaigns. The inter-professional challenge of the former is to learn how to 'reduce' (ibid., 108) the differences between specialisms so members of the team can draw on one another's insights to reconfigure extant or create new software. In contrast, the latter challenge is to 'bridge' (ibid., 108) the different foci and concerns that exists between members of the same project team so that they can convince clients of their capability to respond to evolving needs.

It should therefore be relatively clear that the sub-sector specific circumstances and *project-purpose* requirements, generate slight but significantly different challenges in interprofessional learning for the professional engaged on projects. With the above in mind, we turn next to highlight our model in brief and within that, focus specifically on aspects of interprofessional judgement. At the start of the next sub-section, we will also provide a few definitions for our core terms to assist in the clarification and discussions, later on.

Sectoral Upskilling for Interprofessional Learning and Judgement

On a most simple conceptual level, interprofessional working, including on and in projects are about professional collaboration. Collaborative efforts bring together experts from different domains, firms, and professional bodies/communities to initially frame, and then set about solving a specific problem, and to provide a strategic advantage over single discipline or single firm offerings. Professional collaborations, including in-projects, often start by involving entities that possess different expertise and skill sets. In sum, we collaborate to frame (i.e. ask the appropriate question) and tackle problems which are deemed too large or complex for a single individual, team or firm, and to utilise multiple expertise. The increasing breadth, depth, and complexity of the creative sector projects now usually require interprofessional collaborations, with a wide range of complementary skills.

Various definitions of skill abound and yet the term remains stubbornly slippery both in practice and policy domains. We have reinterpreted and recontextualised the concept of 'skill webs' (Ashton et al. 2009, 2010) first introduced in exploring the strategies of multinational/transnational corporations (MNC/TNCs), within their knowledge and skill sourcing activities. We have re-applied the concept in the context of small firms, particularly digitised creative sector (such as in new technology-based firms—NTBFs) which at times, tend to mimic some of MNC/TNCs' innovative practices around '*bridging, linking and bonding*', in order to survive and prosper. Small digitised technology firms learn to innovate by connecting and weaving their skill webs, via bridging, linking and bonding (BLB) activities. Additionally, skill webs as a concept is useful in highlighting an analytical and empirical tension on the concept of learning in distributed and project-based activities the firm, including the *expansive and contractive* features of skill webs (Alyani 2017). In exploring the 'skill' in the 'skill webs', we remain conscious of its personal and collective dimensions, whilst retaining its productive and expandable nature (Green 2013).

In our re-definition, we have relocated the concept of 'skill webs', at a micro and meso level of firm's operation. Similar to the original usage, we define and employ the concept of 'skill webs' as a means to enable the researchers 'to focus on the ways in which companies chose to generate and use skills and knowledge they require' (Ashton et al. 2009, p. 329). Whilst Ashton and colleagues deployed the concept at a macro level of 'skills arbitrage' processes, we have refined and re-appropriated the concept to in-project resourcing, in smaller firms.

In our empirical observations, we have also used the notion of learning episodes, as a primary unit of analysis within our model, outlined later: they are here defined as "an occasion in which a [project] team learned something significant that advanced the project" in line with previous studies (Sole and Edmondson 2002, p. S20). Within the episodes, our attention was directed at identifying circumstances when, where, and how an interprofessional project team reaches a 'break-through' and/or a 'cul-de-sac', falling within the spheres of explorative or exploitative learning spheres.

Exploitation refers to the firm's refinement and development of existing knowledge with predictable outcomes, whereas exploration refers to the pursuit of new knowledge with uncertain outcomes (March 1991). We further noted that the nature of interprofessional learning is in the form of generative interactions between individual and collective inquiries (Elkjaer 2004).

As well as 'collaboration' activities, previously mentioned, interprofessional interactions and transactions also include 'coordination and control'. Within our model, we define coordination and control, in line with the literature, broadly as management of processes to enable effective work as well as *managing dependencies between activities.*

It may be useful to clarify our use of two further terms before outlining the details of the model with a case vignette, and follow-up commentary. These are 'interprofessional' and 'professional judgement'. In line with previous studies, interprofessional (not hyphenated here), in our work,

> refers to the way in which people from different occupational specialisms come together to work on common projects and, in the process, learn how to make the implications of their insights and judgements explicit to other members of the team of people they are working with. (Guile 2012a, p. 80)

Defining professional judgement (and later, interprofessional judgement) requires a bit more time and space. As there is a dearth of studies on interprofessional judgement generally and within the evolving digitised creative sector, we have had to turn selectively to features of two recent studies (Foss and Klein 2012; Ranzilla et al. 2013) in an effort to shed light on the processes at play in the development of the capability for professional judgement in practice, and subsequently, potentially draw comparable insights for our circumstances.

The choice of the two studies above is not random; not only both studies are relatively recent but they are also complementary. The first, is broadly a theoretical study with multi-layered issues of entrepreneuriality in its core and the second, is a practice-based synopsis and recommendation, with its sight set firmly on operationalisation of capability for judgement.

Foss and Klein's recent work has advanced an interesting way to explore entrepreneurship activities, building on the underlying theoretical work of Frank H. Knight who emphasised the development of judgement as a core component of entrepreneurship. Their conceptualisation links entrepreneurship with the resource-based theories of the firm and views entrepreneurship as a particular type of action, particularly, the entrepreneurial exercise of judgement regarding the utilisation and use of resources, under conditions of uncertainty. They thus view judgement as

> ... residual, controlling decision-making about resources deployed to achieve some objectives; it is manifest in the actions of individual entrepreneurs; and it cannot be bought and sold on the market, such that its exercise requires the entrepreneur to own and control a firm. (Foss and Klein 2012, p. 78)

It may also be interesting to note that in some entrepreneurial activities, professionals may have to exercise 'meta-judgement', which could be described as "judgment about other people's judgment" (Foss and Klein 2012, p. 216).

As a contrast to the first study's in-depth theoretical positioning and integration, the second study that we draw on is essentially a synthesis of recent practice and theory, organised and advocated by KPMG auditing and consulting firm (produced together with Brigham Young University faculty), specifically on formation of professional judgement. Whilst the study is pitched as a practice-based modular compendium for trainees and practitioners, it covers a number of interesting features, especially on operationalisation of professional judgement. Their definition of professional judgement, grounded in their sector, is

> the process of reaching a decision or drawing a conclusion where there are a number of possible alternative solutions. [...] [and which] occurs in a setting of uncertainty and risk. [and is] typically exercised in three broad areas:—Evaluation of evidence ...—Estimating probabilities ...—Deciding between options ... (Ranzilla et al. 2013, p. 2)

With those terms covered, we now turn to outline our model and a case vignette in brief.

A Conceptual Model

As described earlier, the empirical work on our geographical focus and city level remains in progress. We have therefore chosen to draw on a previously formulated model, constructed based on primary data in the form of firm-based organisational ethnography, in a highly abridged version of previous work (Alyani 2017). Whilst there are, and will clearly be some contextual differences, we propose that our model will have enough conceptual insight and fidelity to apply, with some minor adjustments as necessary, to these new sectoral situations.

The model and related case vignettes are reported in detail elsewhere (cf. Alyani 2017; Alyani and Guile 2017). For our purposes here, it suffices to outline that the underlying research examined the digitised creative sector in London and Tehran in a qualitative longitudinal research design, involving five waves (one pilot and four actual) of data collection, covering a period of 10 years between 2004 and 2013. This was broadly in line with a 'panel design', where as far as possible, the same people are contacted, observed and/or contacted and interacted with more than once, with the orientation and focal thematic questions mirroring previous research.

The organisational ethnographic immersion periods, at the firm and/or attached to related project meetings, derived from the five waves, investigated sharing of problem-reframing/-setting and problem-solving project and interprofessional judgement on the issues that emerge out of daily business challenges in projects, which is both of a technical (software) and a commercial (business model and service design) nature. Despite the potential attrition rate, the study's longitudinal design strengthened the shortcomings of a case study method and is of particular value when time-critical processes such as learning, human capital, and capability development are observed. The projects were undertaken under local and later distributed scrum, trying to introduce new and innovative services in the banking, advertising and public sector, via mobile platforms.

Scrum methodology refers to an agile and lean-inspired software development model based on multiple small teams working in an intensive and interdependent manner. The term is named for the scrum (or scrummage) formation in rugby, which is used to restart the game after an event that causes play to stop, such as an infringement. Scrum employs real-time decision-making processes based on actual events and information. This requires well-trained and specialised teams capable of self-management, communication, and decision-making.

We outline just one case vignette in the interest of brevity in this chapter, in the banking sector to ground the later discussions on our model.

In this vignette, the service developers faced major issues in creating 'generative metaphors' in problem-setting, to make the banking staff, of either a technical (i.e. Financial Technology—*FinTech*) audit or marketing/branding background, to 'recontextualise' the issues. A breakthrough was an initial inquiry leading to an agreement to allow a prototyping phase, overseen by a single Tehran-based bank's ICT department, to go ahead. Once the prototyping was a success (cutting customer queuing time from an average of 15 minutes, to conducting most transfers in 2–4 minutes), it was quickly taken up as a serious and viable service-channel option. The application was modified over a number of years and has rolled out with many Iranian national and private banks, a number of which are still using an evolved version of the solution.

Essentially, the team members, as well as the different professionals within the teams, had to find ways to mutually understand and grasp the potential and limitations of service design, given the local conditions. As it was well summarised by a team member 'Our learning here is all about 'beta': learning and innovation are coupled and yet learning comes first'.

We next turn our attention to outline our analytical model. Condensing the large project teams' activities data by data compression methods, a number of trends became apparent. At the heart of the activities, we noted a range of processes which we labelled as *DEAL*, as an acronym that stands for the cycle of *Design, Execute, Adjust* and *Learn*. Within the DEAL model, various activities were enhanced via formal and informal knowledge brokering and knowledge sourcing via, in, and between projects and firms. A sample series of questions, relating to each problem or inquiry, which are tackled at the different stages include:

- **D**esign: What is desirable and viable, and how feasible is it?
- **E**xecute: What are the processes involved, and how are they to be undertaken for a smooth (and lean) execution? What is the expected outcome and impact of the processes/artefacts?
- **A**djust: What worked, what did not, and why? (such as problems in prototypes)
- **L**earn: What is or remains to be the core problem and cause? How can we frame and reframe to improve continuously? What is the processes and technologies range of tolerance (allowance), before failure?

The cycle in the model continues with framing and reframing of the new problem and inquiry, which then leads to a new design imperative, transforming prototype to archetype, till an adequate and functioning solution is formulated. Brokerages and sourcing, in the form of bridging, linking and bonding (BLB) activities may occur initially via formal means (e.g. contractual domains) but are mainly conducted informally, developing diverse project skill webs, with trust gradually gained in time, by

- Visits to technology fairs and workshops, nationally and internationally;
- Exposure to global/glocal professionals or R&D networks and ecosystems; and
- Participation in online developers' space on specific technical problems.

The figure below attempts to schematically outline the above description, expanded further below.

As previously outlined, and now outlined in the model, exploitation refers to the refinement and development of existing knowledge with predictable outcomes, whereas exploration refers to the pursuit of new knowledge with uncertain outcomes. Additionally, the nature of in-project interprofessional learning is in the form of generative interactions between individual and collective inquiries, whilst engaged on performative learning (i.e. learning that directly derives out of performance), in order to innovate. These are placed on the horizontal and vertical axis of the model's schematic respectively, as outlined in Fig. 6.1.

In the centre of the Fig. 6.1, drawing on the 'learning episodes', we noted the zone of 'collaboration' and 'coordination and control' activities within project tasks, as articulated and facilitated by interprofessional interactions (and in the technical teams' vocabulary, the reflective phases of the cycles of 'Scrums and Sprints').

Thus, in formulating the analytical framework, derived from the data and enhanced by the literature, we attempted to ground our observations and theorisation. As no single strand of literature provided the necessary

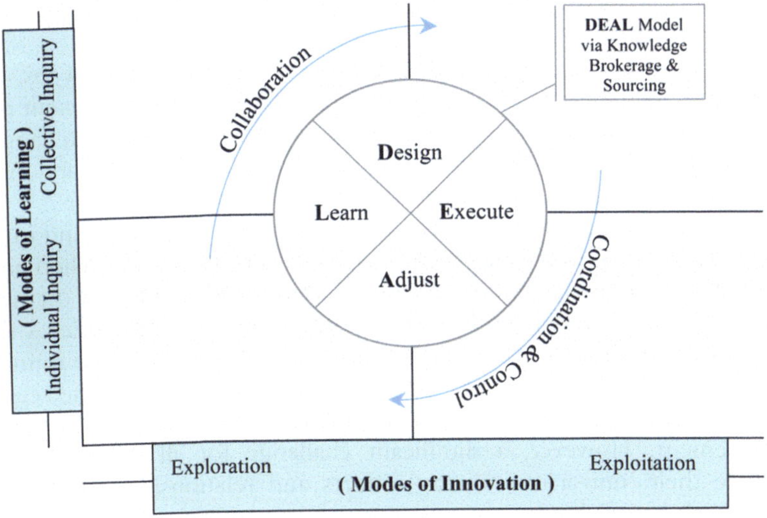

Fig. 6.1 DEAL analytical model: learning and innovation processes in digitised creative sector projects (Source: Alyani 2017)

theory, we brought together arguments of several theories and soon traced patterns of cyclical exploitation and exploration, within inquiry-based activities.

The potential output of this work and our model can be summarised in two strands: at a micro level (strand 1), we focus on the strategies that enable the firms to discover, develop, and commercialise their digitised technologies (as in the case of the vignette, in the form of software and services). In particular, whilst unpacking the 'black-box' of brokerage, we have come to consider the importance of the development of interprofessional learning and particularly, interprofessional judgement, in pursuit of innovation, as an important area for attention and further investigation. The goal is to better understand how entrepreneurial digitised creative sector firms, establish and utilise brokerage and intermediation, to build an interdisciplinary, and thus interprofessional capability so as to be more successful at innovation, and pursue the successful commercialisation of their new services and products, and along this journey, further upskill and develop their human talent, as a core asset.

In addition, the introduction of the DEAL (design, execute, adjust, learn) model was a way to identify and disaggregate non-linear processes, which in situ, draw on interprofessional learning and judgement, demonstrating a re-iterative and cyclical—rather than linear—nature in actual practice.

Whilst all the stages of the DEAL processes draw on skill webs, the 'prototypes to archetypes' transition phases as outlined above, benefit particularly from the interprofessional judgement and related exchanges. These findings can thus be offered as practical insights at a micro and meso level, to other firms via a potential 'sectoral platform' policy.

At a meso level (strand 2), there are also possibly important and interwoven educational implications embedded within the above. Whether in the Gulf's hub cities, London, or Seoul—as cities with significant digitised creative sectors—there is no longer a shortage on the supply side. A significantly large number of teaching and research universities, and training and vocational institutions now operate within the cities and the region with different levels of specialisation and at different stages of quality enhancement. However, a significant challenge for all of them is to enhance their 'university-industry' efforts and relationship, within and between the specialised sectors, and industry and ultimately graduates' job-market. This is so that their curriculum content and pedagogy can be kept relevant and up to date. This is no small undertaking in a region that has seen near exponential growth in its higher education in the last two decades.

Whilst similar to 'entrepreneurship', and 'innovation' (as separate undergraduate or graduate school courses and topics), interprofessional learning and judgement cannot (easily or directly) be taught, a capability development framework could be facilitated by the way the courses are structured. Insights from our study (and a small but growing literature) are issues that universities, educational institutions and policy analysts ought to be taking into account, if they are going to sustainably support the need for new forms and models of learning, closer to the practice-based requirements of the workplaces within the specialised and fledgling, yet growing, sectors. Whilst there is an increasing level of policy hype on the emergence of the *Creative Economy* within the region, there also needs to be grassroots and incremental reforms on the practice side.

Equally, the insights from the study's tools and methodology, refined as necessary, could assist in the universities and related institutions knowledge transfer and consultancy activities, to aid in initially unpacking the shortcomings and then upskilling their own staff and their target audiences' lifelong learning efforts. This inquiry-based mode of engagement, based partly on the needs of practice, could potentially further enhance the knowledge transfer in other settings and sectors, so as to support genuine lifelong learning mechanisms, beyond a 'check-list' or a fad. The study's insights on skill webs processes for example, support knowledge transfer in different sectors and settings, so this work has a more general argument which is about the necessary 'architecture' of lifelong learning in professional settings, particularly through university or professional programmes as a resource to pass on to others entering into, or operating within practice-based settings.

Coming out of the above primary focus at a micro level of the firm (strand 1), our planned work, at a meso (sectoral and regional) level (strand 2), plans to explore issues around entrepreneuriality and innovation capability development for new sectors, in aid of sustainable 'decent' job creation, and related meso-level policy and practice interventions.

Drawing from policy studies and economic geography in this strand, we have narrowed our remit on the city-level SMEs and within that, retain an interest on developing implementable policies. This could be timely for two reasons: firstly, if small and medium enterprises are to develop and play a more important role in the industrial policy and (as part and parcel of value chains of) foreign direct investment (FDI) policies, the way they enhance their learning and innovation capabilities must be better comprehended. Secondly, this meso-level engagement may then provide another avenue to consider the sustainability of the region's current creative 'start-up spring', on both the north and south side of the Gulf.

Concluding Remarks: Digitised Creative Sector Upskilling

The nascent digitised creative sector in the Gulf, with its growing interconnections globally, both in terms of policy and practice, is increasingly capturing the attention of the policy makers as a viable vista for new sectors, and with it, potentially new and sustainable private-sector employment creation. Our chapter has explored this (drawing on an analytical model, with longitudinal empirics, at a micro and meso level) and reiterates the importance of practical means to better link academic, TVET programmes, and workplace learning with the practical and evolving needs of the firms within these fledgling sectors. Our observations confirm that the sector is in pursuit of global interconnections for quality and niche specialisation (specificity).

The current regional efforts, in the form of strategic plans on a policy level, and practical brokerage on a practice-at-firm and -sector level, are welcome moves. Sectoral interconnections, globally and locally, and within the sector—in pursuit of quality and specificity—need to be carefully thought through with potential policy risks and unintended consequences identified and addressed, so as to be *implementable* with an enhanced engagement and coordination between key stakeholders (i.e. firms in the private and public sector; education and training providers; and government and other oversight/advisory agencies). Policy design therefore is much more than policy borrowing, and in practice, *policy amnesia* should not be allowed to disable and disband *policy memory*, so as to build on unique national and city contexts.

Our exploration on the formation and cultivation of interprofessional judgement, required for innovation, has led us to foreground the role of facilitating brokerage (i.e. BLB) mechanisms. With innovation remaining high on the economic, sectoral and firm-based agenda, workplace learning mechanisms can contribute to the development of workers' essential performative learning and sector knowledge.

Taken together, these factors point to a move away from relying on the credentialist approaches (ironically both dominant in the Gulf region's societal and educational fabrics, and—till recently, at least—highly embedded in various international advisory body's solutions), where qualifications are viewed as a proxy for vocational or professional skills, and towards acknowledging the multi-faceted role of social capital in *learning by doing* (Cherif and Hasanov 2014, pp. 12, 24), and specific to our earlier conceptual argument on interprofessional judgement, nurturing a transition;

> from conceiving learning as consisting of the accumulation of prespecified outcomes to seeing it as the development of judgement. [by undertaking practice-based inquiries, and rehearsing and revising procedures, mid-stream]. (Livingstone and Guile 2012, p. 357)

Whilst strategy making is an important prerequisite, it is these gradual firm- and sector-specific capability-building processes, at a practice and policy level, which will ensure the success of a fledging sector with significant regional potential.

In sum, in the language of a recent World Bank analysis, as the demand for skills in the age of innovation (Kutznetsov 2010) gathers further pace, an in-depth and join-up look at ways to develop a consistent sectoral skills policy, along with a congruent incentive system, would be required.

What would also be of immense value in crafting a smart 'skills development policy' in the region, is to take account of the overlapping layers and the logic of *strategic incrementalism*, as outlined in Fig. 6.2 below. Strategic incrementalism refers to developing and facilitating methods of gradual change by which many small policy changes are enacted over time in order to create and facilitate a larger broad based policy change, increasing confidence in the implementation and realisation stages.

Whilst the ambitious strategic agenda may be for a radical shake-up of multiple macro social and incentive systems, a more nuanced method could be to explore, experiment with, and exploit policy designs coherently which allows for an initially small but near-certain change. Social systems (such as education and training, skills development, and employability incentives) are stubbornly 'path dependent' (and largely resist and defy new 'path creation') which means that they intrinsically carry a significant amount of inertia.

The question of recreating and reframing a new system of incentives for new sectors and the necessary skills development, both on a personal (i.e. individual) and collective (i.e. sectoral cluster, city, regional, and national) level and particularly for the upcoming Saudi and Emirati working

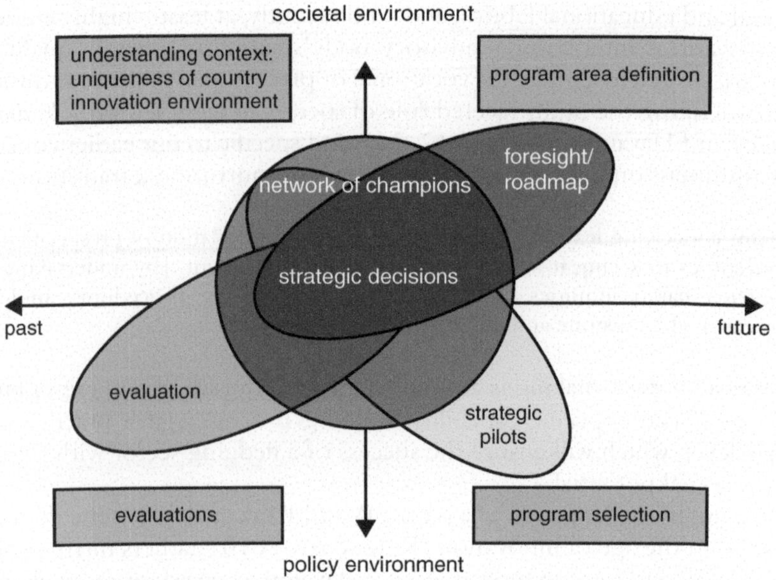

Fig. 6.2 Core elements of strategic incrementalism in policy implementation (Source: Kutznetsov 2010, p. 264)

generation, must be explored imaginatively as an integral part of other systematic economic diversification and specialisation overviews. Otherwise, KSA and UAE will need to finely balance the policy risk of diversifying its economy only to quickly realise that the national citizens are unprepared or unwilling to engage with some segments of the diversified economy, and thus, the lion's share of the new industrial and sectoral positions would have to be filled by skilled migrant workers (Kapiszewski 2001, p. 73). The challenge for Iran, however, is not the issue of migrant workers, but to make critical decisions around a reorientation towards a coherent industrial policy, by gradually building-up the evidence-base and promoting policy entrepreneurs to make the case for letting go off a number of *middle-aged 'infant' industries* and form a strategic focus on selected existing and new sectors. This is paramount if Iran is to close the gap in productivity and quality, exacerbated by decades of embargoes and sanctions, insularity of economic sectors and isolation from robust competition in international trade. This could also call for a reorienting the thrust of modern industrial policy in Iran so as to better facilitate learning to innovate, making smarter use of the potential inward FDI into the country's industrial and service base, in the next decade to come. Be it in Iran, KSA or UAE industrial policies, new ideas on *smart specialisation* within a regional policy context (OECD 2014) could also be worth some analytical attention.

These are complex and multifaceted policy decision conundrums that require systematic, small-scale policy reframing, design, and experimentation to test the responses and more importantly, other 'unintended consequences' of any new policies on incentives, while utilising rapid mapping tools for evidence-based policy (re)design. On this note, there is some preliminary and anecdotal evidence that the national citizens of KSA and UAE and the younger digital generation of Iran, particularly the segment of university-educated young female labour force, are particularly keen on the creative sector activities.

A strategic diversification agenda without significant buy-in from multiple stakeholders on the skills side, including the employers and firms, is likely to get into major difficulties in programme roll-out, implementation and realisation stages. For a labour market model to treat the local nationals as if they are self-adjusting *plug-and-play* workers is not only unrealistic but also unproductive and unsustainable due to conflicting social incentive systems. Systematic support in the form of a more coherently joined-up national and sectoral skill policy can assist the policy makers in exploring future scenarios, where new policy incentives are better weaved into the existing and emerging socioeconomic fabrics.

References

Alyani, N. (2017). Learning to Innovate Collaboratively with Technology: Exploring Strategic Workplace Skill Webs in a Telecom Services Firm in Tehran [unpublished] (PhD Thesis). University College London, London.

Alyani, N. (2018). *Igniting Innovation: Brokering Learning in Tehran's New Technology Firms*. Washington, DC: Westphalia Press.

Alyani, N., & Guile, D. (2017). Learning to Innovate By Connecting Interprofessional Judgement: Exploring the Digitised Creative Sector in the Gulf. In M. Pilz (Ed.), *Vocational Education and Training in Times of Economic Crisis: Lessons from Around the World, Technical and Vocational Education and Training: Issues, Concerns and Prospects Series*. Dordrecht: Springer Science & Business Media.

Ashton, D. N., Brown, P., & Lauder, H. (2009). Developing a Theory of Skills for Global HR. In P. R. Sparrow (Ed.), *Handbook of International Human*

Resource Management: Integrating People, Process, and Context (pp. 321–339). Chichester, West Sussex: John Wiley & Sons.

Ashton, D. N., Brown, P., & Lauder, H. (2010). Skill Webs and International Human Resource Management: Lessons from a Study of the Global Skill Strategies of Transnational Companies [Article in Special Issue: "Critical Reflections on HRM and Its Possible Futures"]. *The International Journal of Human Resource Management, 21*, 836–850. doi:10.1080/09585191003729325.

Baqadir, A., Patrick, F., & Burns, G. (2011). Addressing the Skills Gap in Saudi Arabia: Does Vocational Education Address the Needs of Private Sector Employers? *Journal of Vocational Education & Training, 63*, 551–561. doi:10.1080/13636820.2011.589533.

Bhargava, J., & Al Kaabi, N. (2014). How Young Arabs Are Fuelling the MENA Media Market [1st edition: Arab Media Perspectives Report at Abu Dhabi Media Summit 2014]. Strategy&, PwC & Abu Dhabi Media Zone Authority (TwoFour54), Abu Dhabi, UAE.

Cherif, R., & Hasanov, F. (2014). *Soaring of the Gulf Falcons: Diversification in the GCC Oil Exporters in Seven Propositions* [IMF Working Paper] (No. WP/14/177). International Monetary Fund, Washington, DC.

Creative Industries UK. (2014). CI: UK to the World [Creative Industries UK: Facts and Figures, Including Recent UK-Based Sectoral Research And Publications] [WWW Document]. Creative Industries UK. Retrieved May 31, 2015, from http://www.thecreativeindustries.co.uk/uk-creative-overview/facts-and-figures

Elkjaer, B. (2004). Organizational Learning: The "Third Way". *Management Learning, 35*, 419–434.

Financial Times. (2014). Abu Dhabi Feels the Force of Blockbusters to Lift Economy: UAE—The Oil Emirate Is Seeking to Build a Film and Digital Media Hub to Create Jobs [Report by Simeon Kerr for FT in UAE, 13th May 2014]. *Financial Times* 2.

Foss, N. J., & Klein, P. G. (2012). *Organizing Entrepreneurial Judgment: A New Approach to the Firm.* Cambridge and New York: Cambridge University Press.

Galal, A. (2008). The Road Not Traveled: Education Reform in the Middle East and North Africa (MENA Development Report). World Bank Publications, Washington, DC.

Grabher, G. (2004). Learning in Projects, Remembering in Networks? Communality, Sociality, and Connectivity in Project Ecologies. *European Urban and Regional Studies, 11*, 103–123. doi:10.1177/0969776404041417.

Green, F. (2013). *Skills and Skilled Work: An Economic and Social Analysis.* Oxford and New York: Oxford University Press.

Guile, D. (2010). *The Learning Challenge of the Knowledge Economy, the Knowledge Economy and Education.* Rotterdam and Boston: Sense Publishers.

Guile, D. (2011a). Interprofessional Learning: Reasons, Judgement, and Action. *Mind, Culture, and Activity, 18*, 342–364. doi:10.1080/10749039.2011.573045.

Guile, D. (2011b). Workplace Learning in the Knowledge Economy: The Development of Vocational Practice and Social Capital. In M. Malloch, L. Cairns, K. Evans, & B. N. O'Connor (Eds.), *The SAGE Handbook of Workplace Learning* (pp. 385–394). London and Thousand Oaks, CA: Sage.

Guile, D. (2012a). Inter-Professional Working and Learning: "Recontextualising" Lessons from "Project Work" for Programmes of Initial Professional Formation [Special Issue on: Reconceptualising Professional Learning in a Changing Society]. *Journal of Education and Work, 25*, 79–99. doi:10.1080/13639080.2012.644908.

Guile, D. (2012b). Working and Learning in the "Knowledge-Based" Creative and Cultural Sector: Vocational Practice, Social Capital, and Entrepreneurability. In D. W. Livingstone & D. Guile (Eds.), *The Knowledge Economy and Lifelong Learning: A Critical Reader* (pp. 301–316). Rotterdam and Boston: Sense Publishers.

Handke, C., & Towse, R. (2013). Introduction. In R. Towse & C. Handke (Eds.), *Handbook on the Digital Creative Economy* (pp. 1–6). Cheltenham, UK & Northampton, MA: Edward Elgar.

Hausmann, R. (2015). The Education Myth: Governments Are Agreed on the Importance of Education, But Increased Schooling Is Not Enough to Boost the Wealth of Individuals or Nations [The Knowledge Perspectives Section]. The New Economy [The Quarterly Digest of Technology, Innovation and Business] (Summer issue), 22–23.

Hausmann, R., Hidalgo, C. A., Bustos, S., Coscia, M., Simoes, A., & Yildirim, M. A. (2014). *The Atlas of Economic Complexity: Mapping Paths to Prosperity.* Cambridge, MA: MIT Press.

Hvidt, M. (2013). Economic Diversification in GCC Countries: Past Record and Future Trends [Report by LSE's Kuwait Programme on Development, Governance and Globalisation in the Gulf States] (No. 27). London School of Economics and Political Science, London.

Hvidt, M. (2015). *Transformation of the Arab Gulf Economies into Knowledge Economies: Motivational Issues Related to the Tertiary Education Sector.* Doha, Qatar: Arab Center for Research & Policy Studies.

IMF Survey. (2014). Gulf Development Conference [co-hosted by IMF & Kuwait's Ministry of Finance]: Gulf Economies Should Diversify to Sustain Strong Future Growth [Article in "IMF Survey Magazine: Countries & Regions"] [WWW Document]. Retrieved May 25, 2015, from http://www.imf.org/external/pubs/ft/survey/so/2014/car060314a.htm

Jamjoom, Y. S. (2012). Understanding Private Higher Education in Saudi Arabia: Emergence, Development and Perceptions [Unpublished] (PhD Thesis). Institute of Education, University of London, London.

Kapiszewski, A. (2001). *Nationals and Expatriates: Population and Labour Dilemmas of the Gulf Cooperation Council States*. Reading: Ithaca Press.

KDI. (2012). Toward Knowledge-Based Economy of the Kingdom of Saudi Arabia [a Knowledge Sharing Program report by Korea Development Institute (KDI) and Ministry of Strategy and Finance (MOSF), Republic of Korea, for Ministry of Economy and Planning (MOEP), Kingdom of Saudi Arabia]. Knowledge Sharing Program, Center for International Development, Korea Development Institute, Seoul, Republic of Korea.

Kutznetsov, Y. (2010). Policy Implementation: The Art and Craft of Innovation Policy Making. In The World Bank (Ed.), *Innovation Policy: A Guide for Developing Countries* (pp. 237–269). Washington, DC: The World Bank.

Lauder, H. (2014). Economic Development and Education. In D. C. Phillips (Ed.), *Encyclopedia of Educational Theory and Philosophy* (pp. 249–252). Thousand Oaks, CA and London: Sage.

Livingstone, D. W., & Guile, D. (2012). Conclusion. In D. W. Livingstone & D. Guile (Eds.), *The Knowledge Economy and Lifelong Learning a Critical Reader* (pp. 349–360). Rotterdam and Boston: Sense Publishers.

Lundvall, B.-Å. (1999). Technology Policy in the Learning Economy. In D. Archibugi, J. Howells, & J. Michie (Eds.), *Innovation Policy in a Global Economy* (pp. 19–34). Cambridge and New York: Cambridge University Press.

Lundvall, B.-Å., & Johnson, B. (1994). The Learning Economy. *Journal of Industry Studies, 1*, 23–42. doi:10.1080/13662719400000002.

Malerba, F., & Nelson, R. R. (2012). Introduction. In F. Malerba & R. R. Nelson (Eds.), *Economic Development as a Learning Process: Variation Across Sectoral Systems* (pp. 1–20). Cheltenham, England & Northampton, MA: Edward Elgar Publishing.

March, J. G. (1991). Exploration and Exploitation in Organizational Learning. *Organization Science, 2*, 71–87.

McKinsey Global Institute. (2015). Saudi Arabia Beyond Oil: The Investment and Productivity Transformation. McKinsey & Company, Global offices [Principal Offices in North America, Europe and Asia/Pacific].

Nelson, R. R. (2000). Selection Criteria and Selection Processes in Cultural Evolution Theories [Previous Working Title: "Different Perspectives on Technological Evolution"]. In J. Ziman (Ed.), *Technological Innovation as an Evolutionary Process* (pp. 66–74). Cambridge and New York: Cambridge University Press.

OECD. (2014). Cluster Policy and Smart Specialisation [STI Policy Profiles: Networks, Clusters and Transfers]. In OECD Science, Technology and Industry Outlook 2014 (pp. 221–225). OECD Publishing, Organisation for Economic Co-operation and Development, Paris.

Ranzilla, S., Chevalier, R., Herrmann, G., Glover, S., & Prawitt, D. (2013). Understanding and Developing Professional Judgment in Auditing and Accounting [Summary of "Elevating Professional Judgment in Auditing and Accounting: The KPMG Professional Judgment Framework"—Recipient of the 2013 AAA/Deloitte Wildman Medal Award]. KPMG, Global Offices [Principal Offices in North America, Europe and Asia/Pacific].

Smith, K. H. (2007). Innovation and Growth in Resource-Based Economies. CEDA Growth [Committee for Economic Development of Australia] pp. 50–57.

Soete, L. (2005). On the Dynamics of Innovation Policy: A Dutch Perspective. In P. De Gijsel & H. Schenk (Eds.), *Multidisciplinary Economics: The Birth of a New Economics Faculty in the Netherlands* (pp. 127–149). Dordrecht: Springer.

Soete, L. (2007). From Industrial to Innovation Policy. *Journal of Industry, Competition and Trade, 7*, 273–284.

Sole, D., & Edmondson, A. C. (2002). Situated Knowledge and Learning in Dispersed Teams. *British Journal of Management, 13*, S17–S34.

Strategy&, PwC. (2013). The Digital Future of Creative Europe: The Economic Impact of Digitization and the Internet on the Creative Sector in Europe [Report Commissioned by Google Inc. and Independently Researched and Written By Booz & Company]. Booz and Company [now "Strategy&" PwC], Düsseldorf, San Francisco, Berlin and Zurich.

The Economist. (2012). Micro Stars, Macro Effects. *The Economist, 405*, 69–70.

The Economist. (2013). New Model Army [Economics after the Crisis: Efforts Are Under Way to Improve Macroeconomic Models]. *The Economist* 406.

UNCTAD. (2008). Creative Economy Report 2008—The Challenge of Assessing the Creative Economy: Towards Informed Policy-Making [By United Nations Conference on Trade and Development]. United Nations [UNCTAD & UNDP], Geneva and New York.

UNESCO-UNEVOC. (2014). UNESCO UNEVOC World TVET Database—Country Profiles [Provided by the International Centre for Technical and Vocational Education and Training] [WWW Document]. UNESCO UNEVOC. Retrieved May 31, 2015, from http://www.unevoc.unesco.org/go.php?q=World+TVET+Database

UNIDO. (2012). *Diversification vs. Specialization as Alternative Strategies for Economic Development: Can We Settle a Debate by Looking at the Empirical Evidence?* [Working Paper by Florian Kaulich, for UNIDO's Development Policy, Statistics and Research Branch] (No. 3/2012). United Nations Industrial Development Organization (UNIDO), Vienna, Austria.

World Bank. (2015). The World Bank's Data: Countries and Economies [WWW Document]. The World Bank's Databank: Countries and Economies. Retrieved May 31, 2015, from http://data.worldbank.org/country

CHAPTER 7

Success Factors of Saudi-German Joint Ventures: A Meta-Analytical Approach

Maike Laska-Khalil

Introduction

Coming out of the recent recession, small- and medium-sized enterprises (SMEs) have historically proven themselves as essential drivers of job creation and inclusive economic growth around the world (Eden et al. 1997). According to the Organisation for Economic Co-operation and Development (OECD), small- and medium-sized enterprises represent over 95 percent of all businesses and account for 60–70 percent of all new jobs created in OECD member countries (2009). Likewise the majority of enterprises in MENA are SMEs, estimated at 19–23 million (formal and informal) in number and comprising 80–90 percent of total businesses in most countries (SUSRIS 2011). The MENA region comprises Algeria, Bahrain, Djibouti, Egypt, Iran, Iraq, Israel, Jordan, Kuwait, Lebanon, Libya, Malta, Morocco, Oman, Palestine (Gaza Strip and West Bank), Qatar, Saudi Arabia, Syria, Tunisia, United Arab Emirates and Yemen (OECD 2009). Due to the relevance of SMEs as the economy's backbone in terms of employment as well as economic stability, institutions and policy makers were dedicated to support the development of new markets for SMEs to grow and achieve economies of scale which cannot be reached when operating in the domestic market alone (OECD 2009). While the

M. Laska-Khalil (✉)
Chair of Management, University of Fribourg, Fribourg, Switzerland

A. Mishrif, Y. Al Balushi (eds.), *Economic Diversification in the Gulf Region, Volume II*, The Political Economy of the Middle East,
DOI 10.1007/978-981-10-5786-1_7

formation of International Joint Ventures (IJVs) has grown into an important and widely used tool for the market development of international operating companies, SMEs seem to be left behind due to their limited resources—in particular their limited financial, managerial and information resources and their attitude to risk (cf. Morschett 2005, p. 379)—and are more likely to fail than large firms (Eden et al. 1997). Nevertheless, a growing number of SMEs choose IJV as their preferred mode of expansion and have proven that limitations can be overcome (Isidor et al. 2012).

Given the failure rates of IJVs, their increasing popularity triggered several studies focussing on IJV performance. Currently around 130 independent primary studies can be identified, which have empirically studied the impact of selected factors on the success of IJVs. However, research remains fragmented and often controversial (cf. Reus and Rottig 2009). Accordingly, studies tend to highlight individual facets of the management of IJVs, such as partner choice, contractual conditions or continuous control, with individual success factors being arbitrarily selected and examined in isolation (Teusler 2008). Moreover, many studies tend to focus on international joint ventures established by large firms. These findings are not necessarily applicable to SMEs, given the significant differences between smaller and larger firms (Morschett 2005; Buckley 1997). Finally, the results of the studies are cast in doubt by measurements of the success of international cooperations that are often contradictory or lack precise definitions (Larimo 2007, p. 396).

This seemingly contradictory nature of the research field is criticized by many reviewers, who demanded a merging of existing research results, with a sound clarification of any discrepancies, as well as the integration of the results of any future research into the interactions of international cooperations (Beamish and Killing 1996). Attempts to consolidate the previously examined success factors of IJV performance can be found in several narrative reports (e.g. Reus and Rottig 2009), as well as in tabular presentations, which tried to distinguish between significant and non-significant results by using the so-called vote-counting method (Robson et al. 2002). Although such qualitative literature studies make an important contribution to the reappraisal of the research field, the analysis of success factors often lacks in an economically sound and cohesive concept (Teusler 2008, p. 94). Furthermore, the clarification and review of the success factors are often confined to anecdotal evidence. Reliable statements about the mode of action as well as the effect size of the examined success factors are nowhere to be found.

To fill this crucial research gap, a quantitative synthesis of the previous studies is required. The first attempt of a quantitative consolidation of previous IJV research was undertaken by Reus and Rottig in 2009, who conducted a meta-analytic integration of 61 IJV based on agency theory and behavioural perspectives.

A clear theoretical foundation allowed the authors to consolidate the so far heterogeneous findings on a theoretical basis and to integrate them meta-analytically. However, the narrow theoretical focus proved to be detrimental, in that ultimately only four success factors were examined to reduce complexity. In contrast, previous research of IJV success is characterized by an abundance of success factors, hailed as beneficial in various research works (cf. Robson et al. 2002).

The existing inconsistencies in the research field could be further reduced by a theory- and phase-independent meta-analytic study, which comprehensively examines influential IJV success factors, selected based on their frequency of recurrence and priority ranking in existing quantitative empirical studies.

The current chapter draws on the previous issues with the aim to:

- Develop a meta-analytical approach with the integration of quantitative IJV success factor research results which considered small- and medium-sized enterprises with large cultural distance
- Identify specific success factors of IJVs over great cultural distance

Section 2 gives an overview of literature research into success criteria used for evaluating IJVs. Section 3 introduces the meta-analysis and explores the methods and variable definitions used to construct it. Section 4 wraps up with an overview of German-Saudi economic cooperation, which serves as a focusing scope for our research. Finally, a summary and overview of future work is given in Section 5 (Fig. 7.1).

German-Saudi Arabian Joint Ventures

With its rich history and colourful present, the MENA region is very diverse in its social, political and legal structures. Despite rapid economic growth, the region is still characterized as one in general need of economic development. With a gross domestic product of almost 540 billion US dollars in 2011, Saudi Arabia (KSA) is the largest economy in the MENA region; no other country is currently investing more in the diversification

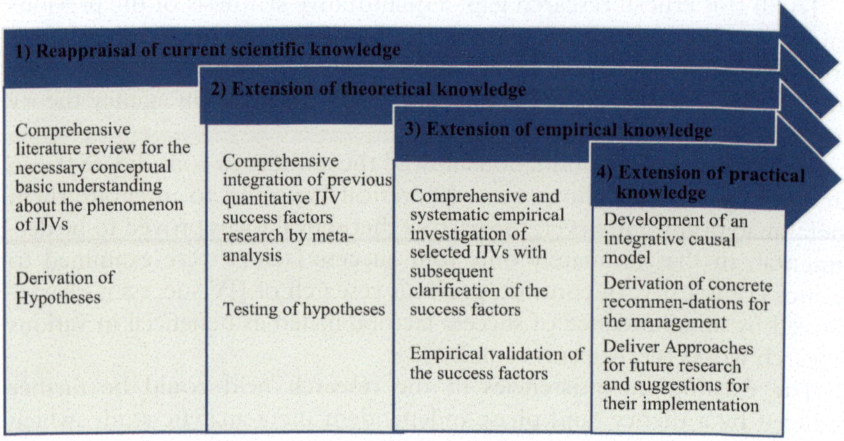

Fig. 7.1 Summary of research objectives and the process steps

of its economy and its infrastructure. 70 billion US dollars were invested directly into new projects in 2012 alone, a sum necessary to continuously counteract the negative consequences of demographic change. Saudi Arabia has a population growth of 2.2 percent (SAGECO 2011). According to Saudi Labour Minister Adel Fakieh, around 500,000 new jobs would have to be created annually to provide employment opportunities to the younger generations. To meet the demands of an ever-growing industrial society, investments to the tune of 900 billion US dollars in infrastructure development and 300 billion US dollars for petrochemical, energy and water projects, as well as 100 billion US dollars for transport and logistics, are planned till the year 2020.

The ambitious development plan offers German companies excellent business and investment opportunities. German industry and services, with an export volume of nearly 5 billion euro in the year 2009, represent the most important European supplier to Saudi Arabia. The relation is reciprocal, with Saudi Arabia being Germany's most important trading partner in the Arab world (OECD 2005). More than 400 German companies, nearly half of them joint ventures, are currently represented in KSA (see Table 7.1). The cooperations include direct investments, training on the spot, as well as the transfer of technology and know-how and therefore successfully contribute to the scientific development of Saudi Arabia (AHK Newsletter Jan. 2012, http://saudiarabien.ahk.de/en/).

Table 7.1 Development of Saudi-German joint ventures

German share %	*Saudi share %*	*Capital SR—Mio.*	*No. of JVs.*	*Year*
38	62	450	5	Up to 1975
41	59	113	14	1976–1979
26	74	274	24	1980–1989
30	67	1027	29	1990–1999
32	68	4639	41	2000–2004
50	50	24,903	64	2005–2009
50	**50**	**31,406**	**177**	**Total**

Source: SAGECO, December 2009

Saudi Arabia, with its mix of tradition and modernity and its prominent position in Middle Eastern affairs, presents a unique case of political, juristic, social and cultural conditions, which can be difficult to navigate for outsiders. These unique conditions, combined with its extraordinary economic and social importance, make Saudi Arabia an ideal candidate for the scoping focus of the research questions identified in this study.

Success Criteria for International Joint Ventures

In the organizational research, success ("performance") is one of the probably most commonly used dependent variables; nevertheless, till today there is no consensus on how success should be operationalized (Isidor et al. 2012).

Choosing a suitable success criteria for IJVs is even harder considering the plurality of interest within the partner company (Oesterle 1995, p. 990). The spectrum of applied success criteria in the literature ranges from the very existence of companies about financial indicators to assessments of the management with regard to the success of the IJV. Inspired by Robson et al. (2002), it will be distinguished between financial success indicators (profitability (cf. Artisien and Buckley 1985)), revenue growth, market share (cf. Luo 1999), stability (changes of ownership, survival (cf. Killing 1983), duration of the partnership (cf. Kogut and Singh 1988) and multidimensional success indicators (satisfaction (Dhanaraj et al. 2004) and goal attainment (Krishnan et al. 2006).

Financial Oriented Success Criteria

Financial success criteria include indicators such as profitability, sales growth and market share. These criteria are, however, not without limitations when applied to IJVs. IJVs are created for multiple objectives, whose level of achievement cannot be measured solely through financial criteria (Mohr 2006, p. 250). For instance, if an IJV is set up with the intention of developing new technologies or opening new markets in the long term, the necessary adaptation processes and ramp-up phase will make it difficult for the IJV to generate substantial profit, if any, in the first years (Geringer and Hébert 1991, p. 251). Similarly, an IJV can still be considered very successful for a partner not making financial gains if the IJV, for example, provides them access to critical resources or the transfer of otherwise unattainable technological knowledge. In contrast, shifting interests and different strategic priorities, or insurmountable conflicts between the partners, can cause even financially successful IJVs to fail (Schaan 1988, p. 5 f.). In addition, traditional financial indicators, such as profit or profitability, are an inadequate measure of success, if the IJVs' gains are mainly made in intellectual properties and their licensing and royalties (Geringer and Hébert 1991, p. 250 f.)

Stability-Oriented Success Criteria

The previous remarks demonstrate that financial criteria capture only one facet of IJV success (Anderson 1990, p. 22) and not the heterogeneous—potentially conflicting—individual and collective goals of the partners. Accordingly, literature provides approaches for the performance measurement of IJVs, which give greater value to the plurality of the partners' interests and goals. Such IJV specifics include longevity but also especially the stability of the IJV. The stability is operationalized by the changes of ownership or the liquidation of the IJVs (Inkpen and Beamish 1997, p. 181). Stability-oriented success criteria therefore also describe the quality of the cooperation, with stable IJVs considered successful. However, the use of stability-oriented success criteria also has disadvantages. For example, if the IJV was founded with the intention of being a temporary cooperation, then the resulting dissolution should not be interpreted as a failure (Inkpen and Beamish 1997). This also applies to the acquisition of the IJVs by a partner. Here, the IJV is completed, but the acquisition can also be interpreted as the application of a "real option" and thus represent a sign of a successful IJV (Kogut and Singh 1988). In addition, stability proves to be an indirect operationalization of the IJV's success. Thus, if an IJV is dissolved because the financial expectations of the partners were not met or because there were some insurmountable problems of coordination between the partners, IJV stability would gain validity at the very least as ex post indicator of success (Oesterle 1995, p. 992). Conversely, it is difficult to extract conclusions about the success of an IJV from its mere existence or the duration thereof (Mohr 2006, p. 250). The existence of an IJV, regardless of its success, can rather be a sign of high market exit barriers (Parkhe 1993, p. 302).

Multidimensional Success Criteria

A third group of approaches dispensed with both financial and stability-oriented success criteria in favour of a direct survey of management as a means of determining success. Such a subjective measurement of success is usually performed when the success criteria the study is trying to determine cannot be quantified. According to Schaan (1988, p. 319), only this approach can provide information about whether the IJV has met the expectations or criteria for success of the partners. However, the level of detail varies widely across studies employing multidimensional performance measurement (Robson et al. 2002, p. 397). For instance, in some studies, the degree of target achievement is used interchangeably with the degree of satisfaction with the overall success of the IJVs as a measurement of success. Yet, the degree of target achievement should be regarded as the more accurate measure of success, especially since the degree of satisfaction is not only more of a result rather than an indicator of IJV success, that is, it follows rather than is the cause of success, but is also influenced by other non-performance-related factors (Hatfield et al. 1998, p. 364).

Subjective measurement is an attempt at tackling the multidimensionality of success (Luo 1999, p. 21) and allows the evaluation of success in relation to one's competitors (Teusler 2008). Yet, its strength is also its weakness, and hence the risk of subjective distortion and the associated lack of validity of the statements constitute clear disadvantages of this method (Eisele 1995, p. 86).

Although numerous studies have documented significant correlations between objective and subjective success criteria (cf. Dhanaraj et al. 2004; Geringer and Hébert 1991; Hatfield et al. 1998; Pearce 1997), some researchers claim that the different operationalization (financial, stability-oriented and multidimensional success dimensions) are not readily substitutable. Hatfield et al. (1998, p. 357) demonstrated that no measure of success can explain more than 43 percent of the variance of another dimension. They suggest instead that a causal relationship exists between these success criteria. Thus, the positive perception of the IJV's success induces a higher willingness to continue ongoing cooperation, which is in turn expressed in the IJV's continued survival (Hatfield et al. 1998, p. 358; López-Navarro and Molina-Morales 2002, p. 121).

The demonstrated issues make it clear that a complex concept like success cannot be adequately covered by a single approach. Rather, a combination of different approaches seems to best compensate for the weaknesses inherent in each one (Luo 2002, p. 2; Yan and Gray 2001, p. 311). Oesterle (1995, p. 992 f.) points out, however, that an aggregation of various success criteria, while indeed reducing the influence of strongly distorted values, simultaneously dilutes correct values. Nevertheless, these aggregated values should have a higher general validity in the measurement of IJV success than the values created by the use of any one single approach (Oesterle 1995, p. 992 f.).

IJV Success Factors and the Development of Hypotheses

The identification as well as causal classification of success factors, which form the basis for an accurate operationalization of IJV success, are among the largest hurdles in IJV research. In co-operative research, there are several works which examined success factors (cf. the narrative literature review by Robson et al. 2002). However, due to inconsistent results, no reliable statements about the profit contribution of individual factors can be made as yet (Child and Yan 2003, p. 284).

On the one hand, the ambiguity of the results can be attributed to the different construct operationalizations. As surmised by López-Navarro and Molina Morales (2002, p. 115), "... different subjective indicators used in the literature actually measure different phenomena and, consequently, are affected in a different way by variables used as determinants of the joint venture performance". On the other hand, the divergence of the results can also be interpreted as a sign of the multidimensionality of IJV success factors.

To overcome this, we chose to combine all potential success factors by means of a systematic analysis, with their frequency of appearance in relevant literature serving as the main differentiating factor.

As a description of all hitherto examined success factors would go beyond the scope of this work, only those factors will be presented, which were tested empirically more than five times—otherwise a meta-analytic analysis wouldn't be justified. This resulted in 14 success factors. According to Robson et al. (2002), these success factors can be divided into two categories: the partner and the joint venture level. This classification is also followed in the present study.

Partner Level

The partner level describes the attributes and characteristics of the partner companies. In particular, these include the compatibility as well as the experience of the partners. Taking into account the partner attributes, the choice of the "right" partner plays an especially crucial role, since the success of IJVs depends on combining the resources of the partners, as well as on the availability of these resources for the joint undertaking (Geringer and Hébert 1991, p. 42).

Partner Fit

The "Fit" between partners has often been identified as an indicator of success. Partner fit refers here to the compatibility and complementarity of the partners. Adarkar et al. (1997, p. 124) describe this fit as "... balance that is the hallmark for successful and enduring alliances". It is a multidimensional construct that is the product of a variety of different factors (Inkpen and Beamish 1997) and can be achieved on an operational, strategic and cultural level.

The partial overlap of business, functional areas or industries in which the partners are operating is considered operational partner fit. The resulting complementarity of resources within the value chain of the partner enterprises allows an increase in value, according to the resource-oriented approach, as well as synergy effects through the pooling and sharing of complementary resources (Das and Teng 2000, p. 31; Luo 1999, p. 8). The complementarity of manufactured products is increasingly important for the foreign partner in an IJV, because they rely on the existing distribution network, the customer base and the finished production facilities of the local partner to generate economies of scale faster (Luo 1999, p. 651). Furthermore, with a missing complementarity, the foreign partner would lack knowledge of both the local market and the products as well as production technology (Kabst 2000).

Cooperating with a partner from the same industry is however not without its risks, with the underlying rivalry between the cooperation partners incentivizing them to behave opportunistically. Furthermore, the disclosure of company-specific intellectual property involves the risk of unilateral knowledge drain, which in the long run threatens the competitiveness of those companies which disclose their knowledge (Park and Ungson 1997, p. 87). Despite these potentially negative consequences, we agree with the majority of studies that suggest a positive correlation between the operational partner fit and the success of an IJV and consequently propose the following hypothesis:

Hypothesis 1a Operational partner fit is positively associated with IJV success.

The business fields overlap between partners and IJV (operational IJV fit) is considered however consistently positive. Thus, it enhances the transfer of spoken as well as unspoken knowledge (Reus and Rottig 2009), as this is more easily applicable due to the similarity of the activity areas. Cohen and Levinthal (1990) claim that the experience and familiarity that originates in the IJV also rather allows the partner to acquire the knowledge and to transfer back into the company. Merchant and Schendel (2000) postulate that the similarity of the divisions between partners and IJV enable on the one hand the achievement of economies of scale by reduction of expenses. On the other hand, it implies the realization of economies of scope on the basis of the extended learning opportunities. Following the reasoning of these studies, we suggest a positive correlation between the operational IJV fit and the success of the IJV.

Hypothesis 1b Operational IJV fit is positively associated with IJV success.

The compatibility of the strategic objectives of the partner companies is referred to as the strategic fit (Das and Teng 2000, p. 56; Hsieh and Rodrigues 2005, p. 14), where compatibility does not simply mean matching targets. Companies can indeed have different objectives. For instance, a company can seek to enter a foreign market with the help of an IJV, while the other company targets knowledge acquisition through the collaboration. The deciding factor in a successful cooperation is that the partners' objectives be in harmony. This means the targets are not mutually exclusive or conflicting in any manner, so that all partners can work at and achieve their objectives simultaneously (Das and Teng 2000, p. 57). The compatibility of the targets and motives reduces the likelihood of opportunistic behaviour from any partner, and accordingly requires less reciprocal monitoring. The opposite holds true; a mismatch of goals increases the potential for conflict between the partners (Pearce 1997, p. 210). Based on the results of empirical studies we postulate a positive correlation between the strategic fit and the success of the IJV.

Hypothesis 1c Strategic fit between the IJV partners is positively associated with IJV success.

Cultural conformity at the personal as well as the national level between the cooperating partners is referred to as cultural fit. Culture is understood as the wealth of accumulated knowledge and experience affecting the decisions, actions and activities of a social group through thought and behavioural patterns (Kabst 2000). Hofstede (2001, p. 9) defines culture as the collective programming of the mind which distinguishes the members of one group or category of people from another. Cultural distance between the partners is one of the variables that is most commonly examined in cooperation research. The definition of distance is either based on Hofstede's dimensions of culture or captured by the index from Kogut and Singh (1988; Larimo 2002, p. 8). Studies, which use the nationalities of the partner companies as a proxy for cultural distance, are more aptly described as international, rather than intercultural studies, as the nationality is only one factor in cultural distance (Pothukuchi et al. 2002).

To Gatignon and Anderson (1988, p. 311), cultural distance represents a particular form of uncertainty. Hu and Chen (1996, p. 167) claim that the values and norms, applied business practices, and management philosophies of the partner companies match better with a small cultural distance. This reduces the occurrence of conflicts and misunderstandings and thus has a positive influence on the success of the IJVs. According to Perlmutter and Heenan (1986, p. 149), this match of cultural values is a key factor for a successful cooperation. In contrast, a greater cultural distance impedes communication and interaction between the partners (Killing 1983, p. 57; Pothukuchi et al. 2002, p. 245).

Despite the numerous negative effects cited, studies can nevertheless be found, which demonstrate a positive correlation between differing cultures and success (cf., e.g. Park and Ungson 1997). This positive correlation can be justified on the one hand, in the fact, that companies from different countries of origin can learn more from each other and that they show an increased potential for the realization of synergies due to different strengths (Beamish and Killing 1996). On the other hand, Pothukuchi et al. (2002, p. 243) argue that it is not the different cultures of the countries of origin, but rather the difference of the corporate cultures of the partner companies, which determines the success of the IJVs. The influence of corporate culture on the success of IJVs is, however, examined in only a few empirical studies (cf. Aulakh and Madhok 2002; Pothukuchi et al. 2002).

Lung-Tan (2006, p. 439) provides an explanation for the inconsistency in the evaluation of the role of large cultural distances, and lists a number of methodological and conceptual problems that need to be addressed in future empirical research. This article follows the reasoning of the vast majority of studies that posit a negative effect. Therefore, the following hypothesis is:

Hypothesis 1d Cultural fit between the partners is negatively associated with IJV success.

Experience

The relationship between the experience of the partners and the success of IJVs can be explained using the theory of organizational learning, according to which the continuous repetition of an action leads to an accumulation of experience, making it possible to learn from past mistakes committed and avoid them in the future (Inkpen and Beamish 1997). For the success of an IJV, it is therefore crucial that the partner companies already have sufficient experience. The experience may result from previous business relationships with a partner (partner experience), previous inter-organizational cooperations (IJV experience) or from international business operations (international experience).

The advantage of partner experience is that companies which already cooperated with each other in the past have a basic understanding of the corporate culture and the behaviour of the partner company and are aware of its capabilities (Reuer et al. 2002). The experience gained from previous cooperation also creates a basis for mutual trust and reduces the risk of opportunistic behaviour (Hatfield et al. 1998). According to Kale et al. (2000, p. 221), this promotes information and knowledge exchange between the partners. At the same time, the transaction costs of an inter-company cooperation can be lowered both ex ante and ex post, through the reuse of business procedures and processes, well versed by both partners from previous cooperation (Kim et al., 2004). However, Simonin (1997, p. 1150) points that IJV success cannot be indicated by accumulated experience in and of itself. The companies must first internalize this experience and develop a "collaborative culture and know-how" before it can be applied in future cooperation. Reuer et al. (2002, p. 339) further explains, that it is not the extent, but rather the quality of the collaborative experience, that is of particular importance to partner companies. Hence, the mere existence of an earlier collaboration is not always beneficial. In fact, it is also possible that the strategic objective of a partnership has already been achieved in an earlier collaboration—for instance, knowledge transfer from the partner—rendering a new cooperation pointless and unattractive. Despite these potential negative side effects of previous partner experience, we follow the majority opinion from literature and suggest a positive correlation between the experience of partners and the success of IJV.

Hypothesis 2a Partner experience is positively associated with IJV success.

Previous IJV experience can build up a company's reputation as a cooperation partner, and thus increase its attractiveness for other potential partners, as well as guide it when structuring and managing future IJVs (Pearce 1997). Anand and Khanna (2000, p. 313) even claim that companies "... learn to create more value as they accumulate experience in joint venturing". However, the accumulation of partnership experience is only a means to an end and cannot be the sole focus of companies pursuing IJVs. This is especially true, as companies with too large a joint venture experience may leak unfiltered knowledge and intellectual property into the IJVs. We nevertheless assume an overall positive correlation between experience with IJVs and IJV success.

Hypothesis 2b IJV experience is positively associated with IJV success.

International experience is particularly relevant for IJVs, since the legal and cultural conditions, as well as the business practices, in the countries of origin of the partner enterprises can differ from each other significantly (Newbury et al. 2003, p. 405). An accumulated experience with international transactions is beneficial in choosing the "right" partner, as well as country to invest in, and facilitate the acclimatization to the new conditions (López-Navarro and Molina-Morales 2002). It is however noteworthy, that a foreign partner with significant experience in the host country can quickly make the local partner redundant. Although several negative effects to international experience are occasionally pointed out in literature, we agree with most of the empirical studies which postulate a positive correlation between IJV success and international experience.

Hypothesis 2c International experience is positively associated with IJV success.

IJV Level

At the IJV level, the success factors describe the various dimensions of exchange between the individual partners. These success factors include commitment, confidence, control, interdependence, conflicts and conflict management, and organizational learning.

Commitment

According to the theory of social exchange (cf. Blau, 1964), commitment is a key factor for the success of IJVs. Commitment is understood as the sense of inner obligation of cooperating partners to undertake necessary efforts to maintain the business relationship (Morgan and Hunt 1994, p. 23). For Skarmeas et al. (2002, p. 759), the commitment consists of "…a rather diverse set of factors including desire, willingness, sacrifice behavior, expectation of continuity, belief, and importance of the relationship". The development of commitment is an iterative process and will be initiated only when one of the partners signals his commitment, for example, by providing resources. As the benefitting partner does not want to receive more than what they are actually entitled to, they will try to reciprocate the commitment out of a moral obligation (Kabst 2000). This reciprocity in the action of the partners leads to increased IJV specific investments, as well as to the provision and allocation of financial, technical and human resources.

The presence of a similar high level of commitment from all involved partners reduces the incentives for opportunistic behaviour, with partners tending to conduct beneficial transactions, even if they are not secure (Morgan and Hunt 1994, p. 22). Commitment among partners also requires a greater perseverance in the pursuit of common objectives (cf. Morgan and Hunt 1994). Such partners would not look for alternative cooperation partners (cf. Anderson 1990), but instead invest in a long-term relationship, with joint efforts on behalf of the IJV leading to increased success. Hypothesis three thus postulates:

Hypothesis 3 Commitment is positively associated with IJV success.

Trust

According to the theory of social exchange, mutual trust is the second major determining factor of success in IJVs. The development of a trust-based relationship is also an incremental process, continuously improving through repeated and continuous cooperation (Gravier et al. 2006). In addition, Johnson et al. (1996, p. 988) stress the reciprocal nature of confidence. Therefore, existing confidence from one cooperation partner induces the building of trust in the other partner.

With IJVs the establishment of mutual trust on the basis of the inherent uncertainty of any forms of inter-firm cooperation is of great importance (Isidor et al. 2012). Often transactions are carried out in cooperations based on uncertainty and thus provide scope for opportunistic behaviour of the cooperation partner. The development respectively the existence of trust can reduce the risk resulting from the uncertainty perceived of one cooperation partner as far as that transactions can be conducted at all. Furthermore, trust leads to a reduction in transaction costs due to the related waiving of explicit backup and control mechanisms against opportunistic behaviour (Pearce 1997). In such cases, trust functions as a social, informal and cooperation-enhancing monitoring mechanism. Trust as well as formal control is a mechanism to make the behaviour of the cooperation partner predictable. The former through the creation of a moral obligation and the latter by the imposition of sanctions (see Schumacher 2003, p. 7). In their study, Dyer and Chu (2003) noted that partners in trusting IJVs have lower transaction costs, because they waste less time with discussions about the contracts and compliance, as well as with checking-up on and monitoring the other partners. Instead, trust in IJVs leads to increased success, where partners efficiently turn common expenses into joint income (cf. Pothukuchi et al. 2002).

Hypothesis 4 Trust is positively associated with IJV success.

Control

From an agency theoretic point of view, control is the instrument with which the partners check whether the IJV aligns its activities to the objectives of their company (cf. Mjoen and Tallman 1997). Thus, it represents an ideal opportunity to dismantle the existing asymmetries of information between the partners and the IJV. Most of the existing empirical studies attempt to capture control solely through the equity shares of the partner companies (Mjoen and Tallman 1997, p. 258). However, the share-ownership ratio is a rather rough, partly vague operationalization of control, as the proportional control ratio resulting from the "de jure" ownership structure" must not always match the actual "de facto" control relationship (Kabst 2000, p. 120). A minority shareholder can in fact wield more influence than intuited by share ownership, for example, due to contractually fixed veto rights, unequal voting rights distribution among the shares; or a de facto claim on certain key positions or legally capped share ownership (Geringer and Hébert 1991). Thus, we focus only on the perceived extent of control carried out by a partner company on the IJV in our examinations. Control in an IJV is of vital importance for the realization of the strategic business objectives (Geringer and Hébert 1991, p. 237). Clear-cut control and role assignments additionally reduce the inherent uncertainty of cooperation in IJVs by minimizing the chances of opportunistic behaviour and free-riding (Das and Teng 2000, p. 491). Our hypothesis is therefore:

Hypothesis 5 Control is positively associated with IJV success.

Interdependence

Symmetrical "interdependence" refers to the dependency of the inter-organizational cooperation with a cooperation partner for the achievement of the respective strategic business objectives (Hu and Chen 1996). The mutual dependency of the partner companies in regard to resources and capabilities of the cooperation partner is the optimal prerequisite for achieving the best possible success, because the potential loss that the partner companies would take at the termination of the cooperation reduces the incentive for opportunistic behaviour (Hsieh and Rodrigues 2005, p. 13). Partners are thus highly motivated to strengthen and deepen the existing relationship in order to secure access to the resources needed (Hatfield et al. 1998).

In contrast, the existence of asymmetric interdependence has negative effects on inter-company cooperation (Kabst 2000), as they can be used as an instrument of power. That is, companies that are less dependent on the partnership can skew it in their favour (Mjoen and Tallman 1997). Kemp and Ghauri (2001, p. 107) have shown in their study that an asymmetric interdependence undermines mutual trust. Thus, we present:

Hypothesis 6 Symmetric interdependence is positively associated with IJV success.

Conflicts and Conflict Management

Conflicts are an inherent part of every form of inter-firm cooperation (Eisele 1995, S. 177). Agency theory states that conflicts cause partners to increasingly pursue their own goals, implying they become less willing to continue contributing idiosyncratic resources to the joint undertaking (Reuer et al. 2002). Transaction cost theory affirms that conflicts should be avoided, as they are regarded to be economically inefficient (cf. Beamish and Killing 1996).

Although conflicts between the partners may ensure a constant interaction, and promote awareness of the problem, as well as direct focus on efficient solutions (Kemp and Ghauri 2001, p. 103), a high number of conflicts are unequivocally detrimental to the inter-company cooperation. Conflicts draw attention, energy and resources away from the real tasks of IJVs (cf. Johnson et al. 1996). Lyles and Salk (1996, p. 897) explain that conflicts and misunderstandings reduce the flow of information and therefore significantly affect the acquisition of knowledge. In addition, conflicts erode the mutual trust of the partners; increasing the potential for opportunistic behaviour (Cullen et al. 1995, p. 105). Unsurprisingly, Bucklin and Sengupta (1993, p. 42) also find a negative relationship between occurring conflicts and the perceived effectiveness of cooperation. Based on this line of argument we derive:

Hypothesis 7a Conflicts are negatively associated with IJV success.

In order to adequately address conflicts, it is sensible for cooperation partners to establish appropriate tools and mechanisms for conflict management early on (Eisele 1995, p. 177). According to Assael (1969, p. 573), conflict management can influence the relationship between the partners in either a destructive or a constructive manner, depending on the mechanism and its dynamics. For instance, conflict management is destructive, if the proposed solution is forced by the stronger partner—the one with majority shares or control (Assael 1969, p. 579). In contrast, if the problems are solved together through a mutual understanding, conflict management has a constructive influence on the quality of the relationship (Mohr 2006). This requires frequent interaction and open bilateral communication between the partners (Assael 1969, p. 576). These theoretical findings are supported by empirical evidence from the studies of Lin and Germain (1998, p. 187) and Pearce (1997). We therefore assume a constructive conflict management is positively associated with the success of IJVs.

Hypothesis 7b Conflict management is positively associated with IJV success.

Organizational Learning

According to the theory of organizational learning (cf. Argyris and Schön 1978), the main motive for companies to participate in inter-organizational cooperation is the acquisition of competition-relevant know-how as well as the critical skills and abilities of the cooperation partner (Kale et al. 2000, p. 217). These include familiarity with markets and competitors, an existing customer base, existing distribution channels and knowledge of specific management methods, as well as technological intellectual property (Fey and Beamish 2001). In this case, a crucial factor in the success of the collaboration is thus the extent to which the company can internalize the coveted know-how of the partner. In literature, one speaks of the "absorptive capacity" of a company in this context. Cohen and Levinthal (1990, p. 128) define absorptive capacity as the "… ability to recognize the value of new, external information, assimilate it and apply it to commercial ends". From this definition, it is clear that while the acquisition of specific knowledge is a necessary step, it is the subsequent internalization and strategic application of the gained knowledge that makes organizational learning a success. Gravier et al. (2006, p. 17) also conclude that the implementation and generation of knowledge has a greater effect on success, than the mere provisioning of company-specific knowledge. Following this line of argumentation, we suggest a positive correlation between organizational learning and the success of IJV.

Hypothesis 8 Organizational learning is positively associated with IJV success.

Meta-analysis

Meta-analysis appears to be the most reliable method to calculate the influence of the most frequently studied success factors on the different success criteria (Hunter and Schmidt 1990).

The results of the meta-analysis not only provide an assessment of the current quantitative knowledge of IJV success factor research, they also identify additional potential research gaps, serving as a guide for future research efforts. Furthermore, determining the average effect size allows generalizable statements about the "real" connection between individual success factors and the success of IJV (cf. Morschett et al. 2008).

To take a maximum number of primary studies into account and thus avoid a systematic bias of the findings, a broad-based search strategy through various information channels was conducted. Starting with a keyword-based search in various electronic databases, all citations in existing literature overview articles and relevant primary studies are systematically evaluated. In addition, an "issue-by-issue" search was performed in the leading scientific journals pertaining to the investigation. To also include so-called grey literature, such as dissertations, work and project reports, in the meta-analytical evaluation, search engines were used (primarily Google and Google Scholar) to look for relevant articles.

For a primary study to be integrated in the meta-analysis, the following substantial and methodological criteria had to be fulfilled:

To ensure a substantive comparability, the studies must have been written either in English or German.

- The study examines the relationship between different factors and indicators of IJV success either explicitly or implicitly. Because of the intention to consult the published correlations as a measure of the effect size, "Success" must not necessarily be the dependent variable in the studies. Providing an inter correlation between various success factors and the success is sufficient for a meta-analytical evaluation (Hunter and Schmidt 1990).
- The primary studies must have an empirical foundation and use quantitative methods, that is, they have data such as product-moment correlations. If other transferable statistics such as the d-value, t-test or F-test are available, these are transferred in the necessary r-values according to the formulas of Hunter and Schmidt (1990).

In addition, the primary studies must include information on the sample size. This is essential in particular for the calculation of weighted average correlations and the associated variance.

Operationalization of Variables

To allow the integration of different variables from multiple sources into the meta-analytic calculations, a construct definition was set for each variable. This definition was then used to select variables for inclusion from the primary studies, with variables whose content corresponded to the definition being included (see Table 7.2).

Table 7.2 Operationalization of variables

Definition und measurement	*Construct*
Construct definition: Include profitability ratios, sales growth and market share. *Representative measurements*: Kim et al. (2004)	Financial success indicators
Construct definition: Involving changes of ownership, the duration of the partnership or the liquidation of the IJVs *Representative measurements*: Kale et al. (2000)	Stability-oriented success criteria
Construct definition: Include subjective assessments as to the degree of target achievement and satisfaction with the overall success of the IJVs *Representative measurements*: Lin and Germain (1998); Lyles and Salk (1996)	Multidimensional success criteria
Construct definition: Intersection of business, functional areas or sectors in which the partner companies operate, and their size based on sales and number of employees *Representative measurements*: Parkhe (1993)	Operational fit between partners
Construct definition: Intersection of business, functional areas or sectors in which the partner companies and the IJV operate *Representative measurements*: Anh et al. (2006)	Operational fit between each partner und the IJV
Construct definition: The extent to which the partners' goals and motives coincide *Representative measurements*: Newburry et al. (2003)	Strategic fit
Construct definition: The extent to which the cooperation partners come from different cultures (Kogut and Singh 1988), as measured by Kogut and Singh's index or subjective assessment of the cultural distance*Representative measurements*: Anh et al. (2006)	Cultural fit

(*continued*)

Table 7.2 (continued)

Definition und measurement	*Construct*
Construct definition: Previous business experiences with the same partner. *Representative measurements*: Parkhe (1993)	Partner experience
Construct definition: The number of previous IJVs *Representative measurements*: Kim et al. (2004)	IJV experience
Construct definition: Previous international experience of the partners *Representative measurements*: Newburry et al. (2003)	International experience
Construct definition: The perceived importance of the partnership, the willingness to struggle for the preservation of this partnership, as well as the intended long-term cooperation with a partner *Representative measurements*: Cullen et al. (1995)	Commitment
Construct definition: The belief in the reliability and integrity of the cooperation partner (Morgan and Hunt 1994). Trust is often associated with the characteristics: Honesty, fairness, kindness and benevolence. (Aulakh et al. 2002) *Representative measurements*: Krishnan et al. (2006)	Trust
Construct definition: The extent to which one partner exerts control over the IJV *Representative measurements*: Fey and Beamish (2001)	Control
Construct definition: The extent to which a partner is dependent upon the resources of the other partner *Representative measurements*: Pearce (1997)	Interdependence
Construct definition: The number and extent of conflicts and disagreements *Representative measurements*: Ding (1997)	Conflicts
Construct definition: The extent to which problems are solved cooperatively by the partners *Representative measurements*: Kale et al. (2000); Pearce (2001).	Conflict management
Construct definition: The dynamic process of knowledge acquisition and use of knowledge through interaction, communication and interpretation between the partners (Jiang and Li 2008) *Representative measurements*: Krishnan et al. (2006)	Organizational learning

Source: Adapted to own data with reference to Isidor et al. 2012, p. 14

Based on these construct definitions, the primary studies are coded separately by three coders. Cohen's Kappa will be calculated as a statistical measure of the inter-rater reliability of these estimates (see Reus and Rottig 2009). Any remaining discrepancies will be resolved by a discussion among the coders.

Moderator Variables

Moderators can systematically influence the investigation of relationship between an independent and a dependent variable and thus cause a variation in the observed values. If less than 75 percent of the total variance can be explained by sampling error, this indicates the existence of systematically influencing factors, which must be organized into subgroups, depending on their type (study artefacts, moderators). A moderator analysis of each influencing factor subgroup is then carried out, after which the subgroups must individually then undergo a new meta-analysis (cf. Stamm and Schwarb 1995). It should be noted, however, that each subgroup should contain at least three effect levels (k > = 3) (Lipsey and Wilson 2001). The criterion for the verification of a moderator is the decline of two variances (s_r^2 and s_e^2) in comparison to the corrected total variance (s_p^2) (Stamm and Schwarb 1995, p. 18). In addition, a z-test is carried out, which checks effect sizes on significant differences (Hunter and Schmidt 1990, p. 348)

This explains any potentially heterogeneous distribution of the correlation coefficients.

For the present study, the *form of inter-company cooperation* as a moderator variable is taken into account. The total sample is thus subdivided into subgroups depending on whether only equity capital-based IJVs or contractual IJVs are included in the respective sample. One refers to an equity-IJV as at least two legally and economically independent companies from different countries of origin with common equity (Kabst 2000, p. 12). While an equity capital-based joint venture necessarily requires the re-establishment of a legally independent company as a constitutive characteristic term, contractual IJVs are understood as cooperations, which jointly develop, produce and/or distribute develop products and services (Isidor et al. 2012). The primary studies are then differentiated into IJVs belonging to high-tech, low-tech or cross-industry with each respective sampling examined individually to identify any possible effects this factor may have. IJVs from the information, telecommunication, electrical, pharmaceutical industry and biotechnology are classified as high-tech. Samples with IJVs exclusively from the processing industry are coded as low-tech. If the investigated IJVs of a primary study come from diverse industries, this is classified as a cross-industry.

In addition, the *geographical distance* between the countries of origin of the partner entities is examined as a possible moderator variable.

Intracontinental partnerships are coded as short geographical distance, while intercontinental partnerships will be classified as collaborations with large geographical distance.

Finally, the moderator variable of the *size of the partnering companies* was taken. Referring to the definition provided by the OECD (2009), companies with less than 250 employees or a turnover less than €43 million are coded as small and medium sized while those with more than 250 employees or a higher turnover than €43 million are coded as large companies.

Measurement of the Effect Sizes

The overall effect size is calculated in accordance with the procedures of Hunter and Schmidt (1990), where a weighted arithmetic mean with the sample sizes from the correlation coefficients of individual studies is used (Eq. (7.1)).

Thus, greater weight is attached to the primary studies with a larger study population. Hunter et al. (1982, p. 41) weighting generally leads to more accurate estimates of the population correlation coefficient. The corresponding observed weighted variance is estimated using Eq. (7.2) (Hunter and Schmidt 1990, p. 100):

$$\bar{r} = \frac{\sum_{i}^{k} n_i r_i}{N} \tag{7.1}$$

$$s_r^2 = \frac{\sum_{i}^{k} n_i \left(r_i - \bar{r}\right)^2}{N} \tag{7.2}$$

Product-moment correlation coefficient as an estimate of the effect size in study i (i = 1, … , k)	$\bar{r}$
Sample size in study i (i = 1, …., k)	n_i
Total sample size N = n1 + n2 , … + nk	N
Number of independent correlation coefficients (primary studies)	k

In addition, the variance of the sampling error will be calculated (Eq. (7.3)) (Hunter and Schmidt 1990, p. 108). The sampling error is the estimated proportion of variance resulting from the influence of a low sample size. An estimate of this error is important for a future assessment of the presence of heterogeneity or homogeneity of the model:

$$s_e^2 = \frac{\left(1 - r^{-2}\right)k}{N} \tag{7.3}$$

From there, a total variance adjusted to the sampling errors can be determined (so-called population variance):

$$s_p^2 = s_r^2 - s_e^2 \tag{7.4}$$

To determine whether there is a variation (heterogeneity) between the individual correlations of the different primary studies, the 75 percent rule of Hunter and Schmidt (1990, p. 414) will be applied:

$$\frac{s_e^2}{s_r^2} \geq 0{,}75 \tag{7.5}$$

Equation (7.5) expresses that at least 75 percent of the total variance should be explained by the sampling error, so one can speak of homogeneity of effect sizes. If there is homogeneity, the average effect size from the primary studies can be seen as a true estimate of the population effect size. In case of heterogeneity, the effect size is considered as rather average in the studied population (Steinmetz et al. 2011). Furthermore, if the effects do turn out to be heterogeneous, that is, the total variance is less than 75 percent, the influence of moderator variables should be checked (Hunter and Schmidt 1990, p. 414 ff.). In contrast, a moderator analysis is no longer necessary in case of homogeneity of the results, as the observed variance is then mostly due to the influence of uncorrected artefacts.

In addition, the 95 percent confidence interval of the weighted mean effect size will be calculated. In cases where the computed confidence interval includes the value zero, the meta-analytic calculated overall effect size is considered to be not significant.

Finally, the effect of stability will be computed on the basis of the "fail safe-N" according to Hunter and Schmidt (1990, p. 511):

$$FSN = \frac{k}{2706}\left[k\left(\overline{z}_k\right) - 2706\right] \tag{7.6}$$

$$\overline{z}_k = \text{average Z} - \text{value of } k \text{ studies}$$

The fail-safe-N is an index to determine the hypothetical number of studies with an average effect size of zero, which would be required to negate a significant positive overall effect of a meta-analysis. In case the fail-safe-N exceeds the benchmark of 5 k + 10 studies, it cannot be assumed that the significance of the overall effect is due to the selection of non-significant work. At lower values, however, the validity of the significance must be challenged (Steinmetz et al. 2011). The calculation of fail-safe-N takes into account the "dark figure" problem often stated in meta-analyses ("publication bias"). It is assumed that studies with significant results are more likely to be published than studies with non-significant results (Stamm and Schwarb 1995, p. 21).

Summary and Conclusion

The aim of the present study is to carry out an integration of previous IJV success research by means of a meta-analytic evaluation and thus to contribute to reducing the heterogeneity of results of the investigation. In the following the first tendency of the results and progress are discussed subdivided after Robson et al. (2002) into partner and IJV level.

Partner Level

The similarity of the partner seems to have mostly a significant positive effect on the success of IJV. Only the often-postulated negative influence of cultural similarities of IJV's success could not be verified yet.

A possible reason for the lack of success-promoting effect of cultural similarities of the cooperation partners could probably be the operationalization of the cultural construct. A large part of studies only states the weighted average of Hofstede's dimensions of culture. It is possible, however, that only individual dimensions have an impact on the success of IJVs. It could also be that the culture not directly affects the success of IJVs, but has a moderating effect on the relationship between different factors of success and the success of IJV.

Furthermore, the results show that only the partner experience has a significant impact on the success of the IJV. This realization is however not very surprising and was observed by other authors. Previous experience must not necessarily have a positive and successful promotional contribution. Experience can rather be misapplied especially when the substantive difference between the original relationship and the current business relationship is too large.

In such case, prior experience can have no influence or even a negative impact when knowledge is transferred incorrectly. This tendency of the results indicates that the experience gained from previous IJVs or other international activities are very specific and cannot be transferred easily to other IJVs.

Joint Venture Level

A significant scientific progress in the so far conducted meta-analysis is the trend that the variables of the joint venture level seem to have much stronger effects on the success of the IJV as the variables of the partner level. Therefore, soft factors, which determine the process of cooperation between the partners, seem to be critical to success as constitutive characteristics of the partners.

This means that fewer variables—which describe only the partner attributes—are crucial to the IJV success, but rather variables, which determine the cooperation between the two partners (commitment, trust, etc.).

This shows that although IJVs represent an inter-company collaboration that the same variables (trust, commitment, etc.) are crucial for success like with any interpersonal cooperation. The sole consideration of classical economic theories such as the transaction cost theory (Williamson 1985) or the resource-based approach (Barney 1991) appear too limited in this case; whereas behavioural theories seem to have a greater contribution. Since behavioural theories primarily were designed to explain interpersonal behaviour, future research should try to expand the focus of these theories on intercompany behaviour, so that they are suitable also for the explanation of IJV success.

In the next steps, the hypotheses will be validated in selected IJVs in Saudi Arabia. This will be followed by the integration of the consolidated results into a causal model which can be used to derive concrete recommendations for the founding and management of SME IJVs as well as to identify potential research gaps.

This chapter seized upon the opportunity provided by the German Chamber of Foreign Trade in KSA, to use the facilitated access to data to close the identified research gap, and should serve as a guide for German-Arab IJVs, while giving strong boost for IJVs in the MENA region generally.

References

Adarkar, A., Adil, A., Ernst, D., & Vaish, P. (1997). Emerging Market Alliances. *The McKinsey Quarterly, 4*, 120–137.

Anand, B. N., & Khanna, T. (2000). Do Firms Learn to Create Value? *Strategic Management Journal, 21*, 295–315.

Anderson, E. (1990). Two Firms, One Frontier. *Sloan Management Review, 31*, 19–30.

Anh, P. T. T., Baughn, C. C., Hang, N. T. M., & Neupert, K. E. (2006). Knowledge Acquisition from Foreign Parents in International Joint Ventures. *International Business Review, 15*, 463–487.

Argyris, C., & Schön, D. (1978). *Organizational Learning: A Theory of Action Perspective*. Reading, MA: Addison-Wesley.

Artisien, P., & Buckley, P. (1985). Joint Ventures in Yugoslavia. *Journal of International Business Studies, 16*, 111–134.

Assael, H. (1969). Constructive Role of Interorganizational Conflict. *Administrative Science Quarterly, 14*, 573–582.

Aulakh, P. S., & Madhok, A. (2002). Cooperation and Performance in International Alliances: The Critical Role of Flexibility. In F. J. Contractor & P. Lorange (Eds.), *Cooperative Strategies and Alliances* (pp. 25–48). Amsterdam: Pergamon.

Barney, J. B. (1991). Firm Resources and Sustained Competitive Advantage. *Journal of Management, 17*(1), 99–120.

Beamish, P. W., & Killing, J. P. (1996). Global Perspectives on Cooperative Strategies. *Journal of International Business Studies*, (Special Issue), *27*.

Blau, P. (1964). *Exchange and Power in Social Life*. New York: Wiley.

Bucklin, L. P., & Sengupta, S. (1993). Organizing Successful Co-Marketing Alliances. *Journal of Marketing, 57*, 32–46.

Buckley, P. J. (1997). International Technology Transfer by Small and Medium-Sized Enterprises. *Small Business Economics, 9*, 67–78.

Child, J., & Yan, Y. (2003). Predicting the Performance of International Joint Ventures: An Investigation in China. *Journal of Management Studies, 40*, 283–320.

Cohen, W. M., & Levinthal, D. A. (1990). Absorptive Capacity: A New Perspective on Learning and Innovation. *Administrative Science Quarterly, 35*, 128–152.

Cullen, J. B., Johnson, J. L., & Sakano, T. (1995). Japanese and Local Partner Commitment to IJVs. *Journal of International Business Studies, 26*, 91–115.

Das, T. K., & Teng, B. S. (2000). A Resource-Based Theory of Strategic Alliances. *Journal of Management, 26*(2), 31–61.

Dhanaraj, C., Lyles, M. A., Steensma, H. K., & Tihany, L. (2004). Managing Tacit and Explicit Knowledge Transfer in IJVs. *Journal of International Business Studies, 35*, 428–442.

Ding, D. Z. (1997). Control, Conflict, and Performance: A Study of U.S.-Chinese Joint Ventures. *Journal of International Marketing, 5*, 31–45.

Dyer, J. H., & Chu, W. (2003). The Role of Trustworthiness in Reducing Transaction Costs and Improving Performance: Empirical Evidence from the United States, Japan, and Korea. *Organization Science, 14*(1), 57–68.

Eden, L., Levitas, E., & Martinez, R. J. (1997). The Production, Transfer and Spill-Over of Technology. *Small Business Economics, 9*(1), 53–66.

Eisele, J. (1995). *Erfolgsfaktoren des Joint Venture-Management*. Wiesbaden: Gabler.

Fey, C. F., & Beamish, P. W. (2001). Organizational Climate Similarity and Performance: International Joint Ventures in Russia. *Organization Studies, 22*, 853–882.

Gatignon, H., & Anderson, E. (1988). The Multinational Corporation's Degree of Control Over Foreign Subsidiaries. *Journal of Law, Economics, and Organization, 4*, 305–336.

Geringer, J. M., & Hébert, L. (1991). Measuring Performance of International Joint Ventures. *Journal of International Business Studies, 22*, 249–263.

Gravier, M. J., Randall, W. S., & Strutton, D. (2006). *The Role of Knowledge in Alliances: A Meta-Analysis*. Working Paper.

Hatfield, L., Pearce, J. A., II, Sleeth, R. G., & Pitts, M. W. (1998). Toward Validation of Partner Goal Achievement as a Measure of Joint Venture Performance. *Journal of Managerial Issues, 10*, 355–372.

Hofstede, G. H. (2001). *Culture's Consequences: Comparing Values, Behaviors, Institutions, and Organizations across Nations*. Thousand Oaks: Sage Publications.

Hsieh, H. Y., & Rodrigues, S. B. (2005). *Risk Perception and Post-formation Control in International Joint Ventures in Taiwan*. Working Paper.

Hu, M. Y., & Chen, H. (1996). An Empirical Analysis of Factors: Explaining Foreign Joint Venture Performance in China. *Journal of Business Research, 35*, 165–173.

Hunter, J. E., & Schmidt, F. L. (1990). *Methods of Meta-Analysis*. Newbury Park: Sage.

Hunter, J. E., Schmidt, F. L., & Jackson, G. B. (1982). *Meta-Analysis: Cumulating Research Findings across Studies*. Beverly Hills, CA: Sage.

Inkpen, A. C., & Beamish, P. W. (1997). Knowledge, Bargaining Power, and the Instability of International Joint Ventures. *Academy of Management Review, 22*, 177–202.

Isidor, R.; Schwens, C., & Kabst, R. (2012). Die Messung von Joint Venture Erfolg. In J. Zentes (Hrsg.), *Markteintrittsstrategien—Dynamik und Komplexität*. Wiesbaden: Gabler.

Jiang, X., & Li, Y. (2008). The Relationship Between Organizational Learning and Firms' Financial Performance in Strategic Alliances: A Contingency Approach. *Journal of World Business, 43*, 365–379.

Johnson, J. L., Cullen, J. B., Sakano, T., & Takenouchi, H. (1996). Setting the Stage for Trust and Strategic Integration in Japanese-U.S. Cooperative Alliances. *Journal of International Business Studies, 27*, 981–1004.

Kabst, R. (2000). *Steuerung und Kontrolle Internationaler Joint Venture*. München & Meering: Hampp.

Kale, P., Singh, H., & Perlmutter, H. (2000). Learning and Protecting of Proprietary Assets in Strategic Alliances. *Strategic Management Journal, 21*, 217–237.

Kemp, R. G. M., & Ghauri, P. N. (2001). Interdependency in Joint Ventures. *Journal on Chain and Network Science, 1*, 101–110.

Killing, J. P. (1983). *Strategies for Joint Venture Success*. London: Croom Helm.

Kim, H., Hoskisson, R. E., & Wan, W. P. (2004). Power Dependence, Diversification Strategy, and Performance in Keiretsu Member Firms. *Strategic Management Journal, 25*, 613–636.

Kogut, B., & Singh, H. (1988). The Effect of National Culture on the Choice of Entry Mode. *Journal of International Business Studies, 19*, 411–432.

Krishnan, R., Martin, X., & Noorderhaven, N. G. (2006). When Does Trust Matter to Alliance Performance? *Academy of Management Journal, 49*, 894–917.

Larimo, J. (2002). *International Joint Venture Performance: Key Determinants and How Much Do the Results Depend on the Measurement of Performance?* Paper Presented at the 28th EIBA Annual Conference in Athens, Greece, December 8–10.

Larimo, J. (2007). International Joint Venture Performance: Impact of Performance Measures and Foreign Parent, Target Country and Investment Specific Variables on Performance. In G. Cliquet, G. Hendriks, M. Tuunanen, & J. Windsperger (Eds.), *Economics and Management of Networks: Franchising, Strategicalliances and Co-operatives* (pp. 393–418). Springer Verlag.

Lin, X., & Germain, R. (1998). Sustaining Satisfactory Joint Venture Relationships: The Role of Conflict Resolution Strategy. *Journal of International Business Studies, 29*, 179–196.

Lipsey, M.W., & Wilson, D.B. (2001). *Practical Meta-Analysis. Applied Social Research Methods Series*, vol. 49. Thousand Oaks: Sage Publications.

López-Navarro, M. Á., & Molina-Morales, F. X. (2002). On Measurement of Joint Ventures Performance: A Comparative Approach. *International Journal of Business Performance Management, 4*, 115–127.

Lung-Tan, L. (2006). The Relationship between Cultural Distance and Performance in IJVs. *International Journal of Management, 23*, 436–445.

Luo, Y. (1999). The Structure–Performance Relationship in a Transitional Economy. *Journal of Business Research, 46*, 15–30.

Luo, Y. (2002). Product Diversification in International Joint Ventures: Performance Implications in an Emerging Market. *Strategic Management Journal, 23*, 1–20.

Lyles, M. A., & Salk, J. E. (1996). Knowledge Acquisition from Foreign Parents in IJVs. *Journal of International Business Studies, 27*, 877–903.

Merchant, H., & Schendel, D. (2000). How Do International Joint Ventures Create Shareholder Value? *Strategic Management Journal, 21*(6), 723–737.

Mjoen, H., & Tallman, S. (1997). Control and Performance in International Joint Ventures. *Organization Science, 8*, 257–274.

Mohr, A. T. (2006). A Multiple Approach to IJV Performance Measurement. *Journal of World Business, 41*, 247–260.

Morgan, R. M., & Hunt, S. D. (1994). The Commitment-Trust Theory of Relationship Marketing. *Journal of Marketing, 58*, 20–38.

Morschett, D. (2005). Formen von Kooperationen, Allianzen und Netzwerken. In J. Zentes, B. Swoboda, & D. Morschett (Hrsg.), *Kooperationen, Allianzen, Netzwerke* (Vol. 2, pp. 377–403). Gabler: Wiesbaden.

Morschett, D., Swoboda, B., & Schramm-Klein, H. (2008). Einflussfaktoren auf die Wahl einer Markteintrittsstrategie – eine meta-analytische Untersuchung der Entscheidung zwischen Tochtergesellschaft und Kooperation. *Zeitschrift für Betriebswirtschaft, 78*(5), 509–551.

Newburry, W., Zeira, Y., & Yeheksel, O. (2003). Autonomy and Effectiveness of Equity International Joint Ventures. *International Business Review, 12*, 395–419.

OECD. (2005). *SME and Entrepreneurship Outlook* (p. 17). Paris: OECD.

OECD. (2009). Top Barriers and Drivers to SME Internationalisation. Report by the OECD Working Party on SMEs and Entrepreneurship, OECD, Paris.

Oesterle, M. J. (1995). Probleme und Methoden der Joint Venture-Erfolgsbewertung. *Zeitschrift der Betriebswirtschaft, 65*(9), 987–1004.

Park, S. H., & Ungson, G. R. (1997). The Effect of National Culture, Organizational Complementarity, and Economic Motivation on Joint Venture Dissolution. *Academy of Management Journal, 40*, 279–307.

Parkhe, A. (1993). Partner Nationality and the Structure-Performance Relationship in Strategic Alliances. *Organization Science, 4*, 301–324.

Pearce, R. J. (1997). Toward Understanding Joint Venture Performance and Survival. *The Academy of Management Review, 22*, 203–225.

Pearce, R. J. (2001). Looking Inside the Joint Venture to Help Understand the Link Between Inter-Parent Cooperation and Performance. *Journal of Management Studies, 38*, 557–582.

Perlmutter, H. V., & Heenan, D. A. (1986). Cooperate to Compete Globally. *Harvard Business Review, 64*, 136–152.

Pothukuchi, V., Damanpour, F., Choi, J., Chen, C. C., & Park, S. H. (2002). National and Organizational Culture Differences and International Joint Venture Performance. *Journal of International Business Studies, 33*, 243–265.

Reuer, J. J., Park, K. M., & Zollo, M. (2002). Experiential Learning in International Joint Ventures. In F. J. Contractor & P. Lorange (Hrsg.), *Cooperative Strategies and Alliances* (pp. 321–345). Amsterdam: Pergamon.

Reus, T. H., & Rottig, D. (2009). Meta-analyses of International Joint Venture Performance Determinants. *Management International Review, 49*, 607–640.

Robson, M. J., Leonidou, L. C., & Katsikeas, C. S. (2002). Factors Influencing IJV Performance. *Management International Review, 42*(4), 385–419.

Schaan, J. L. (1988). How to Control a Joint Venture Even as a Minority Partner. *Journal of General Management, 14*, 4–16.

Schumacher, C. (2003). *Trust Versus Control in Co-operative Relationships of Small and Medium Sized Enterprises.* Paper Presented at the Annual Conference 2003 of the New Zealand Association of Economists.

Simonin, B. L. (1997). The Importance of Collaborative Know-How. *Academy of Management Journal, 40*, 1150–1174.

Skarmeas, D., Katsikeas, C., & Schlegelmilch, B. (2002). Drivers of Commitment and its Impact on Performance in Cross-Cultural Buyer-Seller Relationships: The Importer's Perspective. *Journal of International Business Studies, 33*, 757–783.

Stamm, H., & Schwarb, T. M. (1995). Metaanalyse: Eine Einführung. *Zeitschrift für Personalforschung, 9*, 5–27.

Steinmetz, H., Bäuerle, N., & Isidor, R. (2011). *Testing the Circular Structure of Human Values: A Meta-analytical Structural Equation Model.* Working Paper.

Teusler, N. (2008). *Strategische Stabilitätsfaktoren in Unternehmenskooperationen.* Gabler: Wiesbaden.

Williamson, O. E. (1985). *The Economic Institutions of Capitalism: Firms, Markets, Relational Contracting.* New York: Free Press.

Yan, A., & Gray, B. (2001). Negotiating Control and Achieving Performance in International Joint Ventures: A Conceptual Model. *Journal of International Management, 7*, 295–315.

Internet Sources

Saudi German Development and Investment Company Limited (SAGECO). (2011). Retrieved November 15, 2011, from http://www.sageco.com.sa/home.html

Saudi-US Relation Service (SUSRIS): A "SME" Authority for Saudi Arabia. (2011). Retrieved February 2, 2011, from http://www.susris.com/

CHAPTER 8

GCC Countries' Diversification and Industrial Development: Looking Beyond the Asian Model

Daisuke Yamamoto

Introduction

The chapter first looks at the shape and background of East Asia's economic development model. Next, it compares situations in the GCC and East Asia and examines paths the GCC should take toward industrial diversification. It then looks at several case studies which, based on the above examination, could serve as models for the GCC while also considering how governments can contribute to the region's industrial development. Finally, the chapter summarizes basic policy and concrete means of diversifying the GCC's economy, as well as listing some points for the GCC to avoid and looking toward what shape the council could take in the future.

East Asia's economic development model has been called the "flying geese" paradigm. While this term originally referred to the mechanisms behind the economic development of a single country, it has come to explain the way that Japan acted as leader of Asia's economic development

D. Yamamoto (✉)
Sojitz Research Institute, Ltd., Tokyo, Japan

A. Mishrif, Y. Al Balushi (eds.), *Economic Diversification in the Gulf Region, Volume II*, The Political Economy of the Middle East,
DOI 10.1007/978-981-10-5786-1_8

through the 1970s and 1980s, followed by similar developments in Korea, Taiwan, Hong Kong, and, eventually, other countries in the region. This "flying geese" model of economic development has been attributed to four factors at the time: the existence of consumer markets for Asian products, the region's plentiful and cheap labor, the transfer of technology from Japan to the Asian countries, and the era's Cold War mentality. After entering the twenty-first century, these factors were joined by the division of labor across countries through global supply chains and the creation of a logistics network which supports these chains.

The GCC nations, on the other hand, have a smaller total population of 50 million people, are already accepting foreign labor en masse, and each have a per capita GDP exceeding US$20,000. This is a very different situation from what Asia experienced during their "flying geese"-based industrialization. The GCC is also lagging behind in terms of both free-trade agreements to support division of trade across countries, as well as the development of a logistics network which stretches outside the region.

Given these conditions, the GCC should not aim for the same industrialization-fueled economic growth that once took place in East Asia. Rather, they should utilize their abundant capital reserves from crude oil and natural gas to promote capital-intensive or knowledge-intensive industries.

This chapter will start by introducing two economic development models which could benefit the GCC: Singapore, which was able to accomplish rapid economic development as a non-resource country, and Norway, which came to operate a welfare state based on capital reserves accumulated through oil revenue. Next, the chapter will examine the role the government can play in promoting new industry, using Finland's SITRA and Israel's YOZMA as examples. All of these case studies show countries which have succeeded through investment in venture companies or venture capital. Finally, the chapter will talk about industrial development through resources and resource-related industries, geography, culture, the environment, and active use of capital as a possible direction for the GCC to take toward economic diversification. In terms of concrete methodology, the chapter will touch on general promotion of industry, strengthening and stimulating oil- and gas-associated industries through M&A, promotion of knowledge-intensive industries, and creation of the soft and hard infrastructure necessary to make these methods viable. Finally, the chapter will highlight some points for the GCC to avoid and talks about what the GCC could be like in the future.

Perspectives on the Asian "Flying Geese" Paradigm

When considering the GCC's future economic development, the economic development model of the East Asian countries including Korea and Taiwan would seem to be a good starting point. First, this chapter will explain the "flying geese paradigm" which serves as an explanation for East Asia's economic growth, analyze the factors behind its success, and verify whether this model is suitable to the GCC countries.

The Flying Geese Paradigm

The flying geese paradigm (the name came from the inverse of the "V" formation, taken by geese flying north in the fall) is one of several general theories of economic development proposed by Kaname Akamatsu. It refers to the process by which the mechanisms behind a country's industrial development (the basic "flying geese" pattern of development) transfers to a higher order of industry (the variant "flying geese" pattern of development). Akamatsu (1974) describes Japan's pre-WWII wool industry as one which underwent two phases of flying geese development: the changing of import commodities according to the country's industrial development and the entire wool industry's growth through implementation of a pattern, from import to domestic production further to export, for each product. The latter in particular helped endow Japanese exports with competitiveness through a process of internal industrial diversification paired with improved and streamlined production methods. This is referred to as "basic flying geese pattern of development," while the former represents the "secondary" or "variant" pattern of development.

Later, Kiyoshi Kojima (2000b) would reformulate the flying geese paradigm of economic development as a framework which he called the "Akamatsu-Kojima Model of Flying Geese Economic Development." In short, it refers to "a model of catch-up industrialization wherein the amassing of capital (and the knowledge gained through that process) streamlines and enables export of an industry. This, in turn, enables the industry to move to a higher order of development, or in other words, increases diversification and sophistication of the industrial structure."

During Japan's postwar period of rapid economic growth, large corporations reigned, having come to self-manufacture their most important parts. Experts have noted that the industrial development which occurred during this period was backed by the effective production relationship created between smaller subcontractors which had organized under the wing of these corporate titans (Kojima 2000b). This is because large companies—these "parent companies"—were catching up to Western technology and had constructed a framework for mass production. This could also be said to be a kind of flying geese model economic development. On the other hand, horizontal relationships between companies had grown more important to the rise in product development which accompanied new tech R&D and new combinations of segmented technologies. One of the reasons for this was the increasing speed at which technology was rendered obsolete, making it impossible for single companies to survive alone. Of particular interest is how this point highlights the limits of the flying geese paradigm.

The flying geese paradigm met its second stage of development after it was presented by Saburo Okita (1985) as the source of the Asia-Pacific region's economic growth. That is to say, the flying geese model which Japan succeeded in utilizing to develop its economy had propagated internationally to reach the East Asian economy, promoting regional integration and bringing rapid economic growth to the less-developed countries. Japan now lead the formation, followed by Korea, Taiwan, and Hong Kong, and behind them, the other countries of the region. Okita (1985) says that the disparity in capital reserves and economic development levels promotes dynamic division of industries over countries and that the capital, support, and technology provided by Japan, as well as Japan's export of cheap capital goods and intermediary commodities, encouraged the industrial growth of these latecomer countries.

A Pattern for Economic Growth

As I mentioned in the previous section, after Japan's industrialization under a period of flying geese paradigm-based economic growth, a similar process took place in East Asia, bringing the same economic growth to the rest of the region. The four factors below have been cited as the factors which made this economic model feasible.

The Existence of Consumer Markets

The USA was the first consumer market for low-priced, mass-produced goods, with Japan later following suit. Graph 8.1 shows the ratio of global GDP held by the USA and Japan. Looking at the graph, we see that from 1963 to 2004, the cumulative total GDP of these two countries equaled roughly 40 per cent of the global GDP. The existence of stable consumer

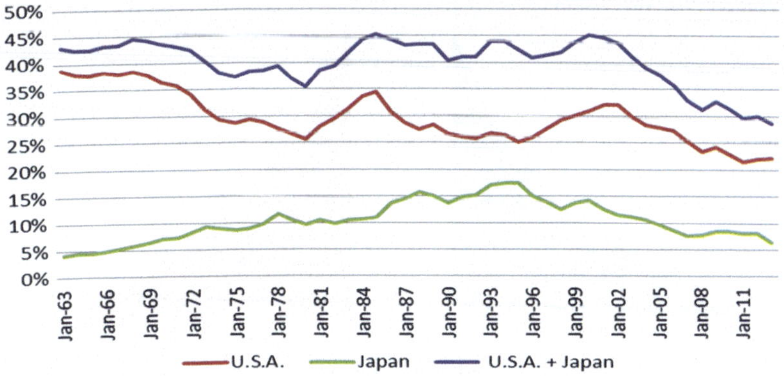

Graph 8.1 GDP share in the world (Source: World Bank)

markets can be said to be one of the factors behind East Asia's gradual industrialization.

Plentiful and Cheap Labor

The second factor was the region's abundant labor. Each of the East Asian countries supported a large, young population, with each country's demography in 1980 maintaining its pyramid shape for the most part. Even as Korea's population began to bell out, their working-age population continued to grow. Indonesia and Korea stand as the most representative examples, and it can be said that this plentiful and cheap labor aided the success of their labor-intensive industries (Graphs 8.2 and 8.3).

Transfer of Technology

East Asia's economic growth was accompanied by an active transfer of technology from Japan. There is no real indicator which can tell us to what degree this technological transfer occurred, so it can be difficult to pinpoint a concrete example. However, we can get some idea by looking at shifts in Japan's foreign direct investment. Graph 8.4 shows how Japan's foreign direct investment shifted over time. As this graph makes clear, the earliest direct investment was in the four ASEAN countries and the Asian NIEs starting in the 1970s, and the stronger yen following the Plaza Accord of 1985 caused this amount to expand dramatically. What is important here is each peak period—when investment in the Asian NIEs peaked in 1989—and how peak investment in the ASEAN countries

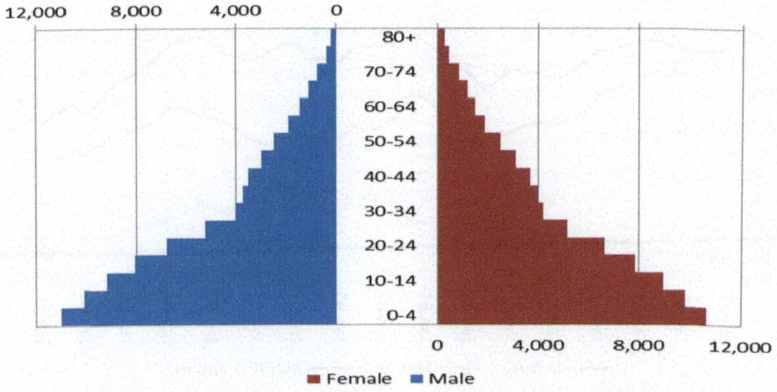

Graph 8.2 Demography of Indonesia in 1980 (in thousands) (Source: UN World Population Prospects: The 2012 Revision)

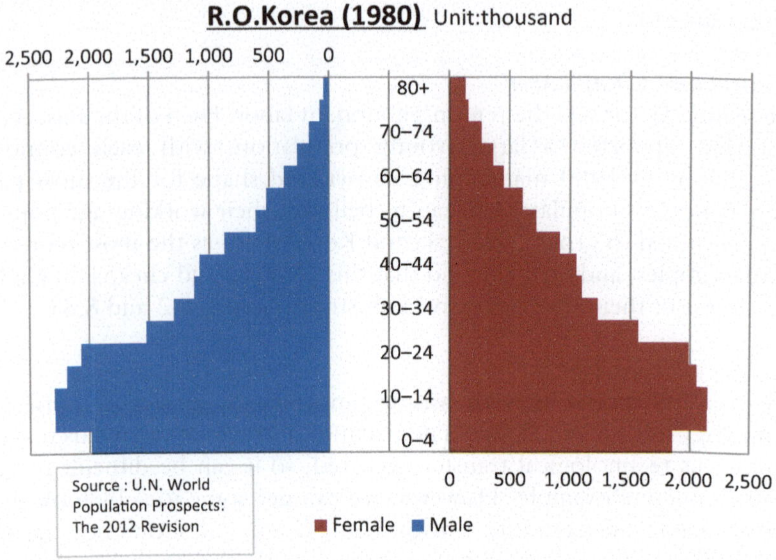

Graph 8.3 Demography of Republic of Korea in 1980 (in thousands) (Source: UN World Population Prospects: The 2012 Revision)

exceeded investment in the NIEs in 1997. Japan's foreign direct investment in China continued to grow through the 2000s, with the country recording US$13.5 billion in balance of payments for 2012.

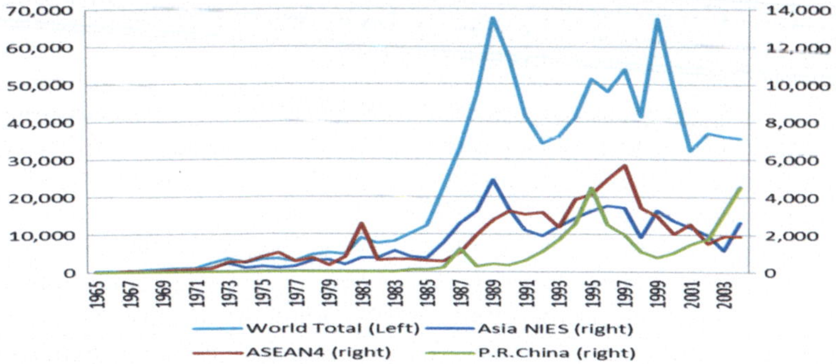

Graph 8.4 Foreign direct investment from Japan based on reports (in US$ million) (Source: JETRO)

The Era's Cold War Mentality

The last background factor which I would like to mention is the Cold War mentality of the time which continued up until 1989. America, in their face-off against communism, sought to support the growth of capitalist economies. For this reason, they actively provided support and cooperated with capitalist nations, with Japan joining suit as soon as they had recovered from their post-WWII depression. According to the Official Development Assistance (ODA) White Paper 2006, Ministry of Foreign Affairs Japan, Japan's ODA started in 1950 as a way to provide postwar reparations and economic support to the Asian countries. The nation started offering full-scale financial assistance after that. By contributing to the revitalization and development of these Asian economies, this ODA was able to restore diplomatic relations between Japan and its Asian neighbors, as well as pull these countries into a capitalist framework during a time of Cold War. While Japan helped finance projects such as the World Bank's structural adjustment facility, they also provided support to these nations based on a singular belief that the government must play an important role in economic development and continue to provide project-based aid. This helped awaken East Asia's economic development. Following the end of the Cold War, China set down a road of liberalization and reform, branding themselves as a socialist market economy. This would add another large bird to the flying geese formation, the effects of which will be discussed in the next subsection.

Changes Within the East Asian Flying Geese Paradigm

East Asia completed its flying geese model-based economic development. Since entering the twenty-first century, however, that structure has continued to evolve. It has been influenced by the way Japanese companies continually raised the ratio of overseas production under the consistently strengthening yen from the 1980s onward, as well as by the advent of a division of labor across countries, particularly in the electronics industry. I would like to touch on the following two points in addition to the four factors I touched upon in section "A Pattern for Economic Growth".

Cross-National Division of Labor Brought on by the Creation of Global Supply Chains

The electronics industry has grown rapidly since the 1990s. By building products out of interchangeable modules, the industry has ensured that

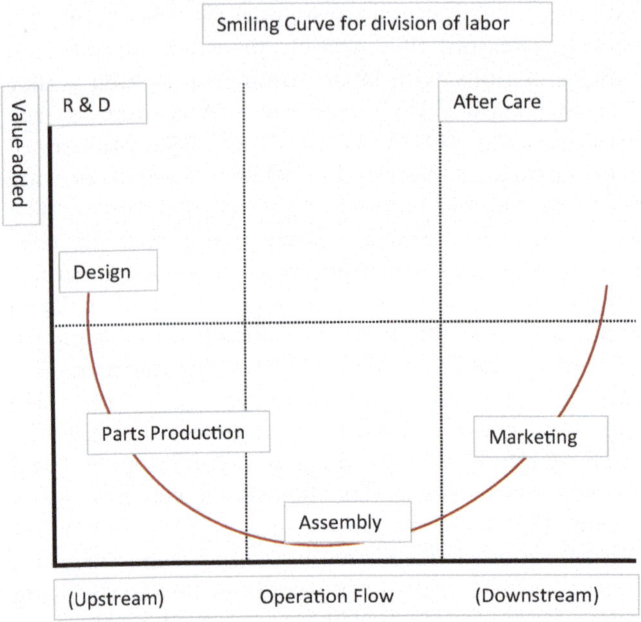

Graph 8.5 Smiling curve for division of labor

Table 8.1 Intra-ASEAN parts trade, comparison between 2000 and 2012 (times compared to 2000, italic values show more than tenfold)

		Importing country							
		Indonesia	*Philippines*	*Singapore*	*Malaysia*	*Thailand*	*Vietnam*	*Cambodia*	*Total*
Exporting country	Indonesia		5.0	1.6	0.9	5.5	*21.3*	3.7	1.8
	Philippines	6.5		1.9	0.5	1.5	*68.4*	*21.6*	1.4
	Singapore	8.4	2.0		1.2	1.2	4.6	2.2	1.7
	Malaysia	7.7	1.5	1.1		2.2	*14.5*	6.4	1.3
	Thailand	*19.1*	2.2	0.8	2.4		27.6	1.7	2.2
	Vietnam	*34.4*	*56.9*	*11.6*	*17.0*	1.8		*61.2*	6.7
	Cambodia	2.0	2.4	9.9	1.0	*315.8*	1.5		*22.0*
Total		*10.7*	2.1	1.2	1.3	1.9	*10.2*	3.4	1.6

Source: Trade White Paper 2014; Ministry of Economy, Trade and Industry, Japan

end products can be utilized no matter the country in which they were manufactured or from what company's parts they are assembled. Thus, the most efficient method of production has become a division of labor between the locations which can produce a given product the cheapest. This is what Stan Shi, chairman of Taiwanese PC giant ACER, is talking about with the smile curve seen in Graph 8.5. The smile curve shows the value added by each phase of PC production. Table 8.1 shows the extent to which parts trading are growing within the ASEAN region. Here, we see that parts trading throughout the region grew 1.6 times from 2000 to 2012, and in some cases, trade between certain countries expanded more than tenfold as the sells painted in yellow. One can surmise that this division of labor is taking place in East Asia due to differences in the degree of economic development within the region.

Creation of an Effective Logistics Network to Support Supply Chains

The creation of an effective logistics network within the region has been cited as one of the conditions which made this division of labor possible. Graph 8.6 shows the increase in global trading volumes. Although global trading volumes have averaged 5.4 per cent growth per year from 1980 to 2015 (recent figures being estimates), growth in developing or emerging nations in Asia has greatly surpassed this number at 9.2 per cent per year.

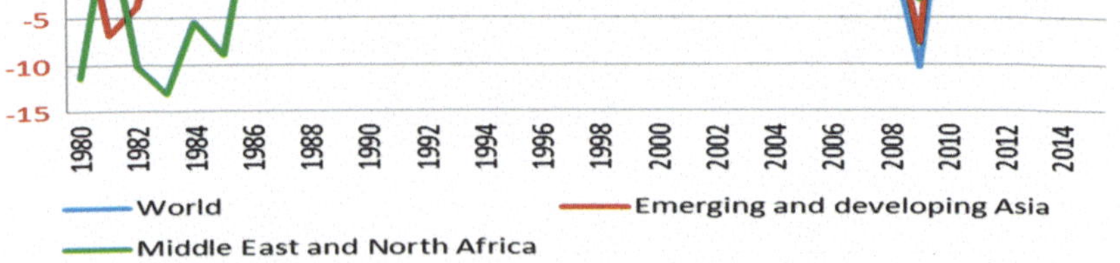

Graph 8.6 Volume of exports of goods and services (per cent change) (Source: World Economic Outlook Database, October 2014; IMF)

This sort of growth in trading volumes suggests that an effective logistics network has been put in place which supports this growth.

On the other hand, China has shown remarkable growth in that time, to become the largest trading partner for not just East Asia, but for countries like the USA and Japan. This massive goose now has the second largest GDP in the world and is continuing to edge toward the front of the formation. Unfortunately, "the world's factory" is currently facing its Lewisian turning point, with population growth placing a drag on the nation's growth and inflating wages. Foreign manufacturers in China are already trying to instigate a movement to displace their myriad production bases to other countries as part of its "China + 1" strategy. Regardless of how this situation may change, when viewed from above, it becomes clear that this framework—wherein intermediate products produced in the location most conducive to their production are then assembled in a different country—has become a fixture of every process in the East Asian region. One could say that each goose, so to speak, has strengthened its mutual ties to every other goose, transforming the formation into a tightly fixed shape.

Industry Condition in East Asia and Europe

Up to this point, we have looked at the theory and background behind East Asia's flying geese paradigm-led economic development, as well as the current situation in the region. Before moving on to talk about the GCC nations, I would like to look at conditions in each of East Asia's and Europe's industries, particularly in regard to industrial development and their production networks. The following points were brought up in a lecture by Fukunari Kimura in 2014.

Economic Development and Regional Integration

To put it another way, "economic development" and "economic integration" could just as easily said to be the product of "spatial and temporal shrinkage"—a process that often happens when least expected. Although experts have difficulty predicting this "shrinkage" since many of the conditions necessary for its occurrence differ, it is ultimately connected to the development of a production network. In Europe, the gap between countries' levels of technology and wages gave rise to a division of labor based on spatial economics—a division of labor between developed countries.

East Asia, on the other hand, has always suffered from industrial disparity. This is why the region continues to develop a production network which takes this disparity into account. What we see occurring now are production processes and tasks divided internationally, with functions simultaneously being displaced and aggregated in what could be called a second unbundling. The dramatic reduction in international telecommunication costs thanks to the spread of internet connectivity has played a large role in this. Still, despite the region's superior labor costs, the division of labor across multiple countries is only feasible providing that costs for consistent communications and logistics decrease.

Situation by Industry

Although international division of labor existed on an industry basis before the 1980s, it was only after that time that division occurred on the level of production processes and tasks (i.e., sections of individual production processes). Particularly of note are the divisions which occurred in the machinery industry. Its production network brings together East Asia, Europe, and North America without extending outside of these three regions for the most part. For comparison, look at the automobile industry. Since the size of auto parts made them unsuitable for long-distance transport and many required precision lapping, most were made locally and completed in-region. Or take the electronics industry, for instance. There is a constantly widening global network for electrical parts, with exports from East Asia to Eastern Europe and Mexico on the rise, thanks to a part's price being inversely proportionate to its size and its ability to be easily transported by plane. The textile industry, on the other hand, has generally divided its labor very loosely. In Uniqlo's case, information regarding top-selling items in the Ginza store is immediately shared with factories so items can be on store shelves only 2–3 weeks later, and the company can increase revenue by cutting down on storage periods. This speed—this temporal shrinkage—could be the twenty-first century's idea of division of labor.

Conditions for Successful Economic Development Model

We have looked at the flying geese paradigm, the factors which make it possible, recent changes to the flying geese model, conditions in Europe, and the situation according to each industry. Assuming the rise of global supply chains is a part of this flying geese paradigm, we can derive the following conditions as requisite for East Asia-type economic development. They are the existence of plentiful, cheap labor which can support labor-intensive manufacturing, the ability to divide labor between countries in a way which utilizes their varying levels of development, a market for manufactured goods existing domestically or in regions connected to the country through distribution channels, and the above conditions enabling the region to lead the market, that is, no real existing competitors such as a major manufacturer like current China.

Meeting the "Flying Geese" Conditions: The GCC Compared with East Asia

In the previous section, we looked at East Asia's flying geese model-based economic development and derived the conditions for its success. In this section, we will consider whether the GCC countries meet these conditions.

Workforce

East Asia's population outnumbers the GCC, with the combined population of the four ASEAN countries in 1980 having already exceeded 250 million (Indonesia: 145 million, Thailand: 47 million, the Philippines: 47 million, Malaysia: 14 million). Furthermore, it is a younger population with a pyramid-shaped population model, or in Korea's case as stated in the previous section, transitioning from a pyramid to a bell shape. The estimated combined population of the six GCC countries as of 2015 is shown in Graph 8.7. As you can see, their combined population totals approximately 50 million people—roughly the same number as Thailand and the Philippines in 1980. Filtering by gender shows approximately 30 million men to 20 million women, and it can be inferred that around 10 million of the men are foreign nationals who came to the GCC for work. Given that there are already more than 10 million foreign nationals working in these countries, the council will need to bring in more foreign workers if they aim to industrialize through labor-intensive industries. Considering that they require a framework for accepting these people, including necessary infrastructure, and that wages will rise in doing so, it is difficult to see this approach as economically reasonable.

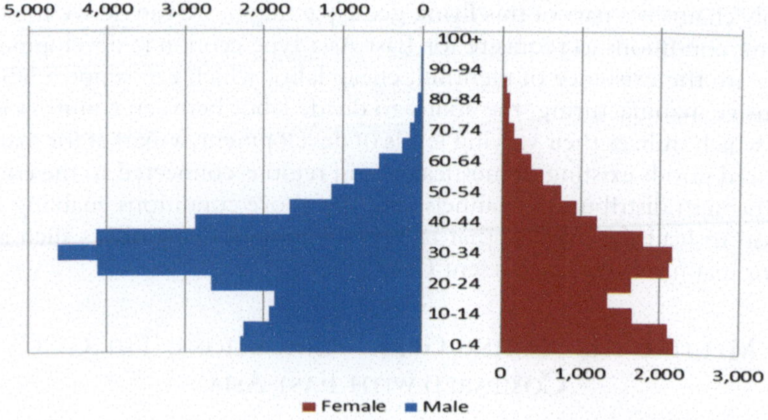

Graph 8.7 Demography of the total of GCC countries in 2015 (in thousands) (Source: U.N. World Population Prospects: The 2012 Revision)

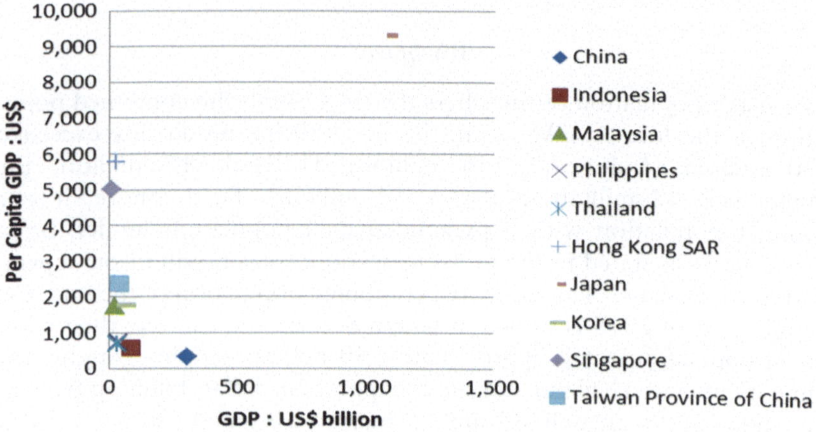

Graph 8.8 Asian countries' per capita GDP and GDP in 1980 (Source: World Economic Outlook Database, October 2014; IMF)

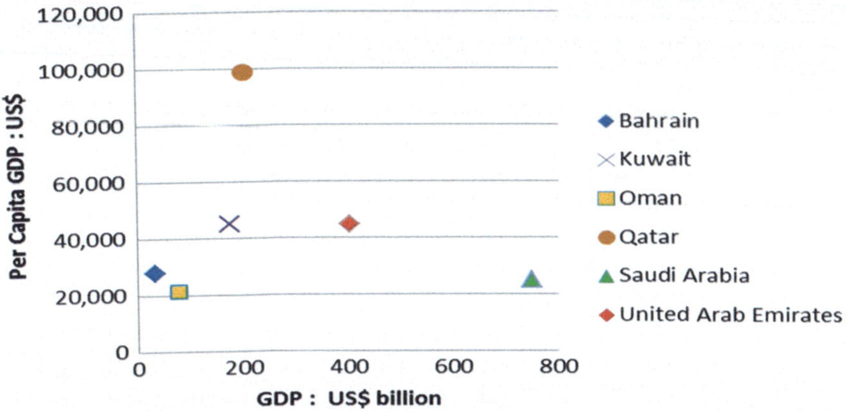

Graph 8.9 GCC countries' per capita GDP and GDP in 2013 (Source: World Economic Outlook Database, October 2014; IMF)

National Strategies for Economic Development

Each East Asian country took different steps toward economic development, but kept as close to the flying geese formation as possible. Graph 8.8 shows each country's per capita GDP vs. GDP in 1980. Here we see Japan's GDP as being far ahead. The other countries, however, have roughly the same size GDP with their per capita GDPs distributed vertically. Compare this with the GCC countries. Graph 8.9 shows the GCC's GDP up to 2015. Each country's per capita GDP is over US$20,000—well in the range of developed countries. The figures would seem to indicate that they are at a level nearing the end of their industrialization. That is, they have reached the stage where they develop high value-added industries rather than relying on competitive wages, to transition to a non-industrial country.

Regional Integration and Free-Trade Agreements

East Asia was able to pull off flying geese-based economic development as a single region, and since then, efforts to unify the region's economies have accelerated, thanks to FTA and economic partnership agreements.

Around the world, international agreements have divided regional economies into roughly the following three zones.

- North America: Canada, the USA, and Mexico joined under the North American Free Trade Agreement (NAFTA).
- EU: Member nations of the European Union abandoned preferential treatment regarding tariffs, import/export volume restrictions, and products between member countries during the EU's previous incarnation, the European Economic Community. This has made Europe a free-trade zone.
- ASEAN + 1: In East Asia, the ASEAN countries have all formed separate free trade agreements with Japan, China, Korea, India, Australia, and New Zealand, making ASEAN something like the hub of a free-trade zone. The first round of negotiations for the Regional Comprehensive Economic Partnership, a holistic economic partnership for East Asia, began in September 2013.

Despite introducing The GCC Customs Union and establishing a region-wide tax (5 per cent) in 2003, the GCC member nations have not made much progress on unifying the region, including the shared currency they named as a goal in 2010.

The ASEAN countries are also gradually concluding free trade agreements with other economic zones. Take, for instance, Korea—a country called a "developed FTA country"—which has already put FTAs into effect with the USA and the EU. Even Japan is currently in negotiations over the Trans Pacific Partnership (TPP) and an economic partnership agreement with the EU, and the USA and Europe have started talks regarding a Transatlantic Trade and Investment Partnership (TTIP).

On the other hand, the GCC has only signed FTAs in their capacity as the GCC with two countries and one region: Singapore, New Zealand, and the European Free Trade Association, respectively. Of these, the only one currently in effect is the agreement concluded with Singapore in September 2013. Japan entered negotiations regarding an FTA with the GCC in 2006, but talks have ceased as of the fourth round of negotiations (the co-chairman level) in 2009. While trade and investment between the GCC countries and the rest of the Gulf States is forecasted to increase, the GCC are still falling behind in terms of achieving regional economic development through unified policy and bolstering their economy through free trade agreements with other regions. Given this situation, even if the industrialization of the GCC were to continue, we cannot expect sufficient development to occur based on the lack of FTA and other policies to support this growth and the delay of logistic infrastructure both inside and outside the region. In other words, the region remains outside of global supply chains.

Can the GCC Rise to Become a Market Leader?

Assuming that the GCC continues its industrialization, the major markets where the council's products will likely find support are Europe, India, and Africa. It will not be easy for the GCC to enter new markets considering the existence of China—a country which already exports cheap products en masse.

Diversifying the Industrial Sector in the GCC

After examining the "flying geese" conditions, we will see the applicability of flying geese model to the GCC, its advantages and disadvantages and then seek for the idea of diversification suitable to the GCC.

Applying the Flying Geese Model to the GCC

The East Asian countries had difficulty in promoting industry through the export of natural resources, with some exceptions. Although the GCC have been able to increase per capita GDP to over US$20,000, they do not exhibit the right conditions for the kind of gradual advancement of industry we see under the flying geese model. If we assume a global flying geese model, we can imagine that parts of Western Europe such as Germany will rise to lead the formation. However, this formation could never include the GCC since Europe already has a production base in Central Eastern Europe, has secured a consumer market within the region itself, and faces geographic restrictions including logistics networks and economic zones. Furthermore, as differences in the degree to which labor is divided between countries become more pronounced (such as the advent of the Chinese electronics industry or clustering of the automobile industry in Thailand), promoting industry without targeting specific sectors or markets has less of an effect. As stated in the previous section, the economy of the GCC countries is supported by over 10 million foreign workers, making it impossible for the GCC to try to transition to capital-intensive industry once development of their labor-intensive industry completes. So these facts and the four points raised in the previous chapter make it clear that East Asia's economic success is not applicable to the GCC.

GCC Advantages and Particular Characteristics

Taking into account the argument in the sections above, the followings are the advantages and disadvantages of GCC countries.

GCC's Advantages Over Other Countries

There are some advantages which the GCC holds over other countries. They are the presence of petroleum and natural gas resources, the ease with which the country can promote petroleum and gas-related industries, the accumulated capital thanks to oil revenue, geographic proximity to Europe, South Asia, and Africa, and its position as a gateway to each, the countries in the vicinity share a common language (Arabic) and religious, cultural background (Islam), and hot sunny climate.

GCC's Disadvantages

There are some points where they could be seen as disadvantageous when compared to other countries such as those in Asia. They are that they have small workforce with a high reliance on foreign laborers which means that the economy is unsuited to labor-intensive industries and that the six GCC countries have a small population which makes it less attractive as a consumer market compared to Asia, North America, and Europe. To offset these disadvantages, the GCC should bring under their influence countries who share a cultural affinity with the GCC—such as the surrounding nations and North Africa—in order to expand the market.

What Kind of Diversification for the GCC

Labor-intensive industry poses little benefit for the GCC. They have already amassed sufficient capital from petroleum and natural gas-based revenue and, therefore, should aim to promote industry which makes full use of these natural resources as well as the GCC's geographical and cultural characteristics, while at the same time promoting capital-intensive and knowledge-intensive industries. In order to promote industry in this way, oil revenue should not be used to subsidize water, public transportation, public service, and gasoline costs; rather, the country should levy a fee for these public services, and capital which had been used as subsidy should be used to bolster investment in fields which straddle the private and public sectors and which will generate long-term profit, such as industrial development, education, and medicine. In recent years, we have seen examples of this, including the abandonment of gasoline subsidies under the Joko administration in Indonesia, changes to rice purchasing policies in Thailand, and the elimination of food subsidies in Indonesia. Placing the cost of public services on their beneficiaries can be an effective way to prevent countries from squandering their precious natural resources.

Government subsidy policies keep the price of public services high and prevent the growth of international competitiveness, ultimately causing long-term financial problems. While providing subsidies to protect the minimum standard of living may be an option for heavily impoverished countries, there is no logical reason for a country with revenue as high as the GCC countries to subsidize services. As a type of interest, subsidiary programs can breed corruption, and in the 2014 version of the "Corruption Perceptions Index" (CPI) published by international NGO Transparency International (TI), the six GCC countries had made it into the Middle East and Northern Africa top 8. Even looking at it from a global perspective, United Arab Emirates (#25) and Kuwait (#67) rank comparatively high on the index. It could be said that now is the perfect time for the GCC to turn away from their subsidiary policies.

Models for Utilization of Capital in the GCC: Domestic Investment

Turning our focus to the GCC's current industries, we see in Table 8.2 that petroleum and natural gas make up roughly 20 per cent of Saudi Arabia and Bahrain's GDP and 30–40 per cent of the other countries. We see a big difference when compared to Australia, a similar natural resource-exporting country, where these resources make up approximately 10 per cent of the GDP. For the sake of economic growth unbound by the price of crude oil or resource scarcity, the GCC must foster the growth of other industries in the future, in order to reduce the GCC's dependence on petroleum and natural gas. Furthermore, considering that they have already amassed a ton of capital through oil and gas-based revenue, they

Table 8.2 Sectorial breakdown of GDP in GCC countries, Australia, and Norway

		UAE	*Qatar*	*Kuwait*
Sectoral breakdown	Oil and natural gas: 18.3% Government service: 15.0% Finance, insurance, and real estate: 14.4% Manufacturing (incl. oil refinering): 13.5% Commerce: 12.7% Transport and telecommunications: 9.8%	Oil and natural gas: 32.7% Real estate: 12.3% Wholesales and retailing: 11.6% Transport, warehousing, and telecommunications: 9.6% Construction: 9.2% Manufacturing: 8.9% Finance: 6.9%	Oil and natural gas: 40.7% Finance, insurance, and real estate: 12.0% Construction: 11.9%	Oil and natural gas: 38.2% Regional/social service: 21.7% Transport, warehousing, and telecommunications: 13.2% Finance and insurance: 10.1% Manufacturing: 6.5% (2011)
GDP US$billion	748	372 (2012)	202	176

	Oman	*Bahrain*	*Australia*	*Norway*
Sectoral breakdown	Oil and natural gas: 43.4% Financial intermediacy: 15.1% Manufacturing: 10.2% Governmental service: 8.0% Transport and telecommunications: 5.6% Construction: 5.6% Real estate: 4.0% (2012)	Oil and natural gas: 21.7% Financial service: 16.7% Manufacturing: 14.5% Government service: 12.8% Transport and telecommunications: 6.9% Construction: 6.6%	Mining: 10.7% Wholesales and retailing: 9.2% Finance and insurance: 8.6% Construction: 8.0% Manufacturing: 7.1% Chemical/technical service: 6.9% Medical and social service: 6.8% Government service: 5.5% Transport, mailing, and telecommunication: 5.1%	Oil and natural gas (incl. related service): 21.5% Medical and social service: 8.9% Manufacturing: 6.6% Wholesales and retailing: 6.3% Construction: 5.6%
GDP US$billion	77	33	1,506	511

Note: All the figures are as of 2013 unless otherwise expressed individually

Source: Japan Center for International Finance, Statistics Norway

should aim to expand capital-intensive industries or knowledge-intensive industries, rather than labor-intensive. (See 5.2.)

This section will first address the situation in Singapore, where the country achieved growth despite being a non-resource country, followed by Norway, a country which successfully utilized its oil revenue as capital.

The Singaporean Model

The Singaporean model has two specific characteristics. One is the policies of its government administration from the day of its independence. The other is Temasek Holdings, an investment company wholly owned by the Singapore Ministry of Finance.

Characteristics of Government Administration

Singapore gained independence in 1965 after being expelled from Malaysia. Government administration in the subsequent years created a prosperous city state which exhibits the characteristics described in the next few paragraphs. Initially, the government adopted policies to develop the country as a center for intermediary trade and to attract domestic direct investment. They implemented a policy of low wages, and when the labor force started to disappear, policy moved toward a more sophisticated industrial structure, aiming to raise minimum wage and leave their labor-intensive industry behind. Furthermore, they were able to supply the funds necessary for investment by utilizing retirement pension and their central provident fund to create development and investment capital. In terms of foreign policy, Singapore has also struggled to create an understanding between its neighboring countries—in particular, Malaysia and Indonesia. This has made the expansion of stable relationships with the ASEAN countries and the USA a pillar of Singapore's regional and security strategies. Additionally, the country has focused heavily on developing human resources through a system, whereby bright and talented students receive government scholarships to attend well-known universities overseas and, after they return, are placed in government positions. At the same time, they also work to recruit talented employees regardless of nationality. In the next subsection, we look at Temasek Holdings, a Singaporean company where one-third of the employees are non-Singaporean.

Investment Company Temasek Holdings

Temasek Holdings is an investment company wholly owned by the Singapore Ministry of Finance (i.e., a sovereign wealth fund, "SWF"). In addition to owning stock in Singapore Airlines Limited, the Development Bank of Singapore (DBS), and domestic infrastructure companies, Temasek also invests in foreign firms. As a holdings company, Temasek Holdings exists outside of the government. However, they do possess and manage shares in government-linked companies. This sort of arrangement is not seen in other countries. According to the Temasek Review 2014, at the end of March 2014, Temasek had S$223 billion in held assets (US$133 billion), and the company's efficient investment over the last 10 years has raised profit on investment by an average of 9 per cent per year. Of their investment, 31 per cent is directed at Singapore, and when combined with their investment in other Asian countries, this number grows to 72 per cent. Breaking down this Asian investment by sector yields 30 per cent finance; 23 per cent telecommunications, media, and technology; 20 per cent transport and industry; and 14 per cent life science and consumer goods. Singapore is a city-state of 5.4 million people (as of 2013), and thus it has been comparatively easier for the country to concentrate its human and economic capital. While it can be said that this method of economic development was once viable, it may no longer be. However, the country has continued to implement these initiatives. Also of note is that Singapore's FTA coverage on trade has reached an incredibly high 76.9 per cent as of the end of 2013, and they remain the only country to have concluded an FTA with the GCC.

The Norwegian Model

Another possible model for the GCC is Norway. An oil-producing country like the GCC, Norway's petroleum and national gas make up 21.9 per cent of their GDP, while exports total 53.7 per cent, according to Jetro. The country's Government Pension Fund (GPF) is the second largest usage of SWF assets after the Abu Dhabi Investment Authority and has made it possible for Norway to fund an advanced welfare state using oil revenue.

Norway's has split its investment between two funds: The National Insurance Scheme Fund for domestic investment and the Government Pension Fund Global for foreign investment. The domestic fund has existed since 1967 and has become the top shareholder in a large number of Norwegian companies. The foreign fund, on the other hand, was originally established as the "Petroleum Fund" in 1990. Following deliberation and approval by the Norwegian parliament in 1998, operation of the fund has been outsourced to Norges Bank's investment division, Norges Bank Investment Management (NBIM). All of the fund's assets are managed overseas. At the end of 2014, their assets totaled 6.431 trillion krone (approx. US$804 billion), their earnings ratio for 2014 alone reached 7.58 per cent, and their annual earnings ratio from 1998 to 2014 equaled 5.81 per cent, according to the 2014 Government Pension Fund Global Annual Report. The number of countries in which the fund has invested climbed to 75, with the breakdown largely being 39.3 per cent Europe, 38.9 per cent North America, and 15.5 per cent Asia; and by types of investment: 61.3 per cent stocks, 36.5 per cent securities, 2.2 per cent real estate. For 2014, profit from real estate investment rose to 10.4 per cent, recording the highest profits of these three investment categories. The fund's stock investments for 2014 covered 9134 companies in 61 countries or 1.3 per cent of all listed stocks globally. Of that, 96 per cent carry less than 5 per cent voting power, meaning that the fund has spread its investment in a bid for profits rather than management of these companies. Securities investment, meanwhile, covers 4256 companies in 31 countries.

Models for Utilization of Capital in the GCC—Investment in New Industries

Let us take a look at how SWF is managed in each GCC country. As far as we can tell from publicly available materials, it is mostly used for foreign investment on a commercial basis and it generates profits higher than the market average. Although we could say that it is managed similar to Norway's Government Pension Fund Global, it would probably be better used for investment in private domestic companies and ventures, in order to promote domestic industry. In that case, what can the government do to help promote the growth of new industries?

Importance of Innovation

In a chapter of *Foreign Affairs* titled "The Innovative State," Mariana Mazzucato (2015) argues that it should not be the government's role to correct market failures or create a level playing field. The market often proves itself to be blind, favoring the beaten path over innovation. The economy needs to be brought to face the new "technological paradigm." However, the market will not do this voluntarily. It must be guided through decisions by the state. The internet started as a research project for the US Department of Defense, and the Apollo missions were only successful, thanks to the initiative of the state. For example, the state could own stock in their own borrowers, similar to venture capital funds. Finland's SITRA and Israel's YOZMA are good examples of this. There are also cases in which investment is made in alignment with government policies, such as with Germany's *energiewende* ("energy transition"). Governments should learn from venture capital funds how to diversify their portfolio and provide capital to numerous projects and technologies. It is interesting to note that in this same issue, Mezue, Bryan C., Christiansen, Clayton M., van Bever, Derek (2015) touch upon the necessity of a platform to accelerate the movement of capital between investors and market innovators. In the next subsection, we will look at SITRA and YOZMA which Mariana Mazzucato mentioned.

Finland's SITRA

SITRA (the Finnish Innovation Fund. Finnish: *Suomen itsenäisyyden juhlarohasto*) was established in 1967 as part of the Bank of Finland. It is now an independent public agency under the direction of the Finnish parliament, operating on the funds returns. SITRA's activities, mentioned in the Annual Report and Financial Statement 2013, The Supervisory Board's statement. SITRA, are outlined below:

> Sitra's special role, as an organization funding its operations from the yield on its endowment capital and working directly under Parliament, gives it an excellent opportunity to drive social change that will shake the status quo and to take risks so that the private and public sectors do not have to. Sitra's task is to promote stable and balanced development in Finland, to enable the quantitative and qualitative growth of Finland's economy and to enhance the country's international competitiveness and co-operation. According to Sitra's vision, Finland will succeed as a pioneer in sustainable well-being. A sustainable well-being model forms the core of this vision, combining ecological, social and economic sustainability. Sitra's operations have been divided into content-based themes. As of 1 January 2014, there are three themes: Resource-wise and carbon-neutral society, Empowering society and Operating models for sustainable well-being and work. The practical implementation of Sitra's specialist work falls under these three themes and com-

prises key areas realised in the form of projects as well as societal training, research and investment activities. Sitra's activities extend to all levels of society: it can act as an expert advisor in preparing legislative proposals in one key area, for example, while carrying out small and agile practical trials in another.

Sitra's investments are carried out in accordance with the policy above. Table 8.3 shows their balance at the end of 2013, and aside from so-called 'endowment capital investments,' they also invest in venture companies and venture funds in what are called 'venture capital investments' in order to promote industry. The ratio of their total investments consisting of venture capital investments has grown to around 9 per cent. For example, one of the companies in which they have invested is Aw-Energy Oy, a venture which is developing equipment to harness tidal energy and which meets Sitra's three focus areas stated above.

In this way, SITRA's investment policy of utilizing national wealth to increase return and invest in business ventures could serve as a model for how the state can promote industry.

Israel's YOZMA Group

Israel has the highest ratio of GDP to venture capital of any member of the OECD. This situation came from the Israeli government's establishment of the YOZMA Group fund and their subsequent investment. Below in an

Table 8.3 SITRA's investment in book value (in EUR thousands)

Endowment capital investments	
Bonds	2,388
Fund investments	580,894
Private equity fund investment	7,979
Shares	7,031
Real estate investment	1,611
Short-term investment	295
S.TTL	600,198
Venture capital investments	
Business development and funding	24,610
Fund investment	39,736
Other investment	258
S.TTL	64,604

Source: Annual Report and Financial Statement 2013; SITRA 2013

excerpt from the OECD's Venture Capital Policy Review by Günseli (2003) which provides a detailed look at the events which led to these conditions.

> The Israeli government supplied US$ 100 million in 1993 to start YOZMA, a venture capital fund investing in high-technology start-ups. Over a period of 3 years, the Group established ten hybrid funds, each capitalized with around US$ 20 million. In parallel, YOZMA started making direct investments in start-up companies. This marked the beginning of a professionally managed venture capital market in Israel. YOZMA is widely given credit for being the catalyst that created Israel's flourishing venture capital industry.
>
> With the backing of prominent American, European, and Israeli investors, YOZMA launched its second fund in 1995. The YOZMA Group invests in all stages of company development with a primary focus on the earliest stages, targeting high-growth companies in ICT and life science/biotechnology sectors. Initial individual investments typically ranged between US$ 1 million and US$ 6 million and additional capital were reserved for follow-on investments. Since inception the Group has managed more than US$ 170 million and has made direct investments in more than 40 portfolio companies, a significant number of which went public on major stock exchanges in the USA and Europe. In addition, the YOZMA Group was instrumental in positioning its portfolio companies for acquisition or an investment by leading multinational corporations.
>
> The YOZMA Group also developed close working relationships with several of the leading academic institutions and technology incubators in Israel. Some of the most promising companies in the YOZMA portfolio have come directly from these institutions.
>
> In 1998, the government decided that private sector venture capital was sufficiently robust for it to sell its YOZMA participation. It successfully auctioned off its direct co-investments in 14 companies and sold its interest in nine YOZMA funds to its co-investment partners. These funds have now been privatized, and the direct contribution of YOZMA-related venture capital funds has been greatly reduced. The government still has a minor interest in two YOZMA-related funds.

Gil Avnimelech (2009) explains that the reason the YOZMA program was successful in promoting Israel's IT industry in particular was not only its timing but its design and the success of its implementation. YOZMA presents a model of how, under a clear implementation policy, the government can invest national wealth to successfully accrete knowledge-intensive industries and sell off a significant portion of the fund in order to exit participation in the fund.

Means of Industrial Development and Diversification: The Way Forward

As the final section of this chapter, we will see the methods of industrial development and diversification backed by the basic policy, pitfalls to avoid, and the possibility of regional expansion.

Promotion of Industries That Could Utilize Comparative Advantages

Taking into account the points made in the previous sections, the following are possible directions which the GCC could take toward industrial development.

Basic Industrial Development Policy

The recommendable basic industrial development policies are the following three points.

The first is the promotion of resources and their associated industries. When we consider the GCC nations' promotion of industry, the first thing which becomes clear is that their abundant petroleum and natural gas obviously form the pillars of their current industrial structure. However, as we saw in Table 8.2, these resources total something in the 20–30 per cent range of the GCC's GDP—a considerable large figure when compared to the 10 per cent of Australia, a similar resource-exporting country. Also, note Australia's automotive market. The 2000s saw automobile production reach the 400,000 level each year despite the country being a resource country with a small population. However, the country is now expected to lose all automobile production by 2017 after Toyota decided to pull out of Australia last year. Toyota's decision stems from the fact that the country can no longer switch to a car-exporting country, given the strong Australian dollar, rise in wages, and small market size stemming from its small population. Meanwhile, the ratio of the GDP attributable to the mining industry is decreasing as industries derived from Australia's resource-based industries advance, including finance, insurance, and logistics.

Therefore, the GCC must aim not only for mere industrialization and division of labor but also focus on the promotion of its superior oil and gas industries as well as industries to be derived from that (petrochemicals and their related industries). Furthermore, they must divide production in order to manufacture goods of a quality suitable for the high-end markets of Europe, while at the same time, manufacture price-competitive products based on pared-down functions which fit the Indian and African markets. It will also be necessary for the GCC to shore up efforts on oil-linked industries including development, finance, insurance, and human resource development.

The second is utilizing geography, culture, and the natural environment. I would like to look at how the GCC could promote industry using its geographical advantages and close cultural affinity with other nations. The GCC's location on a map places it at the midway point for air traffic traveling from East Asian and Oceania (India, Malaysia, Singapore, and Indonesia) to Europe and Africa. This is one of the geographical conditions necessary for it to become an economic hub. In other words, it belies the potential to not only bring in tourism but connecting these countries in a logistics network. An example of this can be seen in Okinawa, which continues to build its position as a hub, utilizing its geographical characteristics as the midway point between Japan and Southeast Asia. In addition, the GCC should leverage the advantages of its cultural affinity to other Islamic countries in the Middle East and North Africa. It should be easier to obtain understanding from these countries compared to those in Europe, China, or Asia. I would also like the GCC to consider the promotion of industries which make use of the GCC nations' natural environment, such as their heavy sun exposure. For example, solar power/solar thermal energy-powered desalination or horticultural business using desalinated water. Assuming the area becomes a logistics hub as I mentioned, these industries could be useful in capturing markets in places like Europe.

The third is the use of capital, that is, the use of their abundant oil revenue. Namely, the key to diversifying the region's industry and developing their economy may lie in how the GCC states use this SWF to promote industry.

Considering Concrete Methods for Diversifying the GCC's Industry Based on This Basic Policy

Based on the basic policy described in the previous subsection, the GCC should promote industry using the four methods below.

The first is general promotion of industry. In many cases, SWF investment is limited to foreign entities. As stated in the section "Norway", however, Norway has divided their SWF into a foreign-targeted fund and a domestic-targeted fund. Kuwait Investment Authority's investment is similarly made up of the General Reserve Fund (GRF) and the Kuwait Future Generations Fund (FGF). The former of these includes contributions to the World Bank and IMF in addition to investment in state-run oil companies. The latter invests in foreign entities. There are some cases, however, such as the Abu Dhabi Investment Authority which do not invest domestically (in this case, no investment in the UAE). While it is not necessarily a mistake for the GCC to invest in foreign businesses in order to make a high return on the foreign capital they receives through oil revenue, it is important for the GCC to use their abundant capital to promote domestic industry.

The second is strengthening and promoting oil and gas-related industries through M&A. The core of the GCC countries' economy consists of their oil and gas-related industries, and many companies within these industries are trusted worldwide. Rather than sticking to simply producing and exporting oil and natural gas, the easier and more reliable path to diversifying the GCC's business lies in expanding these businesses into their surrounding fields: producing necessary equipment in-house, accumulating technology and engineering knowhow, financing and insurance for capital procurement, and so on. However, they should NOT seek the same kind of technological transference which occurred during East Asia's flying geese model-based growth. They should instead take a shortcut toward diversification by buying up foreign companies already operating in their countries and utilize M&A to acquire technology and expertise.

The third is the promotion of knowledge-intensive industry. Since it would not be suitable to develop labor-intensive industry given the current state of the GCC, they should instead promote knowledge-intensive industry using their SWF. Specifically, this means financial services, education, R&D, ICT, and medical services, to name a few. The spread of Islamic finance presents one possible financial service industry. Balances in Islamic finance are in an upward trend and have been estimated at US$1.46 trillion as of the end of 2012, according to UK Islamic Finance Secretariat. Furthermore, it is assumed that this figure surpassed US$2 trillion by the end of 2014. Islamic finance balances by each country at the end of 2011 showed, in weighted order, 36 per cent to Iran, 17 per cent to Malaysia, 14 per cent to Saudi Arabia, 7 per cent to the UAE, 6 per cent to Kuwait, 5 per cent to Bahrain, and 4 per cent to Qatar. Balances in sukuk, the Islamic financial security, totaled US$296 billion as of July 2014, and of the US$59 billion in sukuk issued during the first half of 2013, Malaysia accounts for 63 per cent, followed by Saudi Arabia at 16 per cent, the UAE at 9 per cent, and Indonesia at 5 per cent. Still, most of the sukuk have been issued for domestic finance, in Malaysian ringgit, with the UAE leading in dollar-denominated sukuk for the year prior to mid-2014 at US$25 million, followed by Saudi Arabia at US$16 million, and Qatar at US$8 million.

Although this makes it clear that Malaysia and Iran have the largest amount of money bound up in Islamic finance, the nature of domestic markets will play a larger role in the future. On the other hand, the GCC's amount of dollar-denominated sukuk remains considerably large from a global perspective, and I believe that it would prove effective for the GCC to aim to differentiate itself from Malaysia and develop their financial market to be the center of international Islamic finance. To achieve this, the GCC will need to adopt a strategy to capture financing needs in the Islamic countries of North Africa and South Asia, while also considering ways to cooperate and mutually coexist with European markets (especially London) from a long-term perspective. Additionally, there is the Islamic Development Bank, established in 1975 as an international financial agency for the Islamic world. While mostly it provides infrastructure loans as of now, it may come to compete with China's Asian Infrastructure Investment Bank (AIIB) in the future. As a financial agency for regional development, the Islamic Development Bank will need to consider to whom and under what policies it should provide loans in order to differentiate itself from competitors.

Other knowledge-intensive industries the GCC should focus on are education and R&D. Time Higher Education's World University Rankings for 2014–2015 shows that the universities in the GCC and other Arabian countries unfortunately do not even make it into the top 200. Additionally, the Top 1000 Universities 2014 ranking announced by Saudi Arabia's Center for World University Rankings (CWUR) has only one GCC school able to break into the top 500 (King Saud University (#420)), and in the top 1000, only four schools in Saudi Arabia, four schools in Egypt, one school in Lebanon, and one school in the UAE. While university rankings are naturally not the only way to evaluate a school, having university and research centers which boast superior academics and research can enable a country to gather the talent from around the world. Thus, it would behoove the GCC to use part of their SWF on education and research. This will bring not only economic benefits but also positively impact learning and social aspects of the country in immeasurable ways. Tomsk, Russia, gives an example of a place which has become a hub of education and research in spite of the harsh natural environment.

The forth is the creation of hard and soft infrastructure which will make the above possible. Hard and soft infrastructure, built through government initiatives, will be vital to maximizing the methods above. Zennstrom, Niklas (2015), the founder of Skype, had this to say in his chapter in *Foreign Affairs*:

> Governments can facilitate this (start-ups). In the United Kingdom, for example, the government has been very focused on making the country a terrific tech hub. I wouldn't say that the government has created it, but they've been helpful.
>
> For example, one of big challenges when you start a company is hiring the best people, with the right talent. And the U.K. government had made it easier to hire people from other countries.[…]And the can make it easier to do cross-border business.

In addition, Zennstrom talks about the importance of creating a hospitable environment for private investors—for example, lower taxes on capital gain for start-up investment. For new industries which particularly require innovation, governments must put systems and laws for venture capital into place before diversifying business. We can think of the GCC as a single region, with a common language in Arabic and incredibly similar cultural backgrounds and ways of thinking. The GCC countries now need initiatives which maximize this soft power. Especially in terms of policy, adopting a shared certification system, for example, would help foreign businesses better conceive of the GCC as a single market. If that is too difficult, the GCC should create a shared format for applications and procedures at the very least. This will make the region look dramatically more convenient to foreign investors and companies.

Avoiding Cutthroat Competition

Up to this point, this section has covered the GCC's distinct advantages and the policies which they should consider in order to diversify their industry. The GCC countries have managed to achieve petroleum and natural gas revenue-based economic development similar to other countries, and lack the same staggered economic development seen between the Asian countries. This will lead each of the countries to introduce similar plans for industrial development and foster competition between them. The quintessential example can be found in each country's airlines. Although the GCC currently has three world-class airlines (Qatar Air, Emirates, Etihad Airways), flights between Asia and Europe are all at maximum capacity, leaving the airlines engaged in fierce price competition. A direct flight from Tokyo to London will cost you around JPY.200,000 (approx. US$1700), but a connective flight through the GCC can cost you JPY.100,000 (approx. US$850) or less. Rather than let this kind of cutthroat competition continue, the GCC nations should restructure their airlines into a joint venture with a portion of their flights designated as low-cost carriers (LCC) in order to acquire low-end markets. Scandinavian Air presents a good example of airline created through joint investment by several countries in a region. While Gulf Air was once somewhat similar to this, this changed after the other countries pulled out of the airline. Competition also continues between Dubai, Riyadh, and Kuwait in terms of the financial market. If these three markets were to establish a joint holdings company and standardize listings, issuance of securities, transactions standards and certifications, and so on, they could likely develop the finance sector into the dominant market within the region. They could also consider tie-ups with European and Western markets as a subsequent step.

Inspiring Neighbors

If the GCC is able to diversify its industry through this sort of industrial development proposed above, it could become the next economic zone after East Asia, North America, and Europe, inspiring surrounding countries such as Iran and Pakistan to join together as the GCC grows closer to the global economy. The GCC could also further expand its sphere of influence by making full use of the commonalities it shares with other countries in the Middle East and Africa, such as common cultural backgrounds and religion. The expansion of a GCC economic zone or sphere of influence does not mean putting the GCC in a one-sided position of dominance. Instead, it presupposes a relationship of mutual economic reliance, as well as the exchange of goods and human resources between these entities. A side effect of this should be a lessening of tensions in the region and overtures of peace, which in turn will greatly contribute to making the region one of safety and stability for its people.

References

Akamatsu, K. (1974). *Kinhaika to Kokusai-Keizai* (p. 74). Tokyo: Toyo Keizai Shimpo-sha.

An edited Article. (2015, January/February). The Nordic Model. A conversation with Niklas Zennstrom. *Foreign Affairs*, p. 44.

Annual Report and Financial Statement. (2013). The Supervisory Board's statement. SITRA, p. 6.

Avnimelech, G. (2009). *VC Policy: Yozma Program 15-Years Perspective*. Chapel Hill, NC: University of North Carolina at Chapel Hill.

Baygan, G. (2003). *Box 1. Government Venture Capital Fund in Israel; Venture Capital Policy Review: Israel*. STI Working Paper 2003/3, Industry Issue, OECD, p. 15.

Government Pension Fund Global Annual Report. (2014). Norges Bank Investment Management.

Islamic Finance. (2013, October). UK Islamic Finance Secretariat.

Kojima, K. (2000a). *Ganko-gata keizai hattenron, Akamatsu original: Sekai Keizai Hyoron Mar. 2000*. Tokyo: Sekai Keizai Hyoronsha.

Kojima, K. (2000b). *Ganko-gata keizai hattenron, Saikentou: Surugadai Keizai Ronbunsyu Dai 9-kan Dai 2-go*. Tokyo: Surugadai Syuppansha.

Mazzucato, M. (2015, January/February). "The Innovative State" Governments Should Make Markets, Not Just Fix Them. *Foreign Affairs*, p. 61.

Mezue, B. C., Christensen, C. M., & van Bever, D. (2015, January/February). The Power of Market Creation. *Foreign Affairs*, p. 69.

Ministry of Foreign Affairs Japan Homepage.

ODA White Paper. (2006). Ministry of Foreign Affairs Japan.

Okita, Saburo. (1985). *Special Presentation: Prospect of the Pacific Economies*. Korea Development Institute, Pacific Economic Cooperation: Issues and Opportunities, Report of the Fourth Pacific Economic Cooperation Conference, Seoul, April 29–May 1, 1985.

Temasek Review. (2014). Retrieved from http://www.temasek.com.sg/documents/download/downloads/20140707170404/Temasek-Review-2014-En.pdf

Teraoka, H. (2001). *Chapter 2, Finland; Keizai no hatten, suitai, saisei nikansuru kenkyukai Hokokusyo*. Tokyo: Zaimu Sogo Seisaku Kenkyujo.

Trade White Paper. (2014). Ministry of Economy, Trade and Industry, Japan.

Transparency International. (2014). Corruption Perceptions Index 2014: Results. Retrieved from http://www.transparency.org/cpi2014/results

CHAPTER 9

Economic Diversification in the GCC and the Korean Experience

Minju Lee

Introduction

The GCC economies' journey toward diversification and sustainability has resulted in considerable achievements. For example, the major airlines in the region have been recognized for their high-quality services, and some of the cities are becoming a regional hub for business and tourism. However, the GCC countries' development strategies are now put into question of effectiveness with regard to generating practical progress in the future. In other words, the GCC growth model has reached its limitation as an effective mechanism for bringing diversification and sustainability to the region. Thus, it is critical for the GCC states to prepare a new set of plans to resolve the current hold-up and to complete the journey. One way to enrich the preparation process is to look into the footsteps of others who have overcome comparable challenges.

In that sense, the Korean experience can be a good source of inspiration for the GCC countries. In a half century, Korea has made a remarkable economic development through active policymaking and strong commitment to implementation. Since the 1960s, Korea has set and implemented

M. Lee (✉)
Gulf Studies Program, Qatar University, Chungju, South Korea

A. Mishrif, Y. Al Balushi (eds.), *Economic Diversification in the Gulf Region, Volume II*, The Political Economy of the Middle East,
DOI 10.1007/978-981-10-5786-1_9

a number of economic development plans, with evolving objectives and strategies, which was necessary to adapt process for improvement and further progress. This eventually resulted in a fast and solid economic prosperity from the ashes of the Korean War. Korea tried to upgrade its growth strategy beyond the East Asian development model from the early 2000s, which was led by the former President Kim Dae-Jung. According to Chung (2012), the DJ government constructed its political philosophy based on Alvin Toffler's idea of the 'Third Wave' and Anthony Giddens' concept of the 'Third Way'. This policy direction put cultural industry at the center of their strategy aimed at overcoming the limitations of the economic growth model at that time. With the new policy direction, Korea succeeded to make the challenges into new opportunities for a 'creative turn'. In fact, The United Nations Development Program opened the Seoul Policy Centre in 2011 to work with the Korean government, private sector, and civil society and to share such stories of the Korean experience, centering on the policy dialogue (Taylor, April 29, 2012). This demonstrates the credentials of the Korean experience as an inspiring example for the GCC countries.

Furthermore, Korea has recently embarked on a new array of economic policies to make another leap toward a creative economy. According to a publication of the Korean Ministry of Trade Industry and Energy in 2014, the creative economy discourse led by the former President Park Geun-Hye's Administration aims to establish regional and global cooperation systems in order to impact regional development and secure global markets. Importantly, this strategy makes a meaningful subset, where the GCC economic diversification plans and the Korean economic renovation initiatives make a strong connection to each other under the concept of global partnership.

Against the backdrop of such relevance, the relationship between Korea and the GCC countries are evolving into a more strategic partnership beyond hydrocarbon trading and construction project deals. This recently developing multidimensional aspect of the inter-regional partnership is led by the mutual interests of both sides: The six Gulf Arab states are looking for an effective partner for their economic diversification plans, while Korea is seeking to broaden its global network into the Middle East in an effort to revitalize the economy. The major pact to hold regular strategic dialogue at a foreign minister's level, signed by the GCC Chief Abdullatif Al-Zayani and South Korean Foreign Minister Yun Byung-se at a meeting during the 69th UN General Assembly in September 2014, marked the inception of a new level to the Korea-GCC relationship.

Having such development as a background theme, this chapter aims to examine the current diversification challenges of the GCC countries and relates the Korean experience of economic breakthroughs to the GCC countries' strategic planning for the next phase of diversification toward sustainable growth. To that end, this chapter addresses two main research questions:

(1) Why the Korean experience is a relevant example for the GCC diversification challenges? (2) What suggestions can be made from the Korean experience for the GCC diversification challenges? While answering the questions, this chapter employs a comparative analysis as an overarching methodological framework. In addition, a number of theoretical concepts support the analysis: First, the GCC growth model is examined based on the concept of rentier system and comparative advantage. Then another set of concepts including catch-up development and capability-based view are used to explore the Korean experience. The GCC model and the Korean counterpart is compared from a macro perspective to explain the similarity between the two, and the differences are investigated at a micro level approach. The concept of political economy is also applied in the comparison between these two regions to identify what is delaying the diversification process in the GCC region.

The New Rationale of the Korea-GCC Partnership

The initial relations between Korea and the GCC countries were mainly led by the two fields of cooperation—oil and gas trading and infrastructure project deals. Other than these two economic activities, there has been no active engagement between the two sides. This rare exchange can be attributed to the fact that Korea and the GCC states have not been an immediate focus to each other in building up external relations, as they have had other foreign partners whose economic and political interests are more closely connected to theirs. Despite such remoteness, relations between Korea and the six Gulf Arab countries have started developing into a close interregional partnership in recent years. The 9-day visit of the former president of South Korea, Park Geun-hye, to the four GCC states—Kuwait, Saudi Arabia, UAE, and Qatar—from March 1–9 in 2015 clearly shows the newly evolving nature and scope of cooperation between the two sides. The rationale behind this lately developing partnership could be explained by the combination of the complementarity and timely coincidence of ongoing government initiatives to address the economic challenges on each side.

To see how the combination creates a fertile ground for the formation of the interregional cooperation between Korea and the GCC countries, one first needs to look into the economic challenges of both sides. Korea and the GCC countries are currently facing an urgent need of an economic paradigm shift to sustain the well-being of their economy. Although the detailed objectives and main strategies differ given the different structure and operation of the economy in the two regions, the fundamental goal is the same: to innovate or renovate the current economic system.

Hvidt (2013) explains the core of the two concepts of industrialization and diversification which should be noted for the discussion of economic reform here in this chapter. According to him, diversification aims to spread risk by creating a variety of income sources while industrialization generally means the process of creating these diverse income sources. Thematically, the GCC states' economic restructuring falls into the two categories combined. The ultimate goal of the GCC economic diversification is to broaden the limited scope of national income source based on oil and gas by establishing new other knowledge-based industries.

In fact, the GCC countries have been working on their economic diversification over the past two decades and achieved a quantitative foundation for further progress in a later stage. However, there are many obstacles for them to effectively carry on with the development initiatives. Especially, private sector development is one of the most fundamental issues that complicate the diversification process in the GCC region. Salih (2010) lists the main challenges of the GCC economic diversification: unemployment among local citizens, over-reliance on foreign workers, increasing government budget strain, and outflow of local currency and lack of skilled national workforce. In addition to this, Randeree (2012) points out three more problematic aspects of the local economies in the region: education systems that are still undergoing fundamental development, inadequate gender balance in the workforce, and poor levels of private sector employment of citizens. All these realities can be summarized into three essential matters: education system, labor market, and the private sector.

However, Korea is situated in a different context of economic challenges. Education system in Korea enjoys international reputations. Korea does not have a significant level of concerns for its labor market. Regarding the private sector, various kinds of knowledge-based industries have been operating, in which a number of competent companies and enterprises are performing well both domestically and globally. The fundamental issue for Korea is to get out of the current slump and revitalize the economy. According to a *Korea Herald* news article on January 15, 2015, the Industry Minister Yoon Sang-jick said that the government would make full use of its free trade agreements, promising smaller companies to help them meet their exports target this year and invest in future-oriented services and industries. Given that Korean economy is heavily dependent on foreign trade and the nation's overseas shipments took 42.91 percent of the country's GDP in 2013, Korea must secure a new growth engine and increase its global market share in order to recover from the economic downturn.

Putting the two different contexts together, one can see that there is a complementarity between Korea and the GCC countries, upon which the two sides can cooperate to tackle the critical issues they face, respectively. For example, Korea can share its experience of economic development through the power of education and human resource development with the GCC countries, while the latter has a great market potential for the former. In other words, these complementary aspects between Korea and the GCC states create a conducive environment to the formation of a mutually beneficial strategic ties between the two sides. This new rationale for the Korea-GCC cooperation connects to the relevance between the Korean experience and the GCC diversification challenges, which will be demonstrated in the later sections. For starters, it would be useful to have a look at the details of the historical development and current challenges of the Korean and the GCC economies.

The GCC Economic Development

The Trajectory

With a third of world's proven oil and gas reserves and huge revenues generated from it, the six Gulf Arab states have shown the world its different way of achieving economic development, which employs the unique combination of strong financial capacity and large scale of foreign labor imports. This unique set of development tools of the region has yielded a remarkable economic growth since the 1970s. According to Al-Kuwari (2013), the GCC countries' economies have rapidly developed at an average level of around 8–10 percent from 1970 to 2010. Indeed, the GCC countries are now major exporters of important industrial materials whose demand is high in the global market such as petrochemicals, fertilizers, aluminum, and cement. They have also made noticeable progress in service sectors including banking, shipping, logistics, aviation, and real estate.

Fasano (2003) gives a historical account of the GCC economic development in relation to their economic diversification efforts. According to him, the economic development and diversification of the region have been driven by the capital- and energy-intensive industries with strong government supports during the 1970s and the 1980s. In order to facilitate the process, the GCC governments carried out a number of mega projects to build necessary infrastructure. As a result, many successful state-owned enterprises have emerged such as Saudi Basic Industries Corporation (SABIC) in 1976, Dubai Aluminium in 1980, and Bahrain's steel company in 1985. There has been some progress in the service sectors as well including the establishment of a banking sector in 1975 and the creation of free zones in Dubai since the mid-1980s such as Jebel Ali Free Zone.

During the 1990s, however, the GCC countries were confronted with a rapid local population growth, and the government spending for the national employees' wage bill has reached a worrying level while the oil price was going down. Accordingly, extra efforts for diversification have been made along with the existing economic development strategies. To begin with, the GCC states started working on developing a set of new service sectors such as tourism, trade-related activities, and ICT. On top of that, they opened up their economies to private sector initiatives and FDI, encouraged self-employment and development of small and medium enterprises, and implemented some structural and institutional reforms that aimed at consolidating the foundations for private sector-driven growth.

The Strategy

The GCC development strategies can be summarized threefold: First, the role of state-owned enterprises has been considerable. An OECD report (2013) highlights the contribution of the GCC SOEs to the industrial development across the region while attributing the success of the SOEs to their 'commercial viability' and role as 'incubators' for other companies in the value chain. Hertog (2010) shares the same view on the positive role of the GCC SOEs. He finds that the coherent government policies, great daily autonomy in management, clear focus on profit-making are the main reasons for the successful performance of the GCC SOEs, especially compared to the ones in other resource-dependent countries. Table 9.1 shows some of the names of the GCC SOEs and the associated sectors along with the profit they made in 2008.

Second, the GCC countries have done a great job in capitalizing on their comparative advantages. Ample oil and gas in the region have significantly favored the GCC countries in developing and protecting their key industries such as petrochemicals, aluminum, and ethylene by giving them an easy access to the energy source at a substantially competitive price in those sectors. Also, surplus capital has substantially advantaged the GCC countries as a strategic investment vehicle in the form of a Sovereign Wealth Fund for boosting targeted industries such as tourism and aviation. According to the Facility for Euro-Mediterranean Investment and Partnership (2012), the GCC SWFs' strategy has changed from focusing on a few 'industry bets' to diversifying its portfolio to sectors such as retail, healthcare, and semiconductor technology. It also demonstrates that the GCC countries are taking good advantage of their capital through strategic investment often aimed at acquiring know-hows for building new industry capabilities as well as maximizing returns on investment.

Table 9.1 The leading successful SOEs in the GCC (2008–2009 fiscal year)

2008 Profit	*Sector and year of founding*	*Company*	*Country*
US$5.9b on revenue of US$40.3b	Heavy industry (esp. chemicals) 1976	Saudi Arabian Basic Industries (SABIC)	Saudi Arabia
US$376m	Heavy industry 1971	Aluminum Bahrain (Alba)	Bahrain
US$2.0b on revenue of US$4.1b	Heavy industry 2003	Qatar Industries	Qatar
US$280m on revenue of US$850m	Telecoms 1981	Batelco	Bahrain
US$2.4b on revenue of US$7.1b	Telecoms 1976	Etisalat	UAE/Federal
US$840m on revenue of US$4.4b	Real estate 1997	Emaar	UAE/Dubai
US$270m on revenue of US$12.1b	Aviation 1985	Emirates Airlines	UAE/Dubai
US$530m on revenue of US$3.3b	Logistics 1999	DP World	UAE/Dubai

Source: Hertog (2010)

The third component of the GCC development strategy is the Specialized Cities. Khodr (2011) defines the concept of specialized city as a 'city-in-the-city' that has the main purpose of implementing innovations in selected policy areas, in addition to being a new town. The Masdar City in Abu Dhabi and the King Abdullah Economic City in Saudi Arabia could be the two important examples of the Specialized City initiatives in the GCC region. Kingsley (2013, December 17), illustrates a short anecdote in which the ruler of Abu Dhabi and his advisers discuss the diversification issue:

> The ruler of Abu Dhabi Sheikh Khalifa bin Zayed Al Nahyan knew that the main source of Abu Dhabi's wealth, which is oil, would eventually run out. So he asked his advisers to plot a long-term plan that would allow the country to diversify its economy away from hydrocarbons. The answer was renewable energy.

As implied in the piece of the story, MEED (2015) introduces that Masdar City was created as an effort of the Abu Dhabi government to invest its oil dollars in security of the future in which green industry is expected to replace the hydrocarbon sector. King Abdullah Economic City (KAEC) is a part of Saudi Arabia's diversification plans, which is also one of the largest private sector initiatives in the Middle East. The King Abdullah Economic City was designed to become an extensive strategic area including a variety of industrial and business districts, aimed at providing up to 1 million jobs and homes for 2 million people.

The Challenges

However, the GCC diversification strategies reached its limitations in making further progress. This hold up can be attributed to the peculiar workforce composition of the GCC countries in which foreign labors account for the absolute majority. That is because the demographic imbalance in the labor market eventually makes the whole economy unproductive and inefficient. International Monetary Fund (2013) elaborates on the labor market issue in the GCC states.

> The majority of nationals employed in the public sector and the private sector reliant on an elastic supply of low-skilled expatriate workers, has enabled

> the region to develop rapidly, keep inflation relatively low, and distribute the oil wealth to the population. However, the costs of this model—low productivity and a low responsiveness of the employment of nationals to economic growth—are increasingly becoming an issue as economic diversification becomes more of a policy priority.

As such, the GCC labor market overstaffed by foreign workers became a chronic feature of the local economies, and now it is one of the biggest diversification challenges of the GCC economies.

Randeree (2012) adds some other issues particularly related to the GCC workforce nationalization: transfer of knowledge from expatriate to citizen, better approaches to encourage nationals work in the private sector, and the greater inclusion of women. In fact, the grand economic development plans launched by the GCC governments such as Economic Vision 2030 in Bahrain, the State Vision Kuwait 2035, Qatar National Vision 2030, and the UAE Vision 2021 aim to address those issues. Despite the almost homogenous impressions coming from the titles, there are slight differences in terms of strategic approach toward the same goal between the GCC member states. According to Hvidt (2013), Bahrain and Oman clearly set the direction toward a private sector-led neoliberal free-market economy and plan to introduce meritocracy into the public sector to promote real competition for jobs. Contrary to these two countries' explicit turn, the rest of the GCC countries seem to hold on to the so-called state capitalist approach while expecting the positive role of the private sector in the future.

The reason for the majority of the GCC governments still keeping their diversification policy grounded on the state capitalism is to prevent instability from unexpectedly taking place in their society. Hertog (2013) shares a similar view that the GCC governments continue to lead economic development plans and reforms through dominant intervention and policymaking, while guarantee only a limited level of liberal business activities for 'the defense of the convenient status quo'. One way to understand this conservative trend is to see the context of the political economy in the GCC region. For example, the Arab uprisings in 2011 and the way the GCC governments handled the domino-looking crisis across the Middle East clearly reflect such context. Despite knowing the need to downsize the public sector employment and to reduce government spending, while enhancing the role of private sector, the GCC governments had to resort to the traditional remedy of rentier economy such as salary hike for no reason but to cope with the turbulent waves of the uprisings, in the midst of the diversification plans, and reforms aimed at transforming that rentier system. Such a dilemma is the main cause of the current gridlock in the GCC diversification.

The Korean Experience

Explaining the Korean Model

According to Yonhap News (2012, June 23), Korea became an Organization for Economic Cooperation and Development (OECD) member in 1996, and its nominal GDP ranked the 11th largest in the world in 2002. In June 2012, the population reached 50 million, while the per capita income marked about US$24,000, which made Korea the seventh country to meet the two criteria to enter the 20K-50M Club. The ministry in charge of the country's economic policies celebrated the entry and emphasized the fact that South Korea is the first country that was not an industrialized economy before the World War II to achieve this. The Economist (2015, January 4) remarks on such remarkable performance of Korea as 50 years of economic transformation from a war-ravaged country to a world-class, high-tech OECD economy.

Many have recognized distinct features of the Korean growth model and given several different names to it such as 'government-led', 'export-driven', and 'catch-up development' model. This Korean growth model is primarily characterized by the active role of government. Kwack and Lee (2006) explain the Korean experience of economic development by focusing on the strong leadership of government and give an example of the Korean government's industry targeting policy to elaborate on their explanation. Yet, they argue that the abundant human capital and policies to open the economy and promote competition should be taken into account together to explain the success better. Particularly, Kim and Dahlman (1992) note Korea's heavy investment in human resource development in the early years of industrialization. According to them, with a per capita income of US$90, Korea's educational achievement was fairly parallel to the average result of human resource development for a country with a mean per capita gross national product (GNP) of US$200. Also, Korea's level of human resource development with a per capita GNP of US$107 was equivalent to that of countries with a GNP per capita of US$380. These striking figures alone give a substantial sense of how much Korea dedicated itself to human resource development, which laid a solid foundation for the remarkable economic growth of the country.

On the other hand, Lee (2009) underlines that the 'capability-building' in the private sector rather than state-activism as the real lesson from the Korean experience. He argues that continuous upgrading within the same industries as well as advancing successive entries into new promising sectors is the core of the Korean growth model. He also emphasizes the fact that the firm-level capabilities upgraded from Original Equipment Manufacturer (OEM) to Original Design Manufacturer (ODM) and then to Office of Budget and Management (OBM), while the Korean export structure dramatically changed from the labor-intensive goods (1960s–1970s) to high-margin goods such as electronics and automobiles (1990s onward). He points out that such constant capability-building resulted in Korea's a take-over in the wireless telecommunications industry where Motorola dominated.

This capability-based view connects to the other integral element of the Korean experience, which is technology development. The Korean government has early on recognized the importance of technology development for growth. According to Kim and Dahlman (1992), the Korean government established the Ministry of Science and Technology (MOST) in 1967 as a central agency to coordinate technology-related activities of other ministries. However, another institution, the National Council for Science and Technology, had to be established in 1973 to bring about inter-ministerial coordination because the MOST failed its task. In addition, Jeong (2012) notes that the technology development policy of Korea was set within the whole framework of the economic development plans. In order to move up in the global production value chain and achieve sustainable growth through exports, technology development and innovation was almost a matter of survival for Korea in each developmental stage.

The Strategic Policy Shift as a Way Out

The Korean government has engaged in active policymaking in accordance with evolving structure of the economy. Importantly, the Korean government has made a policy shift in a timely manner to overcome new challenges, which in fact allowed Korea to create a turning point out of the time of crisis for the economy. To begin with, the technology development policy of Korea, which was initially focused on technology learning for the first two decades of industrialization, was swiftly altered with different strategic objectives in order to adapt to the changing environment in the later period of the industrialization.

For example, Korea shifted its technology development policy in the 1980s due to the increasing protectionism in the West, which pressured Korea to open up its domestic market and put Korea in the position to compete with multinationals, regardless of its will or readiness, in both international and domestic markets. Furthermore, the rapid rise of real wage in Korea and entry of low-waged developing countries into the market disadvantaged Korea in terms of price competitiveness (Kim and Dahlman 1992). To cope with such harsh environmental change, the Korean government set a new policy objective and strategy to develop its own technological capabilities.

Accordingly, the Korean government launched the national R&D project in 1982 to support the technology development and formulated various policies to facilitate private firms' R&D activities. As a result, the foreign technology introduction rate compared to R&D was reduced from 40 percent in 1981 to 20 percent in the middle of the 1980s and to 10 percent in the early years of the 1990s. This indicates that Korea began to rely more on its own R&D for technology development. Meanwhile, the R&D investment increased substantially from US$520 million (0.81 percent compared to GDP) in 1981 to US$13,500 million (2.8 percent compared to GDP) in 1996, and US$16 billion (2.6 percent compared to GDP) in 2003. In sum, the R&D investment, for around 20 years, increased 27 times at an annual average rate of 20 percent, which led Korea to rank top six among the OECD countries in terms of the R&D investment size in 2010. Especially, the portion of the government's R&D investment in the IT sector increased from 13 percent in 1997 to 33.5 percent in 2002, which contributed to the IT boom in Korea in the beginning of the 2000s. Importantly, such IT-friendly policy of the Korean government played a critical role in turning Korea into an information-oriented society (Seo 2010).

Particularly regarding the private-level technology-oriented capability-building in Korea, Jeong (2012) and Lee (1992) note the rather unique relationship between the government and the large conglomerates in Korea, in which the government has a certain degree of influence over the big corporates, while the former provides various kinds of institutional supports with the latter. This seemingly against the rule of liberal economy was, in fact, a strategy that the Korean government employed to use the big firms as an efficient unit to push the industrialization process from the stage of light industry to the stage of heavy chemical industry since the early 1970s. Kim and Dahlman (1992) also explain that the Korean government intentionally created the large firms, chaebols, as an instrument to bring about the economy of scale in developing advanced technologies and associated strategic industries for the export-oriented Korean economy.

Consolidating New Policy Regime

Entering the 1980s, the production and peripheral technology of Korea was estimated to have almost achieved the same level of the first industrialized countries' technology. Yet, there was a considerable gap for Korea to catch up in terms of core and high technology. As Korea had to import foreign core technology in order to export finished goods such as computers, machinery, and transportation vehicles, the Korean government and companies were in an urgent need of further technology development, for instance, to localize the parts production. Therefore, the Korean government initiated research funding from 1982 and directed the selection of research subjects. During the mid-1980s, the Korean government created the Credit Guarantee Fund to help financing of small and medium size enterprises and then founded the Technology Credit Guarantee Fund to support capable enterprises receiving loan on security of their technology (Jeong 2012).

In addition, the Korean government increased its investment in the basic science and made a favorable environment where research institutes and private firms can conduct R&D project together since the late 1990s. As entering the 2000s, Korea primarily focused on basic and original technology development. In 2003, the Korean government announced the next-generation growth engine project that involves ten new technology fields: intellectual robots, futuristic automobiles, next-generation semiconductor, digital TV and broadcasting, next-generation mobile communication, display, intellectual home network, digital contents, SW solution, next-generation battery, new biomedicine, and organs (Jeong 2012).

Along with such technology development policies, the Korean government formulated another policy measure, which was aimed at attracting Korean brains abroad back to home. To bring educated and skilled technicians, engineers, and scientists abroad back to Korea, the former President Park Chung-Hee formulated various policies and political support to create a conducive domestic environment such as government-sponsored strategic R&D institution-building, legal and administrative reforms, and the empowerment of returnees via material benefits, guarantees of research autonomy. He underlines the fact that the President Park compromised conventional norms in his own bureaucracy to empower returning scientists (Yoon 1992). As a result, private sector R&D in Korea took off in the 1980s with a rapid expansion of in-house R&D facilities and manpower.

With regard to the reverse brain drain, Song (1997) provides his research findings that shows a shift in the residence choice of Korean scientists and engineers from America to Korea over the three decades from 1970s to 1990s. According to Table 9.2, most of the Korean scientists and engineers (KSEs) who received their doctorate in the 1960s chose to stay in America, and only 16 percent of them returned to Korea. In contrast, nearly two-thirds of the KSEs who earned their doctoral degree in the 1980s came back to Korea by 1987. This can prove that the abovementioned political support and policy measures were effective in creating the targeted outcomes.

Another Turn for Another Challenge

Entering the 2000s, cultural industry has become a new promising growth engine of the Korean economy as the cultural contents such as movies, TV dramas, and even entertainment program platforms are exported to other countries for the increasing demand of foreign audience. According to a *Financial Times* article on November 13, 2013, Korean TV drama exports grew from US$8 million in 2001 to US$155 million in 2011. Although the article admits that this growth of newly emerged industry is not big as much as that of the multibillion-dollar making electronics or shipbuilding, it shows that Korean economy has achieved further diversification.

Table 9.2 Changing trend of KSEs' residence choice (790 survey respondents)

Return to Korea after work in the USA	*Return to Korea just after PhD*	*Stay in the USA*	*Number of respondents*	*PhD year*
12.7%	3.4%	83.9%	118	Before 1970
22.1%	10.1%	67.8%	276	1970–79
29.1%	39.4%	31.6%	396	1980–87
191	188	411	790	Total

Source: Song (1997)

In fact, there was a new policy shift that enabled this 'creative turn' in the Korean economy after the 1997–1998 Asian financial crisis. Chung (2012) demonstrates that the successful performance of the Korean cultural industry is a fruitful result from the political commitments of the two consecutive governments. According to his research, the Kim Dae Jung's administration (1998–2003) prepared the quantitative ground for the cultural industry policies, and the Roh Moo-Hyun's administration (2003–2008) achieved a qualitative upgrade of the previous policy framework. This indicates that the devoted efforts of the two presidents for a decade from 1998 to 2008 have resulted in the establishment of a strong foundation for the Korean cultural industry, which in fact explains the successful performance of the industry since the late 2000s. Table 9.3 shows the specific process of the cultural industry policymaking of Korea during that time. According to the table, the Korean government has made not only plans but also institutional framework to make sure that the plans will be implemented and checked on a regular basis such as the specific mandatory budget allocation and annual paper works on the plan. This shows that the Korean government has made thoroughly organized efforts to implement new policies as well as to set up the policies.

Lately, Korea has initiated a new policy dialogue again in the face of low growth, aging population, and lack of new growth engine. To cope with these challenges, the Korean government launched 'Creative Economy' initiative in 2012. According to Cha and Yoo (2013), the con-

Table 9.3 Major events in the Korea's CI policymaking

February 1998	Establishment of the MCT and expansion of the CI bureau
March 1999	The Five-Year Plan for CI Development as the first long-term government plan
Mid-1999	KOFIC (Korean Film Council), KMRB (Korea Media Rating Board), and KGPC (Korea Games Promotion Centre) were newly established to support and promote the newly rising CI sector
Since 2000	Ensuring 'more than 1%' of the government budget
Since 2000	Publishing CI white papers and statistics annually
June 2004	The new 'vision' for Korean cultural policy 'Creative Korea' was prepared by a newly formed task force composed of a committee of six scholars, a research project team of 16 researchers and experts, and an administrative support team of 14 civil servants. In addition, more than 20 sub-task forces were established, composed of around 200 experts from various cultural sectors.

Source: Adapted from Chung (2012)

cept of Creative Economy has been actively discussed since the late 1990s with the UK and the UN as a center of the debate in the field of cultural industry and city and local policy. Yet, the term reemerged today as an alternative strategic plan for the issue of economic recession and high unemployment rate in the major economies. The US announced a Strategy for American Innovation in February 2011 that aims to reform the ways of government operation and to use creativity in order to maintain competitive advantage and for economic growth. In 2010, the European Commission embarked on the Europe 2020 initiative in preparation for the next 10 years, while the Japanese government started the New Growth Strategy that contains core economic policies set to be implemented by 2020. Such innovation-oriented policy of the major economies mainly aims to nurture creative industries and promote basic research-oriented science and technology policies in order to create jobs and secure a source of sustainable growth.

The Korean government has been also driving the discourse of Creative Economy as a new paradigm for economic growth since 2012. With this new slogan, the government aims to graduate the previous catching-up development and to become a leading player in the world economy. The focus of the Creative Economy policy lies in creating new growth engine and jobs by promoting industry convergence and applying creativity and imagination to every field. One example of the new initiative is the Creative Economy Innovation Center project. According to Table 9.4, there are 17 centers across the nation with the first one established in September 2014, and the centers are expected to become a space where large leading companies support local entrepreneurs to commercialize their ideas and develop it into proper businesses. The primary purpose of this project is to support start-ups, SMEs and local economies through cooperation for technological innovation, thereby creating more jobs.

Besides, the Google Campus Seoul has been established on May 8, 2015 to generate synergy effect with the Creative Economy Innovation Center project by supporting start-ups and entrepreneurs in Korea. The Google Campus Seoul is the third branch abroad and the first establishment in Asia which was the result of the Korean government's enthusiastic commitment to the Creative Economy plans. To invite the campus in Seoul, President Park Geun-hye met Larry Page, the founder and CEO of Google in Cheong Wa Dae, the Korean Presidential residence, in 2013 to discuss ways to establish the campus, and Google officially announced its

Table 9.4 The Creative Economy Innovation Centers across Korea

Filed of cooperation	*Company name*	*Regional CEIC*	*No.*	*Filed of cooperation*	*Company name*	*Regional CEIC*	*No.*
ICT	SK	Sejong	10	IT Service	NAVER	Gangwon	1
	Hyundai Heavy Industries	Ulsan	11	IT Service	KT	Gyeonggi	2
Aviation	Hanjin	Incheon	12	Machinery	Doosan	Gyeongnam	3
Construction and energy	GS	Jeonnam	13	Electronics	Samsung	Gyeongbuk	4
Carbon fiber	Hyosung	Jeonbuk	14	Automobile	Hyundai Motors	Gwangju	5
IT Service	Daum	Jeju	15	Electronics	Samsung	Daegu	6
Solar energy and ICT	Hanwha	Chungnam	16	ICT	SK	Daejeon	7
Digital information and bio	LG	Chungbuk	17	Logistics and Tourism	LOTTE	Busan	8
				Culture	CJ	Seoul	9

Source: Adapted from the Ministry of Science, ICT, and Future Planning blog

plan to establish its third campus in Seoul in August 2014. As such, Korean economy is making another turn toward 'Creative Economy' in response to the challenges emeraged.

Comparing the GCC Growth Model and the Korean Experience

The Industrialization Sequence

The GCC economic development strategies and the Korean experience share both similar and different aspects. First, the similarities between the two growth models lie in the umbrella frame of a government-led catching-up development. To achieve a rapid economic growth, the GCC countries and Korea took a highly centralized development strategy. For example, Dubai has the Executive Office where the ruler manages all development policies regarding megaprojects, state-owned companies, foreign investments, and so on (Hvidt 2009). The Korean government also had the Economic Planning Board for planning and implementation for the Five-Year Economic Development plans. Hertog (2010) also finds the GCC model analogous to the 'Asian developmental authoritarianism', which reflects the common ground that both the GCC countries and Korea had to have a concentrated authority for a fast and coherent policy-making and implementation to make the rapid catch-up happen.

However, the two models differ in terms of detailed strategic approach. First, the differences in the comparative advantage of Korea and the GCC countries can be the starting point of the comparison. The GCC countries have engaged mainly in the capital- and energy-intensive sectors benefitting from the vast size of the oil and gas reserves in the region. This major asset of the GCC states allowed them to achieve substantial economic growth without having to go through the learning by doing hard steps and the regular process of industrialization. The GCC countries could build a solid secondary industrial base, though it is mainly limited to hydrocarbon sector, and now focus on tertiary industry development with tourism, airlines, and banking sector as main target.

Such progress in the GCC industrialization is unique in the sense that the process has been selectively centering on specific sectors that favor the local economies by big margin over international competitors. Overall, the industrialization has been a smooth journey for the GCC countries. This completely contrasts with the Korean experience in which the country went through the whole process of industrialization from the scratch after being destroyed by the civil war in the early 1950s. The industrialization of Korea was a comprehensive and step-by-step process from technology imports to technology learning to finally technology innovation.

Getting the People on Board

The rentier system is another critical factor that differentiates the GCC growth model from the Korean experience. Based on the rentier system, the GCC nationals rely on their government for almost every basic necessity of living such as education, healthcare, and even employment opportunities. Since this system provides citizens with a comfortable life style without asking productive economic participation, the GCC nationals came to develop the so-called rentier mentality which essentially discourages the people making 'standard economic behavior' based on the 'work-reward causation'. This consequently leads to a shortage of skilled national workforce and lack of work ethics as laboring for one's income is considered shameful (Levins 2012). Thus, one can see that the rentier system and the mentality developed out of it becomes a serious obstacle to the GCC countries' economic diversification and private sector development that basically requires productive participation of nationals as a disciplined and skilled workforce.

Contrary to this, Korea's economic development was driven by the enthusiastic participation of the people as much as by the government leadership. To mobilize people in the development plans, the former President Park Chung-Hee initiated the Saemaeul Movement in the 1970s, which aimed to modernize the rural communities by promoting the 'Saemaeul spirit' that consists of three qualities—diligence, self-help, and cooperation. This is because he believed it to be important that people have the right attitude and the right spirit in order for a nation to grow and develop. By promoting the movement, the Korean government nurtured Saemaeul leaders and workforce to have them in charge of the various tasks of Saemaeul project. Not only that, the government also encouraged competition among villages by introducing the principle of 'better support for better performers' upon which it provides additional supports for villages with better performance. This Saemaeul Movement of the 1970s is evaluated as a great contribution to the quantitative growth of Korea during that time around and the spirit and know-how of the movement is exported to many developing countries (Kim 2014) Thus, the Saemaeul Movement can be an inspiration for the GCC countries in formulating policies to encourage nationals' productive participation in the economy.

The Role of Big Business

The state-business relations should be taken into comparison between the GCC model and the Korean experience. Although the practical nature of state-business relations in the two cases is similar as government provides favored supports to large firms and intervenes when needed, technically it is different in that the large companies in the GCC region are state-owned enterprises whereas the Korean counterpart is private business. In addition, it differs again based on how the relations operate, which becomes a substantial distinction between the state-business relations of the GCC region and that of Korea. The big businesses in the GCC states receive generous subsidies and financial backing from the government regardless of their performance. Although Forstenlechner and Rutledge (2010) argue that the GCC SOEs are 'a less unproductive allocation of state resources' and they have the 'potential to be growth-generating investments', they are still heavily subsidized and enjoy government protection, which leads to the lack of competition and discourages national employees realizing the importance of obtaining and developing skills that matches the amount of salary they receive.

However, the Korean government took much strict measures in promoting big business by penalizing poor performers and rewarding only good ones for the purpose of building up their competitiveness in both domestic and international market. Furthermore, the government did not bail out badly managed bankrupt firms, instead selected better managed ones to take them over (Kim and Dahlman 1992). Even more interesting fact regarding the Korean experience is Korean government's so-called 'world-class conglomerates fostering plan' in which the government is expected to support national companies to achieve global competitiveness in the international market but gradually taking its hands off. According to Table 9.5, the plan sets up a time line specifying until when the government supports companies and from when companies should begin to compete on their own feet (Jeong 2012). Such tight control and inducing transition to competition by the Korean government for big businesses clearly contrasts with the GCC countries' soft and over-protective policies toward their SOEs.

Such different state-business relations in the GCC region and in Korea further relate to the gap of private sector development between the two regions. While Korean conglomerates played a leading role in establishing a vibrant private sector in the national economy, the GCC SOEs' focus has been on accommodating nationals in the workforce and keeping the economy working rather than making profits and expanding business. Regarding state-owned enterprises, Lee (2009) stresses the importance of SOEs' ownership privatization and gradual fading out of state activism in order to achieve international competitiveness. This implies that privatization of SOEs is a way for developing private sector in the GCC region.

However, the GCC governments have taken a different approach for privatization of the local economies. Instead of steering toward private ownership, the GCC governments came up with some policy measures such as quotas that impose private businesses a certain number of nationals that they should employ. For example, the Kuwaiti government introduced the concept of Kuwaitization which aims to replace non-Kuwaiti employees by Kuwaiti nationals. Under the program, private companies

Table 9.5 Industrialization policy framework of Korea

Entry into the global market		*Self-help development*			*Industrialization*
World class	*Complete international competition*	*Self-help growth*	*Intensive support*	*Direct protection*	
		Private led, global scale	Government planning, domestic market protection, export promotion	Government planning and subsidies	Policy
Industrializing economy → Advanced industrialized economy					Industrial stage
Economy building → Economy operation/management					Development method
Theory of motherhood → Free-market economy					Theory
MICRO: individual industrialization policy → MACRO, statistical control					Economic policy
Government led → Private led					Leading unit

Source: Oh (1996)

are required by law to hire 2% of their staff as Kuwaitis. Moreover, the Kuwaiti government encouraged nationals to join the private sector by paying them a certain percentage of their monthly salary (Madzikanda and Njoku 2008). However, such policy has not paid off.

The Political Economy

One must consider the unique context of political economy in the GCC region when discussing the soft and, to some extent, spoiling policies of the local governments. Basically, the legitimacy of the political rule of loyal family is primarily supported by the rentier system which distributes oil and gas revenues to its people in the form of various government subsidies and social benefits. Given that the whole point is to satisfy citizens to keep the status quo and internal stability, the GCC governments cannot easily shift the policy supporting generous flow of government spending to its citizens.

Meanwhile, Korea experienced a disparate nature of political economy from the GCC case, which goes back to the President Park Chung-Hee's time. The issue of President Park Chung-Hee's political rule was the fact that he took the presidential office through a military coup in 1961. However, he chose to legitimize his take-over and subsequent rule by rebuilding the national economy through centralized authority. Hwang (1996) argues that the President Park's control over the bureaucracy enabled him to make substantial economic growth happen in Korea, which helped his regime earn political supports from the people. He adds further that the President Park took tight control of Chaebols, Korean big conglomerates, as well to the extent that they were assigned with the responsibility of export promotion to fulfill and pressured not to join the activities of political opposition. Chaebols eventually gained a certain amount of leverage over the government intervention as they became integral pillars of the Korean economy. Consequently, the political economy of Park Chung-Hee government resulted in capacity-building of the private sector.

The GCC leadership is in a fundamental dilemma of diversification challenges. To develop profitable knowledge-based industries, a vibrant private sector should be established, in which nationals run businesses while supplying skilled labor and profitable ideas to the local economy. However, the GCC governments cannot easily do away with the subsidies and public offerings because it may otherwise cause domestic instability. Consequently, the dilemma has been delaying the whole diversification process in the region until today. Therefore, gradual rearrangement of the social contract between state and society in the GCC countries is needed based on considerate negotiations for the rights and duties of both the governments and the people in order to establish a more effective and conducive environment to sustainable growth in the region.

Conclusion

The GCC countries have achieved a rapid economic growth based on the unique combination of oil capital and the large scale of foreign labor imports. Through the growth model, the local economies have made a substantial quantitative progress including the establishment of a modern infrastructure that grabs international attention. In addition, the GCC economies have yielded successful performance in the energy- and capital-intensive sectors primarily through state-owned enterprises. At a later stage, Specialized Cities have been employed as a policy instrument for further diversification across the GCC region.

However, this GCC model reached its limitations as an effective mechanism to achieve sustainable growth as the local economies faced a set of fundamental challenges that include rapidly growing youth population, high unemployment rate, saturated public sector, and underdeveloped private sector. An inclusive solution to all this is to establish a vibrant private sector that can create jobs for nationals and motivate them to compete for reward. Yet, the current GCC growth model that runs on the rentier system can no longer be a valid way for the economic development in the region. Furthermore, the political economy of the GCC countries adds another concern for the local governments. Basically, the state-society relationship in the region is the social contract upon which the governments gain political supports from the people by satisfying the needs of the people through the distribution of oil and gas rents. Although it is a must for the GCC governments to do without the rentier system at some point in order to complete the diversification process, they may risk the status quo for doing that because of the social contract. Consequently, this state-society relationship makes a vicious cycle in which keeping stability involves one of the biggest obstacles to sustainable growth in the region, the rentier system.

Compared to the trajectory of the GCC economic development, the Korean experience has been a quite different path. Korea was a war-devastated land with no natural resources. This humble condition of Korea during that time rather helped the country focus on making the best out of what is given. Korea has gone through industrialization step by step from the scratch, which became a learning by doing process of national capability-building. Korea put the most emphasis on developing human resources through education so that its people can become productive and efficient units to rebuild the national economy and realize further prosperity. Korea has made constant efforts early on for the local capacity building through various policies. According to Lee (2009), the intensification of R&D expenditure and a focus on higher education in the 1980s formed the foundation for knowledge-driven growth of Korea. The results of public R&D were shared with private companies, and private R&D was promoted with tax incentives. In addition, public-private joint R&D was set up for bigger, risky projects. This implies that the Korean government understood the significance of the role of private sector in building national capabilities and facilitating economic growth.

The most critical point of the Korean experience with regard to the GCC diversification challenges should be 'how Korea made a breakthrough at the times of crisis'. Korea has encountered a series of economic challenges. First, the increasing Western protectionism in the 1980s coupled with emerging low-waged developing economies in the international market significantly affected Korea's market competitiveness. To get out of the sandwiched situation, the Korean government formulated various policies to promote in-house R&D and upgrade the national technology capabilities. As a result, Korea achieved better competitiveness in the international market. At the end of the 1990s, the Korean economy was smashed by the Asian financial crisis. To raise up the plummeted economy, two former presidents of Korea, Kim Dae-Jung and Roh Mu-Hyun, made a landmark policy shift particularly in the Cultural Industry policy field where 'Cultural Contents' and 'Culture Technology' became official terms (Chung 2012). Such policy shift and 10 years of political commitment has prepared the foundation for the solid competitiveness of the Korean cultural industry and the growing global reach of the Korean popular culture today.

In conclusion, the moments of crisis eventually became the turning point for innovation in the trajectory of the Korean economic growth. What has made the breakthroughs possible was the threefold political efforts: One is the timely policy shift, two is further consolidation of the policy framework, and three is strong commitment to implementing it. Thus, the Korean experience as a whole can certainly become both a relevant example and inspiration for the GCC countries to find a breakthrough in the diversification dilemma. Specifically, three suggestions can be made for the GCC diversification challenges:

First, the GCC countries' policy objectives and strategies for economic diversification should be established in the long-term perspective, keeping in mind that the goal of sustainable growth involves global competition one way or another. Thus, it is critical for the policymakers to coordinate every policy they design for economic development to be aligned and linked to two essential points—sustainable growth and global competition.

Second, a policy adjustment is needed to enhance the effectiveness of policies concerning chronic diversification challenges such as weak private sector and workforce nationalization. The new policy direction should focus on solving the diversification dilemma that mostly comes from the rentier system and aims to set a new discourse that motivates the members of the GCC society to take part in the preparation for the post-oil era. For this, a redefinition of state and society relationship is also required to help both the governments and the people understand what role they are expected to play to achieve the common goal of sustainable growth.

Third, it is crucial to reduce the gap between the impeccable policy objectives and implementation performance. The GCC countries are now looking for a new mode of economic diversification. There is no denial to the fact that the region is facing difficult challenges on the way. However, the challenges also suggest new rooms for innovation and progress. There is always a breakthrough in a crisis and it is certainly true for the GCC countries. The completion of the task is now halfway done as 'what-to-do' is clearly identified. What is left is only to put it into serious action.

References

Al-Kuwari, D. (2013). *Mission Impossible? Genuine Economic Development in the Gulf Cooperation Council Countries.* Research Paper, No.33, London, UK, Kuwait Programme on Development, Governance and Globalisation in the Gulf States, London School of Economics and Political Science.

Cha, D., & Yoo, J. Y. (2013). *The Concept of Creative Economy and Analysis of Major Economies Policy* (In Korean). Issue Paper, Seoul, Korea, Korea Institute of Science and Technology Evaluation and Planning, Korea. Retrieved from http://www.kistep.re.kr/c3/sub3.jsp?brdType=R&bbIdx=1348

Chung, J.-E. (2012). *From Developmental to Neo-Developmental Cultural Industries Policy: The Korean Experience of the 'Creative Turn'.* PhD Dissertation, Glasgow, UK, Centre for Cultural Policy Research School of Culture and Creative Arts, University of Glasgow.

Facility for Euro-Mediterranean Investment and Partnership. (2012). *An Overview Mobilizing the Potential of the GCC Sovereign Wealth Funds for Mediterranean Partner Countries.* Research Paper, Luxemburg, Luxembourg, European Investment Bank.

Fasano, U. (2003). *Diversification in Oil-Dependent Economies: The Experience of the GCC Countries.* In UNFCCC Workshop, Tehran, October, pp. 18–19.

Forstenlechner, I., & Rutledge, E. (2010). Unemployment in the Gulf: Time to Update the Social Contract. *Middle East Policy, 17*(2), 38–51.

The Economist. (2015, January 4). The Creative Economy Blog Korea Has Achieved an Economic Miracle, But Can It Do It Twice?. Retrieved from http://gelookahead.economist.com/the-creative-economy-2/

Hertog, S. (2010). Defying the Resource Curse: Explaining Successful State-Owned Enterprises in Rentier States. *World Politics, 62*(2), 261–301.

Hertog, S. (2013). *The Private Sector and Reform in the Gulf Cooperation Council.* Research Paper, No.30, London, UK, Kuwait Programme on Development, Governance and Globalisation in the Gulf States, London School of Economics and Political Science.

Hvidt, M. (2009). The Dubai Model: An Outline of Key Development-Process Elements in Dubai. *International Journal of Middle East Studies, 41*(3), 397–418.

Hvidt, M. (2013). *Economic Diversification in GCC Countries: Past Record and Future Trends.* Research Paper No.27, London, UK, Kuwait Programme on Development, Governance and Globalisation in the Gulf States, London School of Economics and Political Science.

Hwang, K. K. (1996). South Korea's Bureaucracy and the Informal Politics of Economic Development. *Asian Survey*, pp. 306–319.

International Monetary Fund. (2013, October 5). *Economic Prospects and Policy Challenges for the GCC Countries.* Paper presented at the annual meeting of Ministers of Finance and Central Bank Governors, Riyadh, Saudi Arabia. Retrieved from http://www.imf.org/external/np/pp/eng/2013/100513b.pdf

Jeong, Y. (2012). *Study on the Spread of Korean Science-Technology Innovation Policy to Developing Countries* (In Korean). Research Paper, No.2, Seoul, Korea, The Export-Import Bank of Korea.

Khodr, H. (2011). *The Dynamics of Policy Innovation and Diffusion in the Gulf Cooperation Council: A Case Study of Three Specialized Cities.* Research, Advocacy, and Public Policy-Making in the Arab World (RAPP) Working Paper Series 7.

Kim, J. K. (2014). A Study on Change and Development of 1970s Saemaeul Movement (In Korean). *Academic Journal of Korea Administration History, 34*, 283–305.

Kim, L., & Dahlman, C. J. (1992). Technology Policy for Industrialization: An Integrative Framework and Korea's Experience. *Research Policy, 21*(5), 437–452.

Kingsley, P. (2013, December 17). Masdar: The Shifting Goalpost of Abu Dhabi's Ambitious Ecocity. *Wired Magazine.* Retrieved from http://www.wired.co.uk/magazine/archive/2013/12/features/reality-hits-masdar

Kwack, S. Y., & Lee, Y. S. (2006). Analyzing the Korea's Growth Experience: The Application of R&D and Human Capital Based Growth Models with Demography. *Journal of Asian Economics, 17*(5), 818–831.

Lee, C. H. (1992). The Government, Financial System, and Large Private Enterprises in the Economic Development of South Korea. *World Development, 20*(2), 187–197.

Lee, K. (2009). *How Can Korea Be a Role Model for Catch-Up Development? A 'Capability-Based View'.* Working paper provided in cooperation with United Nation University and World Institute for Development Economic Research.

Levins, C. M. (2012). Rentier State and the Survival of Arab Absolute Monarchies. *The Rutgers JL & Religion, 14*, 388.

Madzikanda, D. D., & Njoku, E. I. (2008). Employee Attitudes Towards the Privatization of Kuwait Government Departments and State Owned Enterprises. *International Public Management Review, 9*(1), 107–129.

MEED. (2015). King Adullah Economic City: Project Overview. Retrieved April 19, from http://www.meed.com/knowledge-bank/top-100-projects/King-Abdullah-Economic-City

OECD. (2013). The Role of State-Owned Enterprises in MENA Development and Competitiveness. In *State Owned Enterprises in the Middle East and North Africa: Engines of Development and Competitiveness?* Paris, France: OECD Publishing.

Oh, W. C. (1996). *Korean Economic Development Model 2*. Seoul: Kia Economic Research Institute.

Randeree, K. (2012). *Workforce Nationalization in the Gulf Cooperation Council States*. Occasional Paper, No.9, Doha, Qatar, Center for International and Regional Studies, Georgetown University School of Foreign Service in Qatar.

Salih, A. (2010). Localizing the Private Sector Workforce in the Gulf Cooperation Council Countries: A Study of Kuwait. *International Journal of Public Administration, 33*(4), 169–181.

Seo, J. (2010). *The Development of Korean Technology Developing System and the Lessons* (In Korean). Research Paper, Seoul, Korea, The Export-Import Bank of Korea.

Song, H. (1997). From Brain Drain to Reverse Brain Drain: Three Decades of Korean Experience. *Science Technology & Society, 2*(2), 317–345.

Taylor, K. (2012, April 29). UNDP Seoul Chief to Harness Korea's Development Story. *The Korea Herald*. Retrieved from http://www.koreaherald.com/view.php?ud=20120429000325

Yonhap News. (2012, June 23). S. Korea Joining '20-50 Club' Marks New Chapter in Development History. Retrieved from http://english.yonhapnews.co.kr/search1/2603000000.html?cid=AEN20120623001200320

Yoon, B.-S. (1992). Reverse Brain Drain in South Korea: State-Led Model. *Studies in Comparative International Development, 27*(1), 4–2.

CHAPTER 10

Economic Diversification and Empowerment of Local Human Resources: Could Singapore Be a Model for the GCC Countries?

Veronika Cummings (née Deffner)

Introduction

Due to rapid modernisation, a high dependence on foreign imported workforce and expertise both, the economies of the GCC (Gulf Cooperation Council) and the most advanced economies of the ASEAN (Association of South East Asian Nations) are tackling similar political, economic, and socio-demographic challenges. The GCC countries are trying to diversify the economic revenues to reduce the high dependence of the hydrocarbon sector, whereas Singapore, as the most developed economy in the ASEAN community—and desirable "model" for many countries—is implementing policies to diversify from its strong economic foothold, the financial service sector. A key for a successful and, thus, sustainable diversification process for the GCC is the empowerment of their national human capital. Their advanced, swiftly modernised economies require a local workforce which is sufficiently skilled and experienced.

Both regions, the GCC and the ASEAN, are showing mutual interest in enhancing their economic ties, and since the mid-2000s, the relation-

V. Cummings (née Deffner) (✉)
Institute of Geography, Johannes Gutenberg-University, Mainz, Germany

A. Mishrif, Y. Al Balushi (eds.), *Economic Diversification in the Gulf Region, Volume II*, The Political Economy of the Middle East,
DOI 10.1007/978-981-10-5786-1_10

ship between Singapore, in particular, and the Gulf countries has grown both in scope and depth. Singapore represents one of the most sought-after models of an advanced diversified service economy, which stimulated the underlying research project. In some ways, it could offer experiences with general features and practices for the strategic planning and implementation of the diversification process and with the focus on education, research, development, and innovation in utilising its own human resources to fulfil the demands of the workforce. The objective of this study is to provide answers to these questions.

Section 2 will give an overview of the economic structure and diversification process of the GCC countries. This is followed by an examination of the challenges by the GCC in its efforts to restructure its labour markets by empowering its local human resources, a well-known strategy in the region termed "nationalisation" (i.e. Saudisation, Omanisation, Emiratisation, etc.; see, e.g. Hertog 2014a; Randeree 2012; Ramady 2010; Al-Lamki 2000; Al-Ali 2008; Toledo 2013). These nationalisation strategies will be exemplified in Section 3 with specific focus on the Sultanate of Oman. The country has been chosen as an example because it has the second-highest proportion of nationals amongst all the GCC countries (following Saudi Arabia). The pressure of Omanisation is not only high because of the ever-increasing size of the expatriate workforce, (and thus its ever-increasing reliance on foreigners) but also due to natural demographic growth that has prompted the need to create employment for the rising number of young, local job seekers. The country started implementing its nationalisation policies relatively early, which makes it a suitable case study to examine the challenges and obstacles over a certain period of time. The data for this section is derived from two larger empirical study projects undertaken in the capital area of Muscat between 2010 and 2016. Around 150 qualitative interviews were conducted over time with nationals and foreigners working in the private sector in Oman, focusing on their experiences and perceptions, as well as changes of nationalisation policies and practices.

Section 4 provides an overview on the "(success) story" of Singapore, a city-state and young nation that is being confronted with similar structural challenges in diversifying its economy and in dealing with a still high reliance on an international workforce. As indicated above, Singapore represents a highly sought-after model for the GCC. Therefore, this given chapter will be followed by a critical discussion (Section 5) of the question of whether Singapore could be a reasonable template for the Arab Gulf States to follow or which lessons can be drawn, at the very least.

Economic Structures and Diversification in the GCC

The Gulf rentier states have seen a considerable phase of economic reforms and gradual economic liberalisation policies since the 2000s (see e.g. Herb 2014; Hertog 2014b). However, the economic structure of all GCC states is still challenged by two main and well-known aspects: firstly, they heavily rely on hydrocarbon revenues which was above all the starting point, and still is the basis, for the rapid modernisation process in all six countries of the Gulf Cooperation Council. This dominant national income source is mainly managed by international companies, hence accounting for the private sector. Secondly, the proportion of nationals in the labour market is outnumbered by the foreign workforce, as distinctly visible in Fig. 10.1, where the darker grey share of the bars on the right-hand side ("working non-nationals") outstrips the share of the "working nationals" of the bars on the left-hand side. For nationals, the government or public sector is still the major employer. Hence, foreigners constitute most of the workforce that basically runs the private sector economy. This, in turn, accounts for the productivity, which results in the high economic dependence on foreign expertise and workforce.

Consequently, the Gulf States are facing two major challenges: firstly, the need to diversify their economies—in particular towards an *autonomous* diversification of the private sector away from the dominant role and control of the state (Hertog 2014b, 3)—and, secondly, the replacement of foreign employees by a sufficiently skilled and experienced domestic workforce. Both challenges are tied to the push for an improved developed educational landscape, in particular for higher education and vocational training programmes, and further investment into research and innovation, to empower the huge pool of young nationals to strive towards reaching sustainable economic diversification and productivity that is non-hydrocarbon based and less rent recycling.

The high reliance on the hydrocarbon sector simultaneously drives and hinders the diversification process in the GCC countries. An economic turn is being frantically sought due to the finite nature of the natural resources oil and gas. The Gulf monarchies face different estimates as to how long their oil and gas resources will last. Bahrain and Oman, for instance, are estimated to run out of oil in only one and two decades, respectively, whereas Qatar's is estimated to last another century at the current production levels. The estimations for the deposits of natural gas

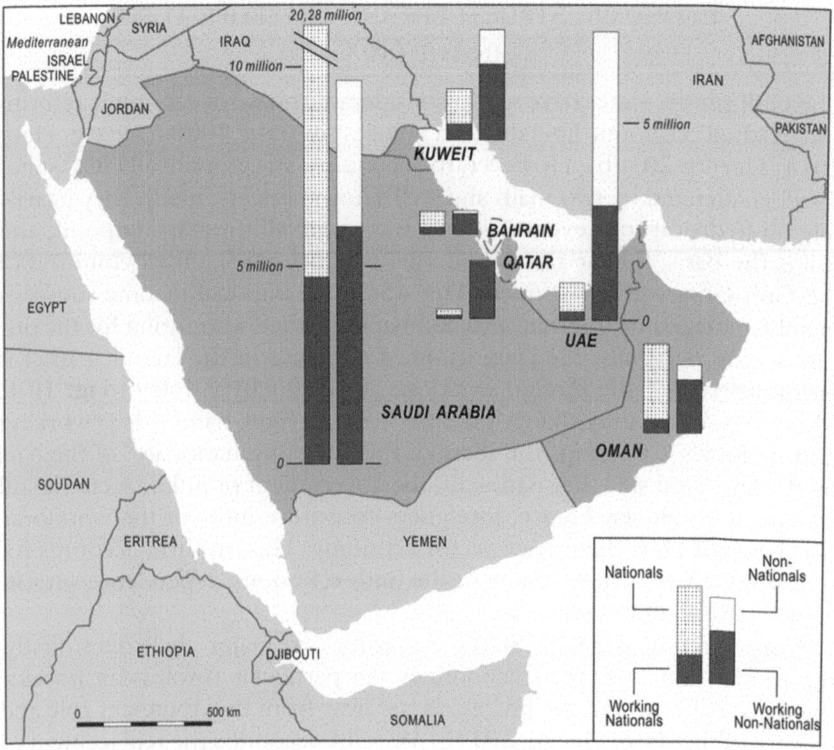

Fig. 10.1 Population and percentage of nationals and non-nationals in the GCC countries (Cartography: H.-J. Ehrig (design: M. Trapp); Data: Gulf Labour Markets and Migration (GLMM) 2015 (according to the latest available data from the national institutes of statistics for the period 2010–2015)

vary widely, but most of the GCC countries are clutching to the hope of substituting oil with gas in the future.

Simultaneously, an economic turn is being impeded by economic vulnerability due to the oil price volatility (Malik and Shawkat 2007). The latter has been affecting the oil-producing countries tremendously since 2014. The level of vulnerability is dictated by three key indicators: the degree of the reliance on hydrocarbon revenues, a fiscal spending policy that exceeds oil revenues, and an inefficient production level in the oil sector which accounts for an overly rapid depletion of the oil reserves (Global Risk Advisors 2015).

Bahrain is one of the more diversified economies of the GCC due to its relatively competitive financial service sector. However, it performs on the same level as Oman, Saudi Arabia, and Kuwait, where oil and gas make up the large majority of the export volume (Hamdi and Sbia 2013).

The UAE hold the best record of export diversification, even though this is solely due to the emirate of Dubai, which has a globally competitive service sector and due to the emirate of Sharjah, which has an advanced manufacturing sector. The largest emirate Abu Dhabi still is highly dependent on oil and gas (Callen et al. 2014, 11ff.). Dubai started relatively early to promote itself as a trade and finance hub in the Gulf region, with modern infrastructure, a business-friendly environment, light regulations, large transport capacities for trade and passengers (two international airports, Jebel Ali Port), and with a rapidly increasing range of offerings for different types of tourism (ibid., 13). While the construction, real estate, and financial sectors were significantly affected by the financial crisis of 2008, the manufacturing and tourism sector kept on growing, as well as the numbers of exports after 2008. However, taking the success of Dubai as a model strategy on a larger scale for the UAE, or even for the neighbouring Gulf States, remains a limited strategy, as Dubai is a city-state with an overwhelmingly expatriate population of 88.5 percent (GLMM 2015).

Oman is focusing particularly on the tourism sector, investment in the banking and finance sector, new special economic zones, as well as privatisation of governmental companies, especially in the energy sector and in the water and electricity supply. Through the latter one, the Sultanate is also aiming for an increase in foreign direct investment. However, the most lucrative national companies are still government-run, such as Oman Air, Omantel, and Oman National Transport Company.

These examples are evidence of the multi-layered need to diversify the sources of economic revenue in the GCC—not only because of the exhaustibility of natural resources, but also because of its political and social consequences. Social disturbance is a threat that can arise more easily in a climate of economic instability and a lack of suitable jobs for nationals in the GCC (Hertog 2010; Valeri 2012, 2015). If the price of imported goods increases, and the governmental costs and subsidies have to be reduced due to the lack of revenues from a consistently low oil price, discontent amongst the population is predictable. The situation becomes especially volatile if this occurs in combination with an already existing sense of resentment from increasing rates of unemployment and when a societal differentiation will start progressing further (Herb 2009; Hertog 2010; Hanieh 2011). The latter one is more predictable in countries with a larger population and where the majority are national citizens (like in Oman and Saudi Arabia; s. Fig. 10.1). A rising middle class is observable which will benefit in the future to varying degrees of the public welfare system.

Restructuring and Nationalising the Labour Markets in the GCC

For a socially stable and economically steady diversification process, a higher participation of the local workforce in the private sector is being widely recognised as an essential prerequisite. Incentives for nationals to aim for a job in the private, rather than in the public sector, might include the strengthening of alternative social safety nets—as the public sector is still recognised as the best "safety valve" for local employers.

Therefore, an immediate consequence of the diversification endeavours is the need to restructure the public and the private sector. To reduce the high dependence of the GCC citizens on their governments for employment, and thereby to lower government spending, a transformation of the public sector and more autonomy of the private sector are widely recognised as the essential starting points. The public sector is still dominating as the main investor, as strongly controlling instance which is enabling (or hindering) and driving business, and as main authority which is regulating, for example, resetting incentives, encouraging collaboration, and providing infrastructure. But the public sector is also still the most attractive employer for nationals as it offers a lot of benefits which the private sector is not providing. Therefore, the private sector has to be strengthened—not only to prepare the ground for a sustainable diversification process, but also to create more incentives for the national workforce to aim for an employment apart from the governmental sector.

The connection between a sustainable economic diversification process and the need to rethink the structures of the labour markets will be examined in the following section, with the example of the Sultanate of Oman. The country represents, together with the Kingdom of Saudi Arabia, one of the only two countries of the GCC that have more nationals than foreign residents.

Case Study: Nationalisation Strategies in the Sultanate of Oman

Sultan Qaboos declared 20 years ago in the "Vision for Oman's Economy: Oman 2020" that development should not only be understood in terms of economic progress, but also as autonomy and independence from a foreign workforce. Thus, in 1995 the Sultanate had already started with the plan to train and qualify native human capital (Al-Lamki 2000, 2) and to improve the educational landscape.

In 2015, 56 percent of the total population of 4.15 million in Oman were nationals and 44 percent were still non-nationals, that is, expatriates (according to the National Centre for Statistical Information (NCSI), homepage as of March 5, 2015). Therefore, the Sultanate of Oman has the second-highest proportion of nationals amongst GCC countries, following Saudi Arabia who has a figure of 67.3 percent (GLMM 2015). Also, the supply of indigenous workers has not remained low in Oman in general. Due to natural demographic growth, the younger generation of Omani nationals has been increasing. Amongst the total population of Omani citizens living in the Sultanate, 34 percent are younger than 15 and 67.5 percent are under the age of 30. Thus, more than two-thirds of the local population are ready to enter the labour market, and therefore request that national citizens be given priority over foreigners with regard to employment (NCSI 2013, 16).

Despite heightened government efforts to restrict the percentage of expatriates in the workforce via policies, the proportion of non-Omani employees in the private sector has continued to rise over the last decades. In 1985, they accounted for 52 percent of private sector employees and, in 1995, 64 percent (see United Nations Expert Group 2006, 16), and 87 percent in 2014. This prompted a new intensification of the Omanisation policies in the last 2 years. Although Oman is heavily reliant on expatriate workers for advanced technical and professional expertise, as well as for manual labour (Aycan et al. 2007, 13), the highest demand for expatriates still exists—as in all GCC countries—in the area of low-skilled occupations, for example, in the construction sector.

Another interesting fact is that Oman is clearly aiming for an "In-Country-Value" strategy that is targeting the generation of income in the national economy that will remain in the country. This is particularly pertinent against the background of the high outflow of remittances which reached 10 percent of the GDP in 2010 (World Bank 2011, 16) and comes hand in hand with the endeavours to nationalise the labour market.

The most important resource for a sustainable nationalisation process is a quantitatively sufficient and qualitatively capable human capital to replace the expatriate workforce. The challenges in substituting foreigners with nationals in the Gulf region in general are, as already mentioned earlier, the preference of the public sector to the private sector amongst job seekers, mostly due to the better working conditions (e.g. regulated working hours, job security, and higher salaries) but also due to frustrations because of overregulation, high bureaucracy, a strong decision-taking leadership, favouritism, and lack of investment opportunities for business start-up's in the private sector—according to interviews with internationally experienced high-skilled Omani nationals (Muscat, February 2015 and January/February 2016).

Therefore, employers face a challenge finding employable staff to fill the manpower quota in the private sector as set within the frame of the nationalisation strategies, particularly in the Saudisation or Omanisation programmes—*and* to meet the demands of the private sector economy.

Figure 10.2 illustrates the continuing high dependence in Oman on international expertise and technically skilled employees who possess ter-

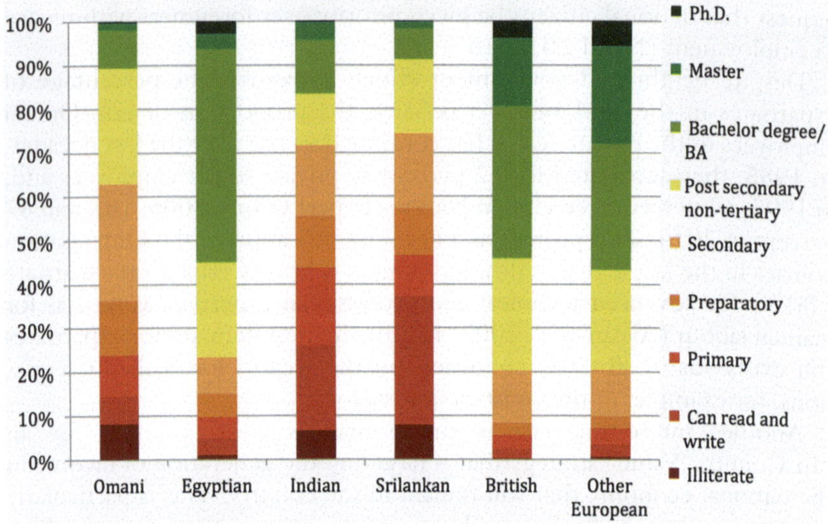

Fig. 10.2 Educational level of selected nationalities in Muscat (Source: Own calculations of census data 2010 by the Ministry of National Economy, Oman (Deffner and Pfaffenbach 2015, 6)

tiary educational degrees (Bachelor, Master, or PhD) or post-secondary/non-tertiary education, which means they hold a secondary education and have enjoyed specific vocational training. The most obvious discrepancy in terms of education levels exists between Omani nationals on the one hand, and Egyptian or "Western" nationals on the other. One caveat, must, however, be mentioned at this juncture: that the age structure of the selected nationalities in the graph varies considerably, but is not respected in the statistical data. Nevertheless, the age has a significant influence on the level of education: while a large proportion of the young Omani population is still in education and training, the overriding majority of the expatriate community are of working age and have therefore already completed their education and training.

To meet the objectives in recruiting an Omani labour force, the nationalisation plan of the Sultanate includes programmes in vocational training, mentoring, training of technical, management, operational skills, and so on. These courses and programmes are accomplished in cooperation with private firms. Several general policies were introduced to replace expatriate labour force successively, which are mainly represented in the following four areas (Al-Hamadi et al. 2007, 105): firstly, in the area of controlling procedures which were implemented and set in occupations of expatriate labour in the private sector, which could easily be omanised, and, secondly, a strategic, efficient, and suitable manpower plan to meet the needs of the private sector. Thirdly, the working conditions in the private sector were improved to increase the attractiveness for nationals. And fourthly, the support of the government to encourage Omanis to establish SMEs—a programme which is directly linked to the economic diversification strategies of the government.

However, efforts at nationalising the workforce appear to be failing, particularly in the private sector, in spite of the introduction of normative quotas for Omani employees in 12 economic sectors ranging from, for example, 20 percent in wholesale to 60 percent in transport and communication and up to 100 percent were targeted in jobs such as department managers, TV cameramen, accounts clerks, or newspaper vendors (see Das and Gokhale 2010). The most attractive jobs for Omani employees are considered to be in the banking, finance, and real estate sectors, as well as in the telecommunication, travel, and tourism sector. In these areas, the Omanisation quota has been set around 90 percent in operating, marketing, sales, supervisory, and other management positions that are generally recogised as representative. Other sectors, which are more difficult to nationalise, in particular due to the technical skill requirements, include the oil and gas sector, which shows a significant lower quota of only 30 percent in 2010. The schooling and educational sector is another area that is difficult to omanise; hence the aimed quota was only 15 percent in 2010 (Ministry of Manpower 2014). Reliable data about the achieved Omanisation quota are lacking. Although all companies in the private sector have to report annually their employment statistics; there is still a high blurring of the de facto replacement of foreign workforce by local nationals. Instead, there are high numbers of double employment, for example, to keep foreign employees to run businesses and to employ Omanis as a matter of form. However, the quotas for administrative occupations in the private sector are successfully achieved in most economic areas.

It should also not be overlooked that a large number of jobs in the private sector are low-skill jobs with pay and working conditions that are unattractive or even unacceptable for Omanis. Consequently, in the aftermath of the Arab Uprisings, the protests in Oman in 2011 addressed, aside from the call for political reforms, the grievances in the public sector. These included unemployment, unsatisfactory employment and income opportunities for Omanis, as well as favouritism (Valeri 2015, p. 10). In response, the government introduced a minimum wage and a 45-hour working week designed to make the booming sectors (construction, tourism and real estate development, electricity and water, environmental technology, etc.) more attractive to the indigenous workforce. The continued growth in the proportion of expatriates in the private sector workforce in 2011 and 2012 could be behind the renewed increase of the minimum wage in July 2013.

The major task for politics is to meet those individual and economic interests and challenges, and to synthesise them in the form of sustainable policies in the framework of the nationalisation programmes. The challenge therein consists in balancing the two sides of the same coin: on the one side, policies have to grant an increase in economic productivity, and to reduce hydrocarbon dependence. On the other side, strict rules have to be imposed on private companies to comply with the Omanisation targets and quotas. State-led changes and adaptations of the working conditions aim to make the private sector more attractive for national job seekers. Therefore, actions were undertaken, for example, the increase of a guaranteed minimum wage, the introduction of a 45-hour working week, and holiday entitlement that was in line with the public sector.

Another mounting challenge is the creation of new jobs in light of the young and growing population of Oman. Qaboos and his government took immediate action after the protest in February and March 2011, which showed the anger of the country's youth about the limited access to jobs in the private sector and the increasing unemployment rate. Around 50,000 new jobs were created, mainly in the public sector (police, military, etc.). However, to meet the expectations of these adolescent Omani citizens, around 60,000 new jobs need to be created each year.

The Singapore Story

The geographically small country of Singapore, with its 5.4 million inhabitants, is characterised and known for its highly developed and, from a capitalist point of view, successful free-market economy. Singapore ranks one of the highest incomes in the world with US$81,300 per capita (est. 2014, Central Intelligence Agency 2015). The GDP is mainly generated in the service sector (74.7 percent), complemented by the industry sector with 25.3 percent (est. for 2014, CIA 2015).

The city-state rose over the last 50 years to become a competitive player in the era of information-driven global economies. Singapore started immediately after its independence from Malaysia in 1965 to focus on its contemporary role as major global hub for finance and trade—which is all the more remarkable given its land scarcity, the lack of any natural resources, and the demographic situation of a population that only immigrated within the last century and didn't share a common history and identity in its founding years.

Nonetheless geography matters (Sparke et al. 2004), though less so in terms of territorial size: Singapore's strategic location and natural harbour at the mouth of the Malacca Strait (the "Suez Canal of Asia"), helped greatly to revitalise its former historical importance as a maritime trading post. It has become a global trading and financial hub in one of the most dynamic regions in the world, connecting the still growing Asian market with established economic regions in the rest of the world. As a pan-Asian business hub, Singapore offers an excellent location, from the perspective of international companies, for the performance of their strategic operations.

The essential elements of Singapore's economic success are mostly described as being the free trade and the rule of law. The latter is based on the tradition of a strong, pragmatic, and stable government that was initialised by Singapore's first Prime Minister Lee Kuan Yew. Referring to his ambitious goal, Singapore turned under his strict laws from "third world to first" (Yew 2000) and became what it is famous for today: order, cleanliness, and discipline. Even though an active government might appear somehow antagonistic for today's global economy, the prudent policies are also responsible for the international reputation as safe, trustworthy, and thus attractive business environment. Transparency International attested Singapore one of the lowest corruption rates worldwide in 2014 (placing seventh out of 175 countries), very low tax rates, and an ease regarding tax forms and visa regulation and acquisition. For 11 consecutive years, Singapore ranked top of the World Bank's "Ease of Doing Business" list that comprised the following categories: starting a business, dealing with construction permits, getting electricity, registering property, getting credit, protecting minority and investors, paying taxes, trading across borders, enforcing contracts, and resolving insolvency (World Bank Group 2015).

Singapore has benefitted thoroughly from globalisation. However, it also showed points of vulnerability towards the global entanglement of its economic activities. The first risk rose on Singapore's booming horizon after two decades of immense growth in the 1970s and 1980s. This growth was basically due to factor accumulation, that is, the input of foreign labour and capital, instead of increasing the factor productivity (with the same amount of labour and capital). Especially for the tremendously booming construction sector, high numbers of low-paid foreign workforce have been employed. Against the background of increased efforts for economic diversification and successful global competitiveness, Singapore's economy has seen increasing productivity. However, this economic growth was also based on the attraction of (new) foreign capital and a highly skilled foreign workforce, for the newly diversified sectors of innovation and new technologies. Critical voices point out that this development easily contains the risk of neglecting the utilisation of domestic resources; furthermore, it could also have the "unintended consequence of 'crowding out' or even 'chasing away' local talent, capital and entrepreneurship" (Lim 2009). The aftermath of the Asian financial crisis 1997–1998 also showed the vulnerability of Singapore's small and open economy in its global entanglements. In particular, because of Singapore's ongoing reliance on the revenues of financial services, which still are about 11 percent of the GDP (Grant 2014, 19). Singapore's exports declined, and the city-state became significantly vulnerable in the volatile electronics and pharmaceutical sectors, which have been the emerging branches of its diversification strategies.

To address these identified risks, the government of Singapore improved its' "Productivity and Innovation Credit Scheme", that aims to provide tax benefits for businesses which invest in productivity improvement and training for their employees. Over the long term, the government seeks to balance the attraction of new economic sectors—and with them a suitable inflow of a skilled foreign workforce—and the creation of diversified job opportunities for its own workforce. Therefore, the current policies acknowledge the importance of foreign talents who bring the required skills for building up new economic sectors, investing capital, and founding enterprises for a more diversified economy. At the same time, the government invests largely in research, investment, and enterprise for its own local workforce: between 2011 and 2015, S$16.1 billion were spent for the educational landscape that try to build strategic links between research and innovation; institutions like the National University Entrepreneurship Centre are often associated with research universities, for example, the governmental National University of Singapore. Singapore has four autonomous universities and five polytechnic colleges. The structure, emphasis, and quality of Singaporeans knowledge landscape hit the target squarely in making Singapore a hub of talent and innovation, enterprise, and excellence. The focus on science and technology to build up "innovative capabilities" (Lim 2009) for high-end manufacturing bears fruit today, in particular in the sector of biomedical sciences, in aerospace, or precision engineering, where the government is aiming to establish research institutes in cutting-edge fields. The biggest project *Biopolis*, on which hopes are pinned, represents a newly built campus that shall combine science and business interests in the fields of biotechnology and pharmacy. The campus hosts a variety of governmentally funded research institutes, in combination with research laboratories of private companies.

This governmentally promoted cultivation of excellence in education has led to a skilled middle class who has provided the necessary manpower for the country's economy. In particular, the efforts in the educational sector have led to a rising entrepreneurial class, that is, an increasing number of Singaporeans who are willing to start a business. In addressing cultural values and mindsets, an Economic Review has been commissioned by the government in 2001, attesting an evolution of "new social values which celebrate entrepreneurship and risk-taking by promoting a culture that accepts diversity and failure, and embraces a broad notion of success" (Lauria 2014).

However, to maintain its capability for economic resilience, Singapore is still reliant on its numerous foreign workforce. According to government statistics for December 2011, 43 percent of foreign workers came from the service sector (foreign domestic workers not included), 30 percent worked in construction, and the remaining 27 percent were in manufacturing. Regarding natural demographic development, the chances of significantly reducing the share of the foreign workforce does not appear to be too high as the Singaporean population is ageing and shrinking. The society is going to experience an unprecedented age shift within the next 15 years: 2020 is expected to be the tipping point, when the number of senior citizens who are entering retirement will outnumber the younger citizens joining the workforce. Since the birth rate is low, the population will also start declining from 2025 onwards, if not offset by immigration into the country (Government of Singapore 2013, 2015). The current policies therefore aim to encourage more women and senior citizens to enter and stay in the workforce. This policy appears somehow ironic, given the already existing difficulty for the elderly; that many have to work far beyond the retirement age to sustain their livelihoods, which is for many not adequately covered by a governmental pension scheme.

But, regarding the reliance on foreign workforce, one important aspect has to be mentioned, too. Singapore is facing a similar situation as the GCC countries: the majority of the high number of foreigners is working in the low-skilled and low-paid sector. They are working for lower salaries than nationals, due to the wage differential between their home countries and the destination countries. The reliance of the latter ones on foreign workforce is not only a question of the quantitative demand of the individual workforce, but also a question of the willingness of national citizens to take over the lower paid jobs (e.g. as domestic workers, in the construction sector, etc.). The most sought-after jobs are the better-paid and recognised "white-collar jobs" (management positions, etc.), where the high presence of high-skilled foreigners starts to be seen critically as a challenge that has to be overcome in the age of nationalisation and the strengthening of national identity (Yeoh and Lam 2016).

Can Singapore Serve as a Model for the GCC?

The attractiveness to look "eastwards" for suitable models for the GCC (e.g. Ministry of Trade and Industry Singapore, 2013) to further diversify their economies and increase their own human capital is based on a variety of reasons that distinguish West and Southeast Asian countries and societies from the highly industrialised countries and normative "Western" concepts of modernity. The Arab Gulf countries share with other Asian countries in particular historical (trading) connections, certain sociocultural values (in particular in distinction to Western societies), but most of all a relatively young history of economic modernisation that only started in the middle of the twentieth century (in the sense of: entering the highly interlaced world economy). Nevertheless, a further look at the economic, political, and social structures of the Arab Gulf monarchies and Singapore makes it rather difficult, eventually impossible, to take Singapore as a model for the development and modernisation goals of the GCC countries, as the following preliminary conclusions on these reflexions aim to highlight.

Concerning the major question of economic diversification, the Arab Gulf countries are facing, to varying degrees, structural obstacles in their endeavours to diversify and nationalise their economies. This is basically due to the antagonist common denominator of strong governments and weak institutions. Most policies of the Gulf monarchies still sustain the dominance of the public sector and the too-long neglected national private sectors; simultaneously, the institutional landscapes are showing weaknesses in the coordination of policy implementations and the efficiency of legal and regulatory systems. Transparency and accountability are important for creating conducive business environments; however, the majority of the Arab Gulf rentier economies still shows impeding cases of favouritism. According to Transparency International (2014), the GCC countries were listed with the following indices for corruption perception in 2014: Out of 175 countries, Kuwait ranked 67, Oman 64, Bahrain 55, Saudi Arabia 55, Qatar 26, and UAE 25.

Singapore has also experienced a governmental (basically "one-party") leadership that is known for being strict in law; but it owes its economic success—and take-off in terms of the diversification away from the strong foothold of the financial sector—to the fact that it enables a reliable business and investment environment that also encourages entrepreneurship for SMEs, due to prudent regulations, low tax rates, free trading structures, and a perceived high level of transparency.

On the subject of the empowerment of national human capital, a comparison would also start from uneven prerequisites and structures. The lack of innovation and limited investment in research *and* development is a weakness that most of the GCC countries are suffering from. Singapore started in its early phase of modernisation already with very strategic investment into a knowledge landscape that specifically targets the combination of research and innovation. The main incentives therefore were to meet the demands of a diversified economy, to play a leading role as an innovation hub, to increase local productivity, and to diversify job opportunities in high-technology branches, but also to offer an educational landscape to build up a well-skilled national workforce (Wiesemann et al. 2014). Singapore was never blessed with natural resources; therefore, the emphasis of its politics has always been on the value of excellence and discipline in knowledge production. But, it also has to be taken into account that Singapore is a city-state with a high percentage of young, dynamic, mobile, urban professionals, respectively, with a high attraction due to lifestyle diversity etc. Moreover, the labour market is highly competitive, which is also crucially distinguishing in its neoliberal order that offers little space and protection for more vulnerable groups (low-income employees, elder or unemployable people, etc.).

While all distinguishing aspects are fluid and still can change over time, one factor can't be changed and has to be taken into account critically: the disproportionate nature of geography that matters. Singapore is a small and limited city-state that has no regional disparities, for example, between a rural and urban population. It has no economic hinterland at its own, but a highly controllable land area. The city itself represents and concentrates all economic activities and is its own consumer for all kind of services. Thus, larger countries like Saudi Arabia, Oman, and Kuwait can hardly use Singapore as a holistic transferable model. A commonly drawn comparison, however, can be found between the "city-emirate" Dubai and the city-state Singapore.

The shared challenges of Singapore and the GCC countries can be seen as a fruitful field to exchange experiences or to cooperate in finding suitable solutions. All considered countries are facing, to varying degrees, the need to diversify their economies further, for example, towards manufacturing and other services, to divert monetary and human capital, and to maintain economic resilience. An important link for exchange or cooperation can be seen in the petrochemical industry, which is in particular important for the economy in Singapore as the country imports a lot of crude oil, using it for refined petroleum products.

But the highest potential for a fruitful exchange of experiences lies in the variety of societal questions that are connected with the emergence of differentiating urban societies, and how they are dealing with identity, citizenship, and diversity—even though these aspects are not high on the agenda of the official and public discourse. It be overseen that all considered countries are currently experiencing an era of strengthening the identification with the nation (e.g. Erskine-Loftus et al. 2016; Cooke 2014; Velayutham 2007). The reasons for the awakening of national identity amongst the GCC citizens can be related to coincidence between the overwhelming presence of foreign employees in their countries with increasing rates of unemployment amongst the youth and the still modest representation of local citizens in the private sector economy. Singapore is experiencing similar tendencies but rather in a way "top-down". The society is showing an impressive level of acceptance and tolerance towards a multi-cultural "living together". However, cultural politics react and are aware of the decreasing birth rate, which has been below the reproduction level of 2.1 for more than three decades with a total fertility rate of only 1.20 children per woman (data for 2011, Government of Singapore, 9), and a persistently high immigration rate. Hence, some see critically an overturning of "the very essence of a Singaporean identity that [the] forefathers built up" (Grant 2014, 19; citing Sudhir Thomas Vadaketh, a Singaporean local writer). The idea of this highly developed country is that a local population that strongly identifies with its own values is the best human capital and success factor to foster economic growth. Hence, the Singaporean government is highly emphasising, in particular this was perceivable within the realms of the 50th anniversary celebrations of the founding of the nation in 2015, the national identification amongst its citizens. At the same time, the Singaporean government is publicly acknowledging its heterogeneity and cultural diversity as a capital for a "global city". This is still a longer way to go for the Arab Gulf countries. But in the aftermath of the Arab spring, the remembrance of a national consciousness has facilitated bottom-up movements and a willingness from the people aiming to strengthen the national identity.

References

Al-Ali, J. (2008). Emiratisation: Drawing UAE Nationals into Their Surging Economy. *International Journal of Sociology and Social Policy, 28*(9/10), 365–379.

Al-Hamadi, A. B., Budhwar, P. S., & Shipton, H. (2007). Management of Human Resources in Oman. *International Journal of Human Resource Management, 18*(1), 100–113.

Al-Lamki, S. (2000). Omanization: A Three Tier Strategic Framework for Human Resource Management and Training in the Sultanate of Oman. *Journal of Comparative International Management, 3*(1), 3–75.

Aycan, Z., Al-Hamadi, A. B., Davis, A., & Budhwar, P. (2007). Cultural Orientations and Preferences for HRM Policies and Practices. The Case of Oman. *International Journal of Human Resource Management, 18*(1), 11–32.

Callen, T. et al. (2014). *Economic Diversification in the GCC: The Past, the Present, and the Future.* International Monetary Fund, Working Paper. Retrieved June 10, 2015, from http://www.imf.org/external/pubs/ft/sdn/2014/sdn1412.pdf

Central Intelligence Agency (CIA). (2015). World Factbook. Retrieved May 20, 2015, from https://www.cia.gov/library/publications/the-world-factbook/geos/my.html

Cooke, M. (2014). *Tribal Modern: Branding New Nations in the Arab Gulf.* Berkeley, CA: University of California Press.

Das, K. C., & Gokhale, N. (2010, February 2). *Omanization Policy and International Migration in Oman.* Middle East Institute, Washington. Retrieved June 9, 2015, from http://www.mei.edu/content/omanization-policy-and-international-migration-oman

Deffner, V., & Pfaffenbach, C.. (2015). Migration, Modernisation, and the Urban Immigration Society in the Sultanate of Oman. *Middle East Insights*, 128, Middle East Institute, National University of Singapore, Singapore.

Erskine-Loftus, P., Al-Mulla, M. I., & Hightower, V. P. (2016). *Representing the Nation: Heritage, Museum, National Narratives in the Arab Gulf States.* New York/London: Routledge.

Global Risk Advisors. (2015). Retrieved May 31, 2015, from http://www.global-riskadvisors.com/oil-price-volatility-and-gcc-countries/

Government of Singapore. (2013). *A Sustainable Population for a Dynamic Singapore.* National Population and Talent Division, Prime Minister's Office, Population White Paper, January. Retrieved June 3, 2015, from http://population.sg/whitepaper/resource-files/population-white-paper.pdf

Government of Singapore. (2015). *National Population and Talent Division.* Prime Minister's Office. Retrieved May 26, 2013, from www.population.sg/vision/economy

Grant, J. (2014, December 2). Singapore Tests Its Success. Syndicates from Financial Times. *Muscat Daily*, p. 19.

Gulf Labour Markets and Migration. (2015). Retrieved May 31, 2015, from http://gulfmigration.eu/total-population-and-percentage-of-nationals-and-non-nationals-in-gcc-countries-latest-national-statistics-2010-2015/

Hamdi, H., & Sbia, R. (2013, September). Dynamic Relationships Between Oil Revenues, Government Spending and Economic Growth in An Oil-Dependent Economy. *Economic Modelling, 35*, 118–125.

Hanieh, A. (2011). *Capitalism and Class in the Gulf Arab States.* New York: Palgrave Macmillan.

Herb, M. (2009). A Nation of Bureaucrats: Political Participation and Economic Diversification in Kuwait and the United Arab Emirates. *International Journal of Middle East Studies, 41*(3), 375–395.

Herb, M. (2014). *The Wages of Oil: Parliaments and Economic Development in Kuwait and the UAE*. Ithaca, NY: Cornell University Press.

Hertog, S. (2010). The Sociology of the Gulf Rentier Systems: Societies of Intermediaries. *Comparative Studies in Society and History, 52*(02), 282–318.

Hertog, S. (2014a). Arab Gulf States: An Assessment of Nationalisation Policies. *GLMM Research Paper, 1*, Gulf Labour Markets and Migration Programme, Badia Fiesolana, Italy.

Hertog, S. (2014b). State and Private Sector in the GCC after the Arab Uprisings. *Journal of Arabian Studies, 3*(2): 174–195. (LSE Research Online. Retrieved from http://eprints.lse.ac.uk/54399/).

Lauria, V. (2014, July 10). What Makes an Asian Tiger? Singapore's Unlikely Economic Success Lies in Its History. *Forbes Asia*, Special Reports. Retrieved May 20, 2015, from www.forbes.com/sites/forbesasia/2014/07/10

Lim, L. (2009). Opinion: Singapore's Economic Growth Model: Too Much or Too Little? *Ethos*, Issue 6. Retrieved May 31, 2015, from https://www.cscollege.gov.sg/Knowledge/Ethos/Issue%206%20Jul%202009/Pages/Singapores-Economic-Growth-Model-Too-Much-or-Too-Little.aspx

Malik, F., & Shawkat, H. (2007). Shock and Volatility Transmission in the Oil, US and Gulf Equity Markets. *International Review of Economics & Finance, 16*(3), 357–368.

Ministry of Manpower, Sultanate of Oman. (2014). Omanisation per Sector. Retrieved June 9, 2015, from http://www.manpower.gov.om/portal/en/OmanisationPerSector.aspx

Ministry of National Economy, Sultanate of Oman. (2010). *General Census of Populations, Housing and Establishment*, Muscat.

Ministry of Trade and Industry of Singapore. (2013, September 1). *Gulf Cooperation Council—Singapore Free Trade Agreement enters into Force*. News Room. Retrieved May 31, 2015: http://www.mti.gov.sg/NewsRoom/Pages/GULF-COOPERATION-COUNCIL-SINGAPORE-FREE-TRADE-AGREEMENT-ENTERS-INTO-FORCE.aspx

National Centre for Statistical Information. (2013). The Statistical Yearbook 2013. Retrieved June 6, from http://www.ncsi.gov.om/NCSI_website/book/SYB2014/contents.htm

National Centre for Statistical Information (NCSI). (2015). Retrieved August 20, from http://www.ncsi.gov.om/NCSI

Ramady, M. (2010). Population and Demographics: *Saudization* and the Labour Market. In *The Saudi Arabian Economy: Policies, Achievements, and Challenges* (pp. 351–393). New York, NY: Springer US.

Randeree, K. (2012). *Workforce Nationalization in the Gulf Cooperation Council States*, Occasional Paper, 9, Center for International and Regional Studies (CIRS), Georgetown University School of Foreign Service in Qatar, Doha.

Sparke, M., Sidaway, J. D., Bunnell, T., & Grundy-Warr, C. (2004). Triangulating the Borderless World: Geographies of Power in the Indonesia–Malaysia–Singapore Growth Triangle. *Transactions, 29*(4), 485–498.

Toledo, H. (2013). The Political Economy of Emiratization in the UAE. *Journal of Economic Studies, 40*(1), 39–53.

Transparency International. (2014). Corruption Perception Index. Retrieved June 2, 2015, from http://www.transparency.org/country

United Nations Department of Economic and Social Affairs, Population Division. (2006). *International Migration in the Arab Region*. UN Expert Group Meeting on International Migration and Development in the Arab Region: Challenges and Opportunities, Beirut, May 15–17. Retrieved June 9, 2015, from http://www.un.org/esa/population/meetings/EGM_Ittmig_Arab/P14_PopDiv.pdf

Valeri, M. (2012). Oligarchy vs. Oligarchy: Business and the Politics of Reform in Bahrain and Oman. In S. Hertog, G. Luciani, & M. Valeri (Eds.), *Business Politics in the Middle East*. Bloomsbury, London: C. Hurst & Co Publishers.

Valeri, Marc. (2015). Simmering Unrest and Succession Challenges in Oman. *Carnegie Endowment for International Peace*, January. Retrieved June 9, 2015, from http://carnegieendowment.org/files/omani_spring.pdf

Velayutham, S. (2007). *Responding to Globalization: Nation, Culture and Identity in Singapore*, Institute of Southeast Asian Studies, Singapore: Utopia Press.

Wiesemann, A., Alromi, N., & Alshumrani, S. (2014). *Education for a Knowledge Society in Arabian Gulf Countries*, International Perspectives on Education and Society, 24, Bingley, Emerald Books.

World Bank. (2011). *Migration and Remittances Factbook*, Washington.

World Bank Group. (2015). Retrieved May 31, 2015, from http://www.doingbusiness.org/rankings

Yeoh, B. S. A., & Lam, T. (2016). Immigration and Its (Dis)Contents: The Challenges of Highly Skilled Migration in Globalising Singapore. *American Behavioral Scientist, 60*(5–6), 637–658.

Yew, L. K. (2000). *From Third World to First: The Singapore Story: 1965–2000*. New York: Harper Collins Publishers.

Index

A. Mishrif, Y. Al Balushi (eds.), *Economic Diversification in the Gulf Region, Volume II*, The Political Economy of the Middle East,
DOI 10.1007/978-981-10-5786-1

The manufacturer's authorised representative in the EU is Springer Nature Customer Service Centre GmbH, Europaplatz 3, 69115 Heidelberg, Germany. If you have any concerns regarding our products, please contact ProductSafety@springernature.com

Printed and bound by CPI Group (UK) Ltd, Croydon, CR0 4YY
30/09/2026
02225440-0001